DISTRIBUTED DATA PROCESSING

Technology and Critical Issues

TRW Series of Software Technology

VOLUME 4

Series Editor
BARRY W. BOEHM

NORTH-HOLLAND – AMSTERDAM • NEW YORK • OXFORD

DISTRIBUTED DATA PROCESSING
Technology and Critical Issues

edited by

M. P. MARIANI
TRW - Defense Systems Group
One Space Park
Redondo Beach, CA 92708
U.S.A.

1984

NORTH-HOLLAND – AMSTERDAM • NEW YORK • OXFORD

ISBN: 0 444 86796 1

Published by:
ELSEVIER SCIENCE PUBLISHERS B.V.
P.O. Box 1991
1000 BZ Amsterdam
The Netherlands

Sole distributors for the U.S.A. and Canada:
ELSEVIER SCIENCE PUBLISHING COMPANY, INC.
52 Vanderbilt Avenue
New York, N.Y. 10017
U.S.A.

Library of Congress Cataloging in Publication Data
Main entry under title:

Distributed data processing.

(TRW series of software technology ; v. 4)
Includes bibliographies.
1. Electronic data processing--Distributed processing. I. Mariani, Michael P. II. Series.
QA76.9.D5D554 1983 001.64 83-16566
ISBN 0-444-86796-1 (U.S.)

PRINTED IN THE NETHERLANDS

To Nancy, Michael and Carrie

CONTRIBUTIONS AND ACKNOWLEDGEMENTS

The contents of this text have evolved over the last four years of research for the U.S. Army, Ballistic Missile Defense Advanced Technology Center (BMDATC). As a result the foundations, concepts, solution approaches and techniques described in the book have been formed through technical discussions, memos and reports of many people both within and outside the TRW. Some of the more major contributors include:

Mr. Hans Agneessens	- Architecture design concepts, parametric payoff modeling
Mr. Syed M. Akbar	- HW Architecture concepts
Dr. Yoichiro Fukada	- Allocation modeling
Dr. Michael L. Green	- Simulation modeling, distributed control
Mr. Stevan Katz	- Analytic modeling, distributed resource management
Dr. Edward Y.S. Lee	- Distributed data base, distributed resource control, simulation modeling
Mr. Samprakash Majumdar	- Distributed resource control
Dr. Michael A. Radke	- Architecture design concepts, distributed control, allocation modeling
Mr. Douglas C. Shannon	- Simulation
Dr. Rein Turn	- Communications
Mr. Tom Wolff, et al. (Univac)	- Distributed Architectures

In addition, many other, too numerous to mention, both within and outside of TRW provided stimulating discussions which have influenced the work presented.

A special acknowledgement is made to Dr. C.R. Vick, Mr. James Williams, Mr. Joseph Scalf, and Dr. Carl Davis, who have followed the Program upon which this text is based, and on many occasions provided technical direction at critical junctures in the research.

Finally, without the administrative support of Ms. Beatrice Sun, Helen Wang and Linda Lin this text would not have transitioned to its final consolidated form.

FOREWORD

The level of system distribution which we address in this text calls for both partitioned and replicated functions and data, which are distributed over a tightly coupled network of heterogeneous computing resources. The systems employ cooperating resources which must be controlled in real time.

A comparison of the centralized software design process with the distributed (HW/SW) design process has revealed the need for a major rethinking of the design, control and processor architectures which have dominated the data processing scene.

In this text we present a synopsis of results, observations, and lessons learned as a result of a multiyear research program* into distributed data processing (DDP) technology. The research program described in this text addresses three major research areas associated with DDP technology; they included,

1) The development of a baseline approach for the design of distributed data processing (DDP) for real time applications. The approach is keyed to the definition of methods and procedures, and the development of tools and techniques which support deterministic mapping of application processes to DDP architectures.

2) The definition and development of solution approaches to issues critical to the design and real time control of DDP architectures.

3) The evaluation of current architectures and associated hardware technology and, where necessary, the definition of new theory and technology to enhance the real time performance of distributed data processing.

The research emphasis was placed on first surveying the current technology state of the art in distributed data processing, second defining deficiencies in current technology which limit the potential of DDP to real time system applications, and finally, where possible, developing solution approaches for resolving key technology deficiencies. Throughout the research, we have concentrated on solution approaches which exhibited the highest payoff potential relative to performance, life cycle cost, reliability/availability, deployability, growth and fault tolerance.

---

* Multiyear contract (DASG60-76-C0088, DASG60-79-C0039) funded by the U.S. Army Ballistic Missile Defense Advanced Technology Center (BMDATC).

In this text we present details of our research resulst in support of three fundamental research areas (Figure F-1): (1) distributed architecture design, (2) critical issues, and (3) advanced architectures.

ARCHITECTURE DESIGN RESEARCH OVERVIEW

Application Representation and Design Methodology

Design of distributed systems provides the potential for tailoring the architecture to the specific needs of the problem addressed. However, the number of architecture design variables involved adds orders of magnitude to the complexity of the design process. Distributed systems conatin concurrent processes which must share data and hardware resources, often without centralized control. Processes and data are often distributed and sometimes replicated at different locations, in different computers at the same location or within different processors of a single computer. Communications and data management now become major design factors.

Currently there exists no single, existing design methodology which adequately treats the extremely complex, varied goals of distributed computing system design. Many critical design issues remain incompletely resolved. For example, methods for control decentralization, data base distribution and management, fault tolerence, and partitioning of functionality for most efficient distribution are still more an esoteric art than a science.

The design methodology must support the transformation of data processing subsystem requirements, generated by the systems engineering activity, to a data processing (DP) architecture specification consisting of hardware, software and firmware. To accomplish this transformation the design methodology must accommodate both the functional and nonfunctional requirements. In addition, the methodology must explicitly provide solutions to the critical operational issues of distributed data base management, distributed control and communications which arise as a result of distribution of the requirements and associated data. The design methodology must also include parametric models of key payoffs (reference paragraph 2.1) upon which the design tradeoff will be based. An overview of such a design methodology framework is provided in Figure 3.1

Key to the success of such a design methodology is the ability of the systems engineering activity to produce requirements for the data processing subsyste which have preserved the natural problem structure defined by the data flow and DP subsystem interforces (e.g. data arrival, or potential multiple asynchronous subsystem interfaces). Such preservation must be insured by not imposing design restrictions which unnecessarily constrain the application of distributed processing.

Payoffs

At the root of all deterministic design approaches lie parametric models of system effectiveness. One of the key areas of research for the Phase I study was the work in formal definition and development of payoff models which support distributed data processing (DDP) design.

Early research recognized the inherent complexity of the basic payoff measures which provide the driving force behind DDP design for Bal-

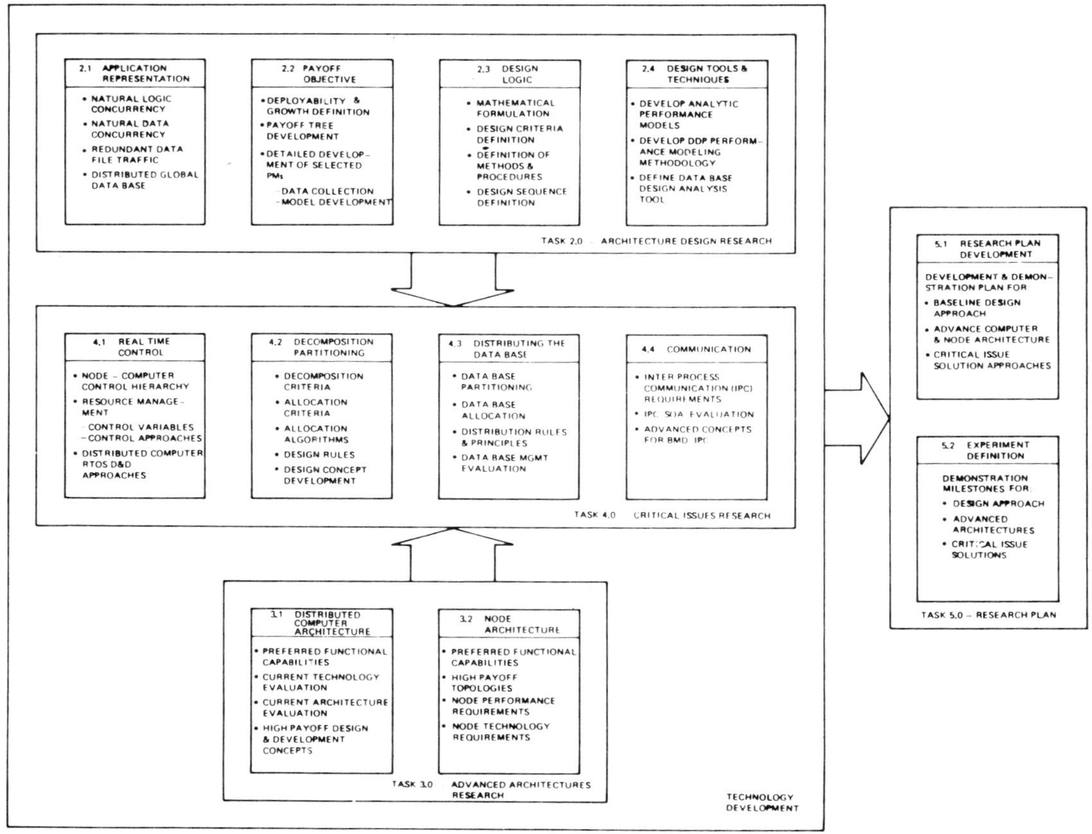

Figure F-1. DDP Technology Program

listic Missile Defense (BMD). This complexity exists both within the structure of each payoff measure and also between payoff measures in the form of trades. Successful development of parametric payoff models requires that each payoff measure be defined completely in terms of contributing design variables, and that those highly influential design variables be expressed as parameters within the payoff model. TRW successfully implemented an approach to payoff modeling which is based on a technique of structuring payoff trees.

The research concentrated on developing cost and reliability payoff models. Model development is based on three activities: 1) completion of development of payoff trees and the identification of the highly influential design variables; 2) collection of cost and reliability field data and data projections; and 3) derivation through regression of analytical payoff models based on collected data.

Design Tools and Techniques

Throughout the design process, methods and procedures are being developed which require tools and techniques for design support. These tools and techniques fall into three categories:

1) Implementation of the function/data distribution step; usually requiring automation to cope with combinatorial complexity.

2) Analysis of the resultant design product of each step; usually based on one or more payoff objectives.

3) Maintenance of the design process; usually the application characteristics or evolving system design.

Both manual and automated tools and techniques are considered. Primary emphasis during current research is on implementation and analysis tools and techniques. Tools and techniques which simplify the combinatorially complex problem of design allocation are concentrated on during implementation, while tools and techniques for assessing performance are considered in the analysis category.

CRITICAL ISSUES RESEARCH OVERVIEW

Distributing the Data Base

The distribution of the data base is being investigated at the node and distributed-computer levels of design. The research concentrates on establishing principles, concepts and rules which aid the distribution of the data base to support real-time performance and fault-tolerent design.

The performance and resource cost of redundant data base designs are being investigated. In addition, the performance and resource impact of high-potential approaches to distributed data base management at the node level are being analyzed.

Real-Time Control/Resource Management

The issue of real-time control (RTC) at the node and computer level of distributed data processing includes the management of hardware resoures and the execution of the application processes. The control issues of hardware synchronization between multiple computers and within a distributed computer are issues considered in advanced architectures. As a result, the RTC emphasis has centered on the two issues of node-level (multicomputer) resource management and distributed-computer, real-time operating systems (RTOS).

Research into node resource management considers the two real-time issues of resource load balancing and dynamic reconfiguration to support system fault tolerance. Research into RTOS for distributed computers extends past work conducted on design and development concepts such as top down design using virtual and layered design concepts. One of the principal issues of the layered approach to RTOS which is currently unresolved is the additional resource cost and its impact on real-time response. These issues have been investigated through experimentation.

Communications

The distribution of applications to multiple, concurrently executable computing resources will alter the real-time response profile or key computational threads. No longer will computational wait time be the most significant component to response. Distribution can reduce the multitasking environment and also the execution wait time with a dedicated resource environment being the extreme case. As distribution continues the cost of the interprocess communication (IPC) becomes a significant response component. In addition, the need for survivability and improved reliability will further complicate the communications requirements. Data base distribution and in several cases replication will require communications to support remote file access as well as replicated file synchronization. The requirement for distributed control and resource management will result in the requirement that periodic status and control messages be transmitted over the communications network. The characteristics of these messages vary dramatically, and are anticipated to stress correspondingly quite different communications architecture design and protocol.

Research was initiated into approaches for hybrid communication protocols which satisfy the high-response, low-volume communication requirements associated with IPC and system status as well as the low response, high-volume communication requirements imposed by the maintenance of distributed (for reliability) data files.

ADVANCED ARCHITECTURES RESEARCH OVERVIEW

The use of multiple resource systems has evolved over the last decade. The quest for the super computer (e.g. CDC STAR, ILLIAC, STARAN, PEPE, TI ASC, CDC 7600, CRAY) of the 1970's was based on internally distributed computer architectures. These initial architectures were complex, unreliable and extremely costly in terms of their usable throughput. More recently the trend towards multiple processor/computer networks - distribued data processing - offers the "potential" for more cost effective throughput, improved system reliability (through redundancy/fault tolerance), and natural growth paths among other features. However, the "law of diminishing return" (Figure F-2) causes severe limitations on the dimension of such distributed networks.

The nature of this decreasing network performance trend indicates that key-factors in such performance loss must include resource contention, and processor coupling (message traffic). There are two options for reducing such performance loss, (1) partition/allocate the applications and data to reduce the resource contention and message traffic of the system, and (2) redesign the communications and processor HW to reduce the probability of resource contention, and the cost impact of message handling on the applications processes. Advanced architectures will emphasize the second option through the use of new network topologies, communications protocols and processor architectures.

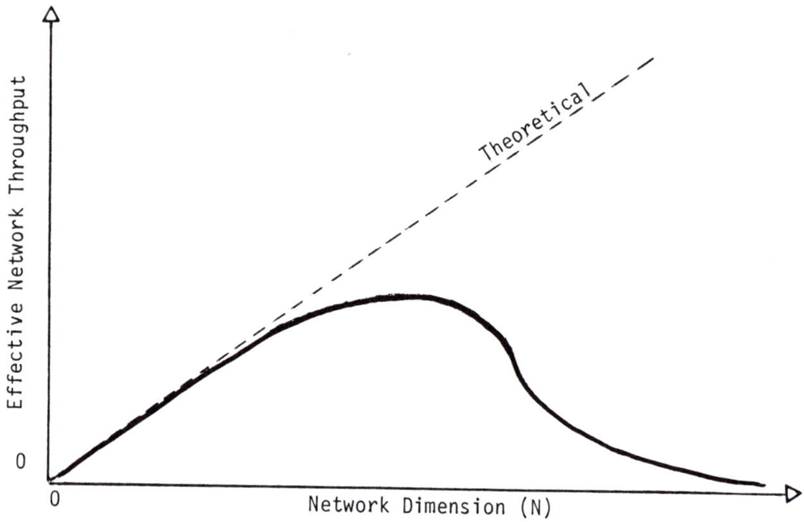

Figure F-2. Network Throughput Growth - "Law of Diminishing Return"

TABLE OF CONTENTS

LIST OF FIGURES

1.0 INTRODUCTION

1.1 DISTRIBUTED COMPUTING SYSTEM - THE SYSTEM CONTEXT

Characterization of the distribution of a computing system may be viewed as involving three basic elements: (1) physical processing hardware and software; (2) data to be processed; and (3) the system control [1-1]. Any computing system (centralized or distributed) may be further classified in terms of its operation; i.e., (1) type of requirements: homogeneous requirements for a single function or heterogeneous requirements for multiple functions; (2) operational speed: real time or non-real time; and (3) operational resource coupling; resorce sharing or resource autonomity. Finally the hardware interconnection can be characterized in terms of being loosely coupled (low bandwidth $\lesssim 10^4$ baud) or tightly coupled (high bandwidth $\gtrsim 10^4$ baud).

A. Distribution Characterization

The use of hardware/software, data and control as a means of characterizing the degree to which a system is distributed is not new. The same notion was used by Flynn [1-2] to develop a classification taxonomy for computer architectures using instruction and data streams. For architectures at higher level of abstraction than computers (that is tightly-coupled multicomputer networks or geographical networks), the physical interpretation of distribution is different. For example, at the computer level of abstraction, distribution of control is interpreted to be the memory fetch of an instruction. At the multi-computer node level, distribution of control may be interpreted to be the dispatch of a complete software process. Data distribution at the computer level are operands, while at the node level will be data records or complete files.

For the levels of abstraction which we refer to, i.e., multicomputer systems, we interpret the characteristics in the following manners:

- HARDWARE/SOFTWARE: distribution of computing resources and the software processes to be executed. Distribution may range from a single uniprocessor computer (totally centralized), to a network of multiple general purpose computers each with identical capability.

- DATA: distribution of shared data within the system which is operated on by software processes. Distribution may range from a single file or file system with a colocated file directory maintained without backups in a central storage medium (totally centralized data base), to a multiple file system with replication of both files and directory distributed across several storage mediums.

- CONTROL: distribution of the process and resource control mechanism which manages the real time operation of the architecture. Distribution may range from a single fixed control point which makes all decisions as to operation based on continual observation of the system performance (centralized control), to a fully distributed set of identical control centers cooperating in the decision process governing the operation of the system.

The characteristics can be visualized as axes of a 3-dimensional cube (Figure 1-1). Such a visualization has been used by Enslow[1-1] and Flynn [1-2]. Distribution can occur along any axis. However distribution along some axes combinations are not logical. For our work we are concerned with only those architecture distributions which include heterogeneous/homogeneous computer networks; with distributed files and directories, under partial replication; and with fully replicated homogeneous, cooperating foci of control (reference Figure 4 shaded area).

B. Operational Characterization

The computing system operation, regardless of the degree of distribution, could also be characterized in terms of three basic attributes; type of application requirements, operational speed, operational coordination between resources.

The requirements may be either, (1) homogeneous: a single data processing problem (e.g., weapons file control system, satellite control system, or bank transaction system); or (2) heterogeneous: integration of several sets of homogeneous requirements which may demand contrary architecture features (e.g., a dual purpose processing center: tactical command and control center which also serves as a batch oriented DP center during peacetime). Homogeneous requirements permit architecture tuning while heterogeneous requirements lead to general purpose architecture solutions - global optimization of the composite problem with suboptimal solutions of the problem subsets.

The system may be required to operate in real time or non real time as measured by the degree of system responsiveness to external stimulus. Typically the system responsiveness is measured in terms of the data arrival rate. For example systems involving man-machine interface may require real-time operation of the order of seconds to minutes, where radar systems often require much shorter response times of the order of fractions of a second. Typically systems which must operate at response times of substantially less than a second require automation of much of the complex control operations that normally are handled manually. As a result such systems can be much more expensive to develop because of the complexity of automated control. Systems which involve less stringent response often employ manual control techniques and as a result can be developed at much lower cost.

Finally, the degree of coupling of system resources implies a great deal about the inherent design and control complexity of the system. Systems can be composed of multiple components each of which operates autonomously. At the other extreme the components may operate at a level in which decisions are made cooperatively. The degree of cooperation between components may vary from occasional information

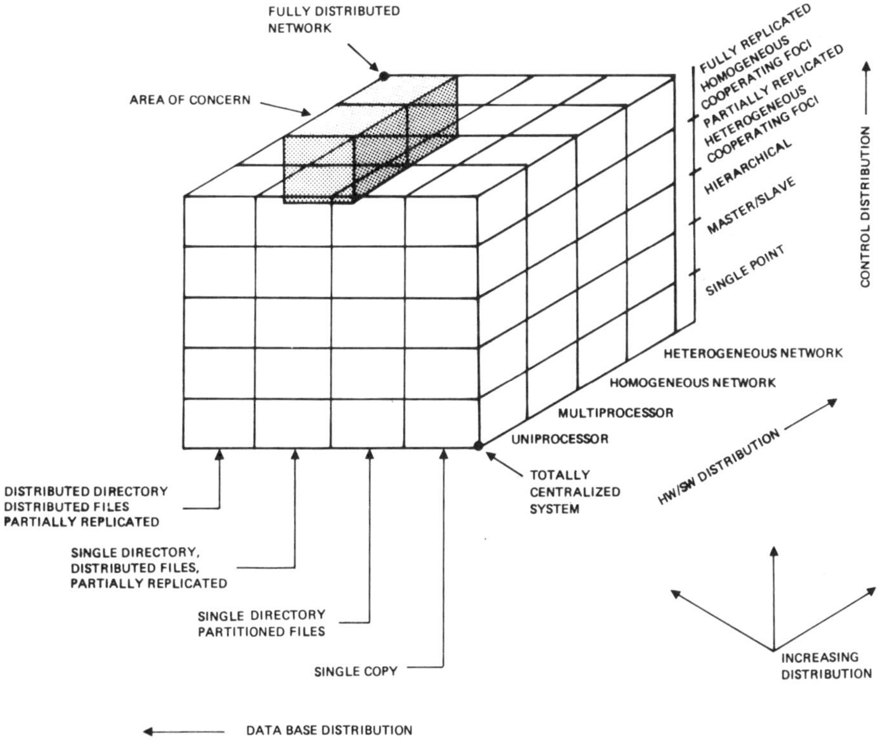

Figure 1-1. Distributed System Characterization

exchange to exchange of information after each decision. The decision to employ a system composed of cooperating components, regardless of the degree of cooperation, immediately complicates the design process - including the distribution of functions and data, the communications network architecture design and protocols employed, and the tradeoff between excess hardware and control software. The higher the degree of cooperation (i.e., frequency of cooperative decisions), the higher the frequency of information exchange and the inter-component message rate. Both the complexity of control and data base are affected by the degree of cooperation.

C. Network* Coupling Characterization

Network hardware architectures can be described in terms of five characteristics; (1) Network components and their individual characteristics (such as links, switches, processor interface units); (2) Network configuration topology - how the network components are configured to support interconnection of the computational resources (processors, shared memories, input/output or computers, special purpose hardware, disc controllers); (3) Network control protocols which support message transmission and resource control; (4) Network performance in terms of bandwidth and message transmission response; and (5) Network cost including both one-time procurement/development and recurring maintenance costs. Local computer networks are usually referred to as tightly coupled networks. Local networks which support distributed processing have been classified by Thurber [1-3] as falling into one of four categories - packet switch (e.g., CM*[1-4]), circuit switched (e.g., C.mmp [1-5]), ring structure (e.g., DCS[1-6]), or I/O channels (e.g., DCN [1-7].

1.2 THE SOFTWARE DEVELOPMENT** PROCESS

The costs associated with contemporary data processing system development (Figure 1-2) is changing drastically from those which governed earlier systems development. Software development for distributed systems must be rethought from what we have practiced for centralized systems. The increased personnel related costs (10-15%/year) will result in the continued increase of software development costs. The rapidly decreasing costs of processor and memory logic (25%/year and 40%/year) will decrease the emphasis of hardware utilization efficiency. Such efficiency has been recognized as being a key contributor to the cost of software development.

---

*We define network as any subsystem which supports information exchange between computing devices using dynamically addressable messages transmitted through the input/output channels of the computing devices. Therefore such subsystems can include shared memories, busses, long range communication lines, satellite links.

**We refer to the software development process as that which commences with receipt of data processing subsystem requirements, and extends through the integration and test of executable software modules which collectively interact with hardware to satisfy the original data processing subsystem requirements.

As hardware utilization approaches system capacity, software must be developed more efficiently sometimes requiring lower level languages and optimization. Distributed systems allows the modular application of lower cost processing and memory logic to incrementally extend system capacity when needed.

The software development process (Figure 1-3) as we have known it for centralized systems will become increasingly more complex for distributed systems. For most centralized systems, hardware was often selected as part of the systems engineering process based on preliminary algorithm sizing estimates. This left the system designer with allocating requirements to software.* Often the requirement allocation process resulted in a more complicated software design and implementation problem. Techniques of structured design were often rejected for real time systems because of their space and time liabilities on pre-selected hardware - hardware whose resource capacity was becoming a major design constraint for centralized systems. Preliminary design emphasized structuring the software process and data base which supported it so as to maximize the total throughput of a resource constrained system. These designs lead to more complex operating systems for improved utilization efficiency. Detailed design often led to code optimization techniques, abandonment of higher order languages in favor of more efficient, more machine dependent software. Distributed system design offers relief to this centralized software development dilemma.

The basic principles which have governed centralized software development must change. We can postpone early commitment to hardware and instead evolve the hardware with the requirements. The use of smaller, less complex components makes such hardware postponement technically more viable because the long lead times may not be necessary; the components may well be readily available from many sources. Now with distributed system design (Figure 1-4) the subsystem design becomes increasingly more complex. Instead of allocating requirements to only software, requirements must be allocated to both hardware and software. The requirements must be decomposed, partitioned and allocated at multiple levels of the architecture before separate requirements on hardware and software are distinguished. This process is referred to as the distributed architecture design process and can be associated with what was previously referred to as preliminary design for centralized systems; i.e., terminating with the Preliminary Design Review (PDR) in the MIL STD 483/490 system development environment.

However, for distributed architectures preliminary design can involve three levels of distribution, the geographical network design, the local network design, and computer design. At each level requirements from the previous design level (e.g., node requirements) must be further decomposed, partitioned and allocated to computational resources (e.g., computer systems) whose internal architecture will be designed at the next architecture design level. At each level, partitioning may be constrained by the communications requirements at that level. However, it is not until after

---

*Note that the driving objectives of this software requirements allocation step was the reduction of the throughput and storage requirements of the total software process and the achievement of system responsiveness.

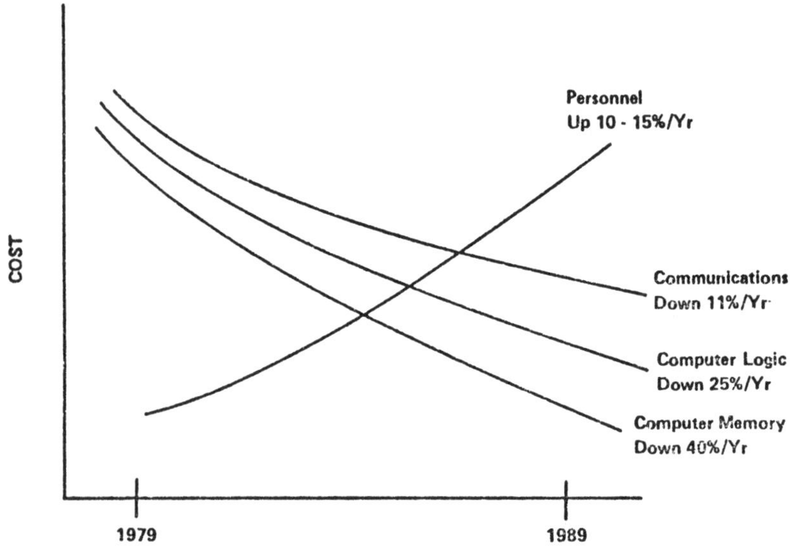

*DISTRIBUTED PROCESSING SYSTEMS: HARDWARE CONSIDERATIONS
ARTHUR YOUNG
DPMA CONFERENCE, 11/14/79

Figure 1-2. Changing Costs Over the Next Decade

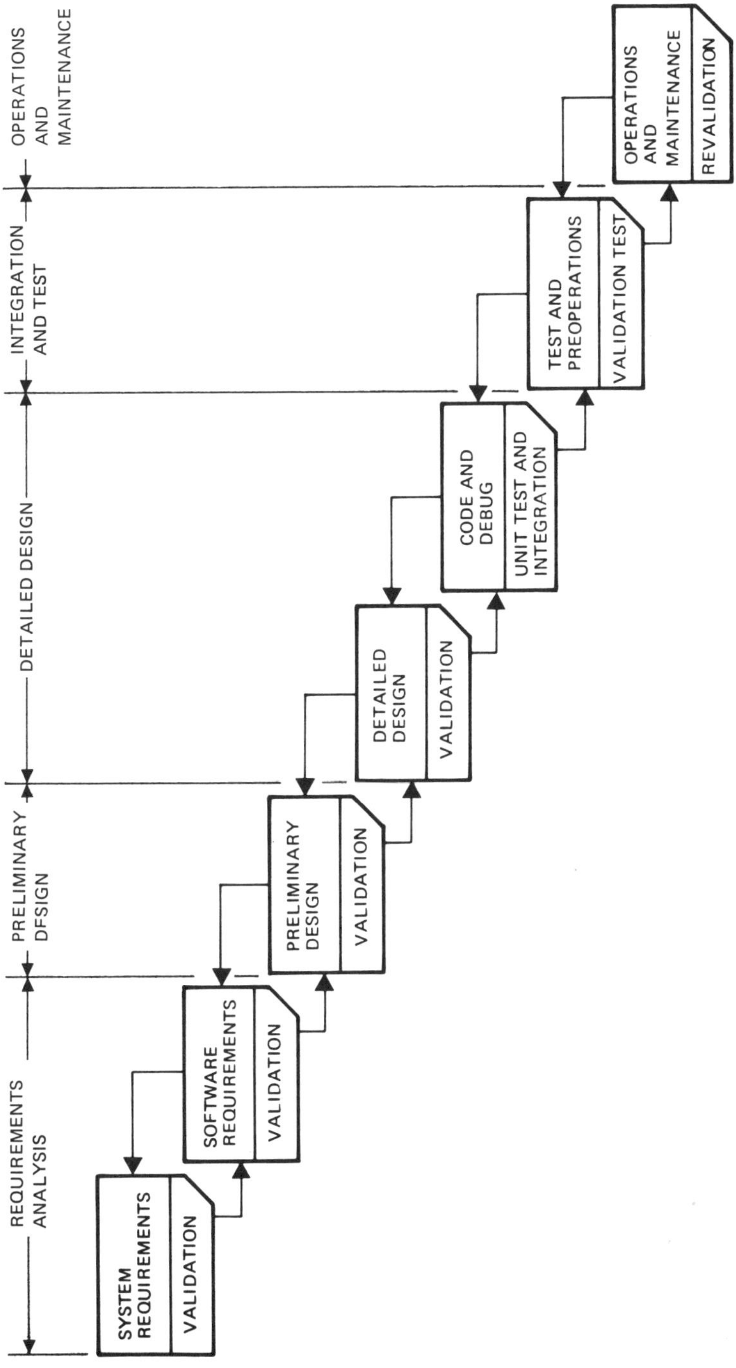

Figure 1-3. The Centralized Software Development Process

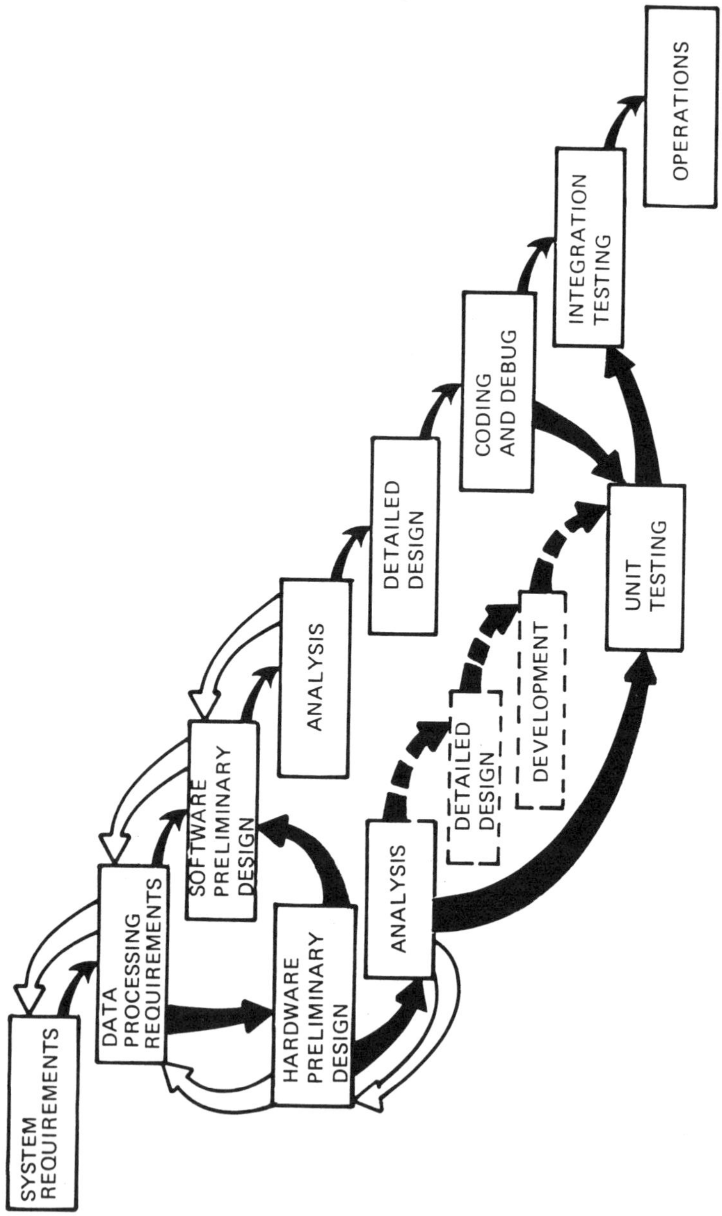

Figure 1-4. Distributed System Design

the computer system level that separate HW and SW requirements (i.e., B-2 and B-5 type specifications) are produced for date processing, and the detailed design phase can start.

With the added complexity of the software design process and the evolution of new basic principles of design, new relationships and sensitivities must be understood, for example:

- SW Design - Data Base Design relationships must be rethought; no longer can the design of the SW processes proceed without consideration of its implication on the data distribution and structure.
- SW Design - Operating System Design relationships must be re-examined both in terms of the control algorithms and overhead implications of requirements, data partitioning/allocation and resulting message traffic.
- SW Design - HW Architecture relationships must be considered in terms of the impact on the selection and/or design of the hardware building blocks; i.e., processors, memory/storage interconnection mechanisms and their control.

The software implementation can now proceed without the constraints of preselected hardware. The ever increasing cost of software relative to hardware (Figure 1-5 [1-8, 1-9]) can now be addressed. By increasing hardware capacity where needed, the designer can afford to use HW inefficiently. Software can now be developed without the HW (processor/memory) utilization constraints which have so severely impacted SW developed costs in the past (Figure 1-6 [1-8, 1-9]).

Early systems of the mid-1950's were driven by HW costs resulting in the predominance of lower-level SW development languages (Figure 1-5, INSERT). In fact, the use of HOL during the 1950's drove HW costs up to the point of causing substantial system costs. The use of lower level machine languages offered reduced total system costs of only a fraction of the system costs under HOL SW development. The use of higher order languages (HOL) such as FORTRAN or PASCAL are now more viable; the time-space penalty can be accommodated with additional low cost computer power and storage. We will continue to see software dominated systems costs. However, the relative system costs (normalized to 1955 dollars) are decreasing with the use of HOL and inefficient, but low cost, hardware.

1.3 THE DISTRIBUTED DESIGN PROBLEM - A PERSPECTIVE

The level of system distribution which we address calls for both partitioned and replicated functions and data, which are distributed over a tightly coupled network of heterogeneous computing resources. The systems employ cooperating resources which must be controlled under stringent real time environments.

A comparison of the centralized software design process with the distributed (HW/SW) design process has revealed the need for a major rethinking of design step. The software requirements and preliminary design steps for centralized systems become a much more complex process as both HW/SW

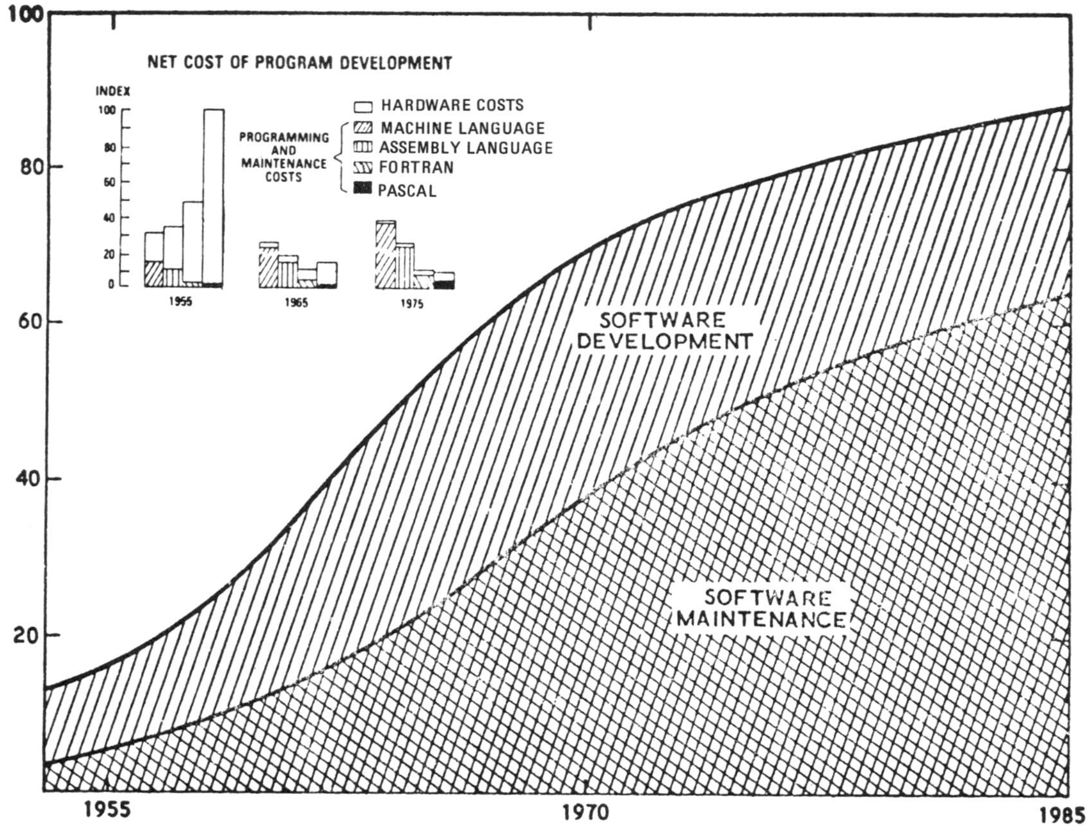

Figure 1-5. Relative Hardware-Software Cost Trends

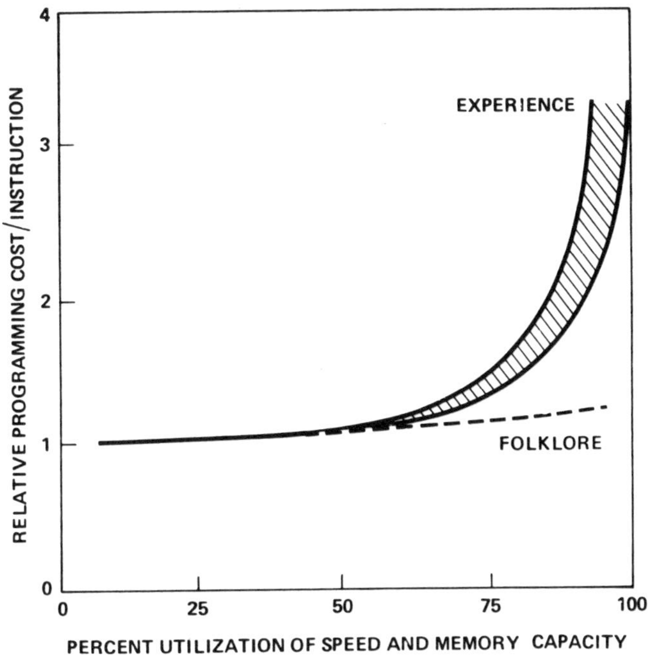

Figure 1-6. Hardware Utilization/Software Cost Relationship

requirements can now be evolved together. This evolutionary design process is a subject of this text. Now in addition to software requirements engineering and software preliminary design, the designers must hierarchically decompose the requirements into "black boxes" at the network, node and finally computer systems levels. This decomposition process is a recursive design process based on a series of four critical steps: elaboration, partitioning, allocation and synthesis.

This recursive process must address several new issues not previously of concern with centralized software development; including,

(1) identification of natural/inherent parallelisms and concurrencies of the problem structure.

(2) function partitioning and allocation to resources.

(3) distributed data base design: file definition, allocation, structuring.

(4) distributed operating system requirements definition.

(5) network specification.

Once the computer system level requirements are defined, the software development process can proceed as we have proceeded with past centralized systems. Of course the computer system may be itself internally distributed and tailored to the problem thus requiring further HW-SW design tradeoffs until SW requirements are defined in a form which we recognize. We will concern ourselves with those design decisions which must take place at the front-end of the distributed design process to translate DP system specifications (A-Spec) into HW and SW specifications for a multi-computer architecture; HW and SW specifications from which computer, communication, applications and system software can be purchased/developed.

1.4 REFERENCES

[1-1] P.H. Enslow, Jr., "What Is a Distributed Data Processing System?", Computer, Janury 1978.

[1-2] M.J. Flynn, "Some Computer Organizations and Their Effectiveness", IEEE Transactions on Computers, Vol. C-21, No. 9, Sept. 1972.

[1-3] K.J. Thurber and H.A. Freeman, "Local Computer Network Architectures", COMPCON 79 Spring, February 1979, pp. 258-261.

[1-4] R.J. Swan, et. al., "CM* - A Modular, Multi-Microprocessor", AFIPS Proceedings, Vol. 46, 1977, NCC, pp. 637-644.

[1-5] W. Wulf and R. Levin, "A Local Network", Datamation, February 1975, pp. 47-50.

[1-6] D.J. Farber, "A Ring Network", Datamation, February 1975, pp. 44-46.

[1-7] D.L. Mills, "An Overview of the Distributed Computer Network", AFIPS Conference Proceedings, Vol. 45, 1976, NCC, pp. 523-531.

[1-8] B.W. Boehm, "Keynote Address to CNR/OAR/AFOSR Symposium on the High Cost of Software", Monterey, Calif., September 1973, TRW-SS-73-08.

[1-9] M.P. Mariani, "Distributed Computer Architecture", IEEE Chapter Tutorial Workbook, Rev. May 1981.

2.0 BASELINE DESIGN TOOLS AND TECHNIQUES

2.1 INTRODUCTION

In this section, the design methods and procedures, and associated tools and techniques are discussed which support the transformation of a DP system specification into HW and SW requirements for a multicomputer architecture [2-0].

The design of distributed systems is heavily driven by a series of four interrelated design phases, i.e.:

Phase 1 - Elaboration,

Phase 2 - Partitioning,

Phase 3 - Allocation,

Phase 4 - Synthesis.

These design phases are apparent at each of the four basic architectural levels of distributed system design:

Level 1 - Geographical Network,

Level 2 - Local Multicomputer Node,

Level 3 - Computer, and

Level 4 - Processor.

The details of the design steps in each of the phases are similar for each of the four levels of the design, only the constraints, payoff priorities, and design parameters change. The elaboration phase is a preparation phase performing the requirements engineering necessary to conduct the design procedure. The partitioning phase is a simplification of the massive requirements and data to reduce the complexity of the subsequent design steps. The allocation phase is one of assigning the requirements to functional, computational and communication resources. Finally, the synthesis phase performs the structuring of the resources into a physical architecture. Each of the four phases consists of several macro design steps.

Figure 2.1-1A provides an overview of the design approach as applied to the node level of design. The four phases and their macro steps are shown. The eleven macro steps which constitutes the design approach is shown in Figure 2.1-1B. Figure 2.1-1B is applicable to all levels of design. Those tools and techniques which are appropriate to each design phase (Figure 2.1-1A) and macro step (Figure 2.1-1B) are indicated by

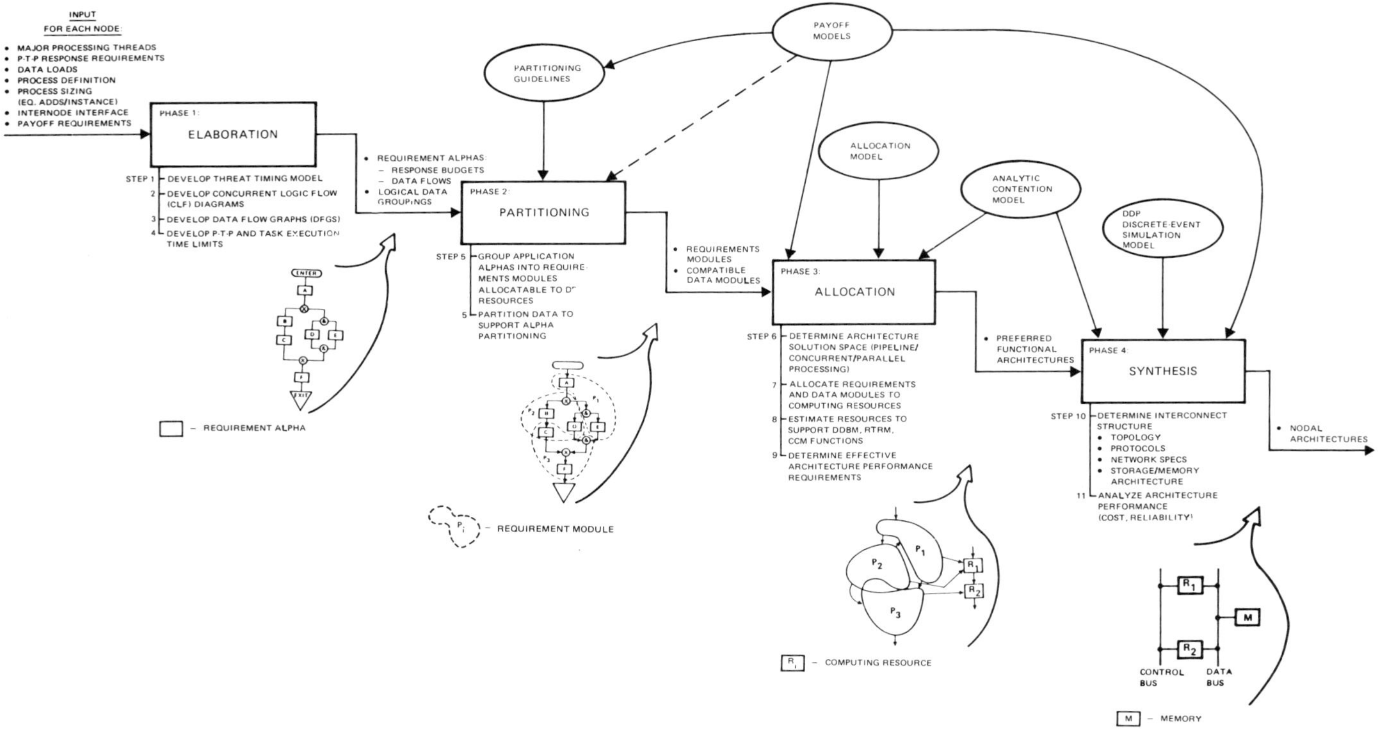

Figure 2.1-1A Node-Level Baseline Design Approach

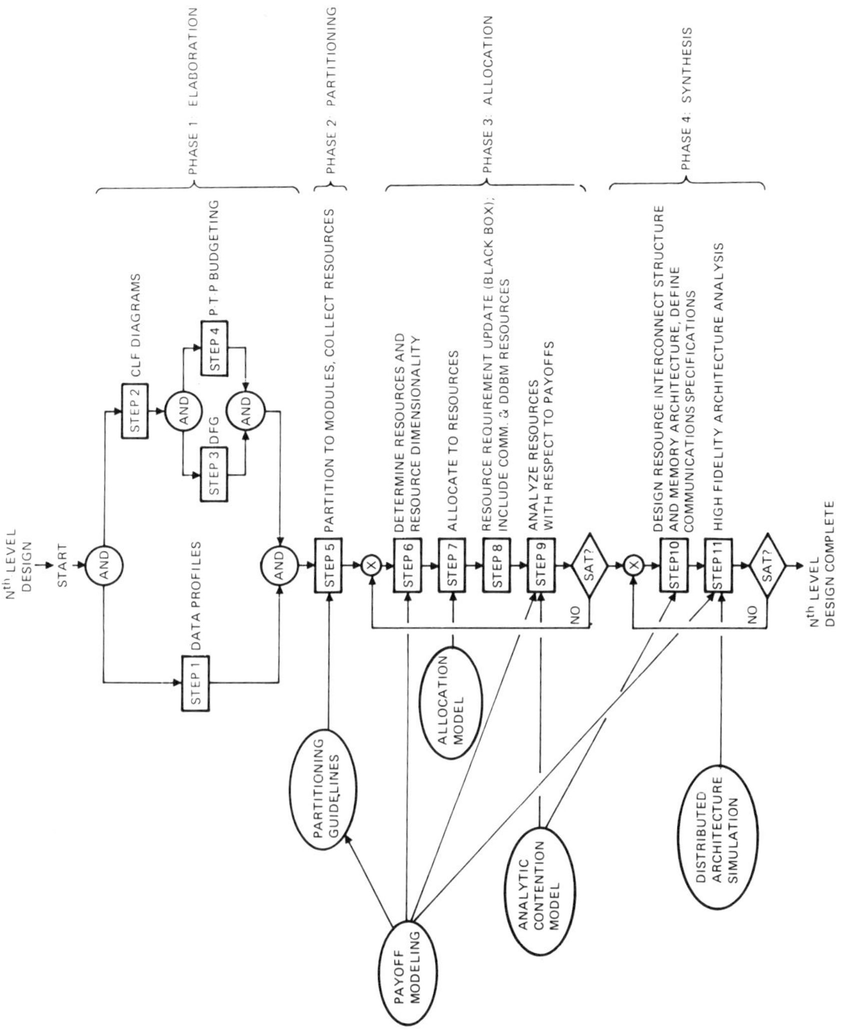

Figure 2.1-1B. DDP Design Approach - Nth Level Overview

means of ovals and the design phase (or macro step) they support by arrows. These tools and techniques include:

- rules and techniques which guide the partitioning of requirements into allocatable modules
- analytic contention models capable of performing preliminary architecture performance evaluation
- allocation models capable of assigning requirement and data modules to computing resources
- parametric payoff models which provide quantitative bases for weighting partition rules and guidelines, and for relative and absolute evaluation of candidate distributed designs.
- distributed architecture simulation models which support detailed analyses of candidate hardware/software architecture designs.

After a short description of each of the four baseline design phases, a discussion of the tools and their use is presented.

2.1.1 Phase 1: Elaboration (STEPS 1-4)

The first phase of design at any architecture level is the elaboration of the requirements. This elaboration phase consists of four macro steps:

STEP 1 - DP driver and environment model development which describes the data loading profiles due to the external stimulus of the applications function over time

STEP 2 - Concurrent Logic Flow (CLF) development which provides a graphical control flow description of inherent parallelisms and logic concurrencies within the applications

STEP 3 - Data Flow Graph (DFG) development which provides an explicit description of data interaction between the application operations

STEP 4 - Port-to-port and task execution time limits development which is based on the decomposition of the system response requirements along the applications logic paths.

In the past, these four macro steps have often been referred to as functional design, and in some instances requirements engineering. In our baseline design approach we use the elaboration phase as requirements preparation; that is, providing explicit description of the application's natural characteristics, data base and response requirements, as well as the external loading profile on the application. Specific emphasis is placed on characterizing the applications and its data access and flow attributes. It is these data attributes on which the partition, allocation and synthesis phases for the corresponding level rely so heavily.

2.1.2 Phase 2: Partitioning (STEP 5)

The second phase of the design process is the definition of requirements modules and data modules which can be allocated to data processing resources. The partitioning process is directed at reducing the inherent complexity of the distributed design problem which is due to the collective considerations of applications requirements, data, concurrency and multiple (payoff) objectives. For even the simplest data processing applications, the design problem may be too complex for conventional manual design techniques. Partitioning offers one approach to simplification of the design problem through a process of grouping of requirements and data into allocatable modules.

The foundation of the partitioning approach lies in the establishment of guidelines which direct the partitioning process. The approach is a two-step approach which first performs partitioning of the applications requirements into modules, then using these results performs partitioning of the data necessary to support the newly partitioned applications modules. The guidelines are derived from the consideration of the multiple objective (payoff) functions which govern the design of the system; including considerations of the payoff of performance, reliability/availability, growth, cost, deployability, form factor, survivability and fault tolerance.

2.1.3 Phase 3: Allocation (STEPS 6-9)

The third phase of the design activity (for the node and computer levels*) is the allocation of both requirement and data modules to functional resources. The allocation process provides initial structuring of the distributed architecture through a preliminary payoff analysis of cost. The allocation process can become combinatorially complex even for moderate design problems when further complicated by the inclusion of design constraints such as resource capacity, placement inclusion/exclusion rules and replication. The baseline allocation phase consists of four macro steps, i.e.,

STEP 6 - Determination of <u>architecture dimensionality</u> which defines the types and number of functional computing resources for requirements and data allocation.

STEP 7 - Allocation of <u>requirements and data modules</u> across the data processing resources identified in prior step.

---

* The allocation phase is not used at the HW/SW (processor) level of design. Instead the two options (HW versus SW) are defined during the partitioning phase (STEP 5).

STEP 8 - Requirement update of functional DP resources to include throughput and storage required to support applications, data base management and communications processing.

STEP 9 - Architecture requirements analysis with respect to performance-cost payoffs.

Collectively these four steps produce a set of preferred functional architectures for synthesis in Phase 4. Three design tools are of use during the allocation phase.

- Payoff models for cost and reliability analyses of candidate configurations
- Allocation model to perform requirement and data module assignments
- Contention model to perform preliminary performance analyses across candidate architectures.

2.1.4 Phase 4: Synthesis (STEPS 10-11)

The fourth and final phase of the design activity is the synthesis phase. This phase performs the physical design of the architecture by developing the resource interconnect topology, physical specifications and protocols. In addition, the storage/memory architecture is developed. The phase consists of two macro steps:

STEP 10 - Design interconnect structure which includes topology, communications protocols and memory architecture for the functional architecture

STEP 11 - High fidelity architecture performance verification at the detailed design level.

Together these two macro design steps produce the architecture specification. The specification developed at one level is used as requirement inputs at the subsequent design level. Three design tools are of use during the synthesis phase.

- Payoff models for cost, and reliability analysis of the selected architecture
- Contention model for preliminary analysis of detailed architecture design decisions prior to simulation.
- Discrete-event simulation model for detailed performance analysis of the architecture

The subsequent sections discusses four key areas of the Design Approach, i.e.,

- Parametric Payoff Modeling
- Partitioning and Decomposition Methods
- Design Allocation Modeling
- Performance Analysis Tools, including
  - Analytic contention modeling
  - Simulation modeling

Research in application representation and analysis have also received extensive attention under requirements engineering [2-7].

2.2 PARAMETRIC PAYOFF MODELS

Parametric "Payoff* Models" support tradeoff analyses between major system level objectives during the architecture design process. The module can be used as a foundation for making/guiding design decisions during the design process as well as verification of the design individual product. The two key issues to the development of such payoff models are their parameterization and quantification.

The selection of those design parameters which have a finite (either positive or negative) influence on the payoff objective can be very difficult, especially for such abstract objectives as deployability or growth. These parameters should include both hardware and software design variables. The development of the analytic relationships of the parameters to the basic payoff can also be extremely complex. In some cases (such as hardware) data can be collected either from previous work experience, vendor supplied information, or experimental results, and regression analysis techniques applied to develop models. In other instances data will be unavailable and subjective estimations of parameter weights must be hypothesized and possibly tested downstream. Subjective weighting techniques must initially be employed for such payoffs as growth and deployability, and currently most parameters associated with software.

Even though analytic models are strived for, their availability is not mandatory. Analyzing the relative weights of all parameters can provide insight into which of the design variables are the key "design swingers". These key parameters can then be used as criteria for function and data partitioning or as the objective function for their allocation to resources. Also parameter tracing can identify tradeoffs which may not have been observed or strengths of tradeoffs based on the payoff sensitivity to changes in the design "design swingers" sited.

2.2.1 Payoff Interrelationships

The hierarchical interrelationships of the payoffs are depicted in Figure 2.2-1 for their hardware and Figure 2.2-2 for their software aspects. From these figures, fault (error) tolerance can be observed to occupy a pivotal position in the payoff hierarchy. This is so because it constitutes one of the two major techniques of achieving low effective failure rates and failure rate is, in turn, a major component of the high level payoffs of availability, reliability and, through the latter, survivability. It can be further noted that fault tolerance can be obtained by redundancy (which also affects survivability via kill probability) or reconfigurability. However, reconfigurability can be defined as the ability to restructure remaining resources in a system not having redundancy and hence implies graceful degradation, or fail-safe behavior, as compared to redundancy which implies overcoming losses (due to failures and/or destruction) without degradation.

Fault-tolerant design is expensive and complicated, but essential for large, complex systems requiring high values for survivability, reliability and availability. Such complex systems can no longer afford to achieve high reliability using more sophisticated HW/SW fabrication techniques to attain higher levels of component inherent fault intolerance.

---

* Performance, survivability, availability, reliability, fault tolerance, growth form factor (power, volume, weight) deployability, and life cycle cost.

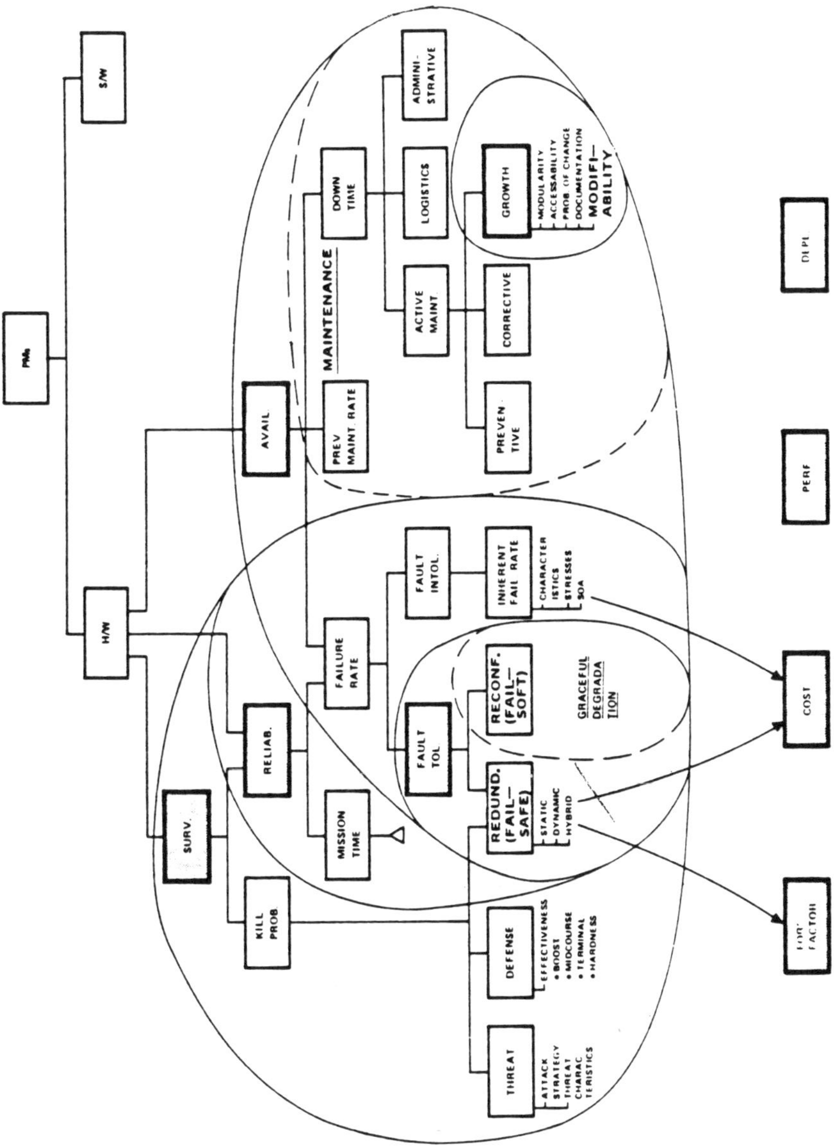

Figure 2.2-1. Payoff Interrelationships (Hardware)

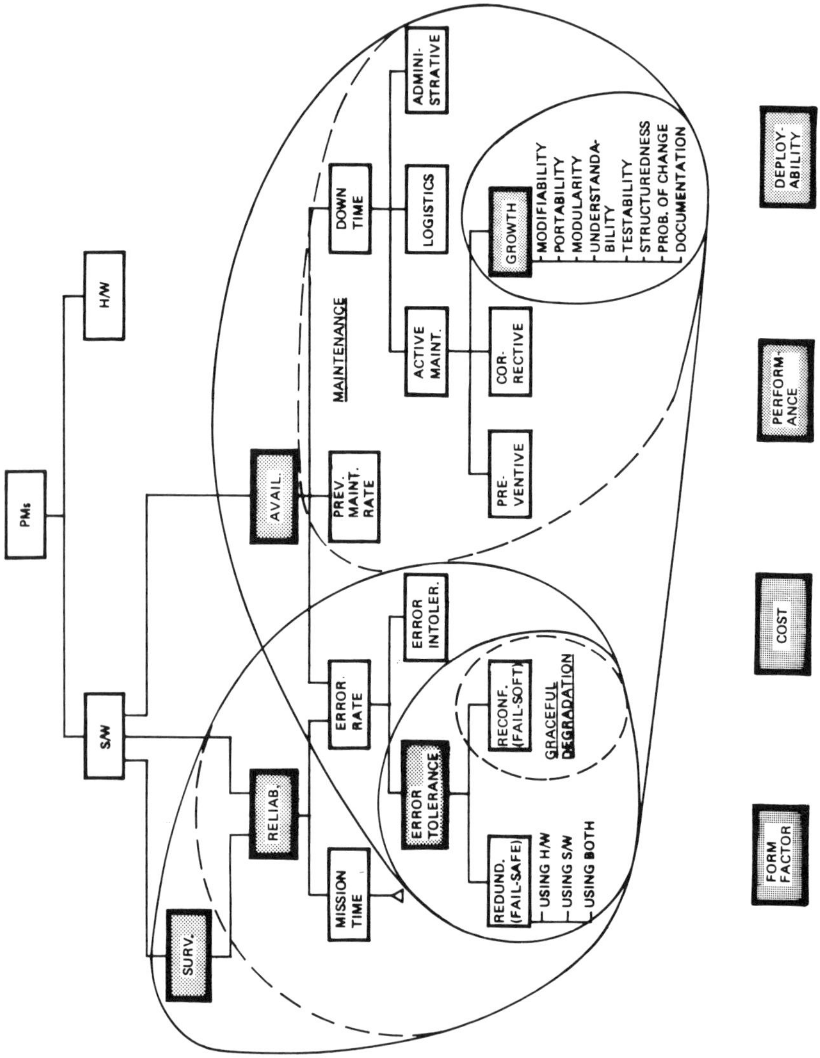

Figure 2.2-2. Payoff Interrelationships (Software)

Instead systems are being developed using a balanced incorporation of fault-tolerant design and fault-intolerant components to meet high-value, system-level payoff requirements of survivability and availability.

The payoff interrelationships for the software aspects (Figure 2.2-2) are very similar to those for the hardware aspects shown in Figure 2.2-1. The major difference is that the software cannot get physically destroyed (killed), other than by destruction of its host hardware, nor "fails" in the hardware sense. As a result software survivability becomes synonymous with software reliability. Software, on the other hand, is well known to contain errors and hence the words "fault" and "failure" in Figure 2.2-1 have been replaced with the word "error" in Figure 2.2-2.

2.2.2 Payoff "Trees"

Delineation of those design variables which affect a payoff model and the subsequent formulation of analytic relationships can be greatly enhanced through hierarchical structuring of the parameters into payoff "trees". (Figure 2.2-3). The "tree" is used to represent functional dependencies between the design variables - variables which are design controllable and/or quantifiable. At the lowest level of the "tree" the basic fundamental design variables are delineated. Each ascending level of the tree represents an aggregation of the previous level into HW/SW building block components of the architecture.

For the hardware aspects of some payoffs (survivability, reliability, availability, form factor, cost) the body of knowledge is sufficiently developed to accomplish the aggregation process in a reasonable manner. Other payoffs (performance, fault tolerance, growth and deployability) and software aspects require extensive research to develop a methodology which can be used with ease and confidence.

To facilitate the payoff measure parameterizing, structuring and decomposition process, payoff measure hierarchical trees could be generated. The decomposition of the payoff measures is further necessitated by the fact that the data required for quantification, if available, is found at the lower component levels.

The basic structure of the payoff tree (Figure 2.2-3) shows the potential dual (hardware/software) nature of payoffs and their hierarchical decomposition by component levels. The basic structure is modified (amplified, reduced, changed) to accommodate specific payoff measure properties. For instance, the life cycle cost payoff tree was modified to permit a cost breakdown by life cycle phases [design, development, verification and validation (V&V), operations and maintenance (O&M)]. Using the information contained in the payoff trees, the next step is to generate models, algorithms or relationships for each component level which allows quantification of the parameter at the next higher level.

The ease with which quantification can be developed varies significantly from payoff measure to payoff measure. Although the formulation of some payoff measures (e.g., survivability, reliability/availability, cost, form factor) is more straight forward than others (deployment, growth, performance), all are very difficult. However, in

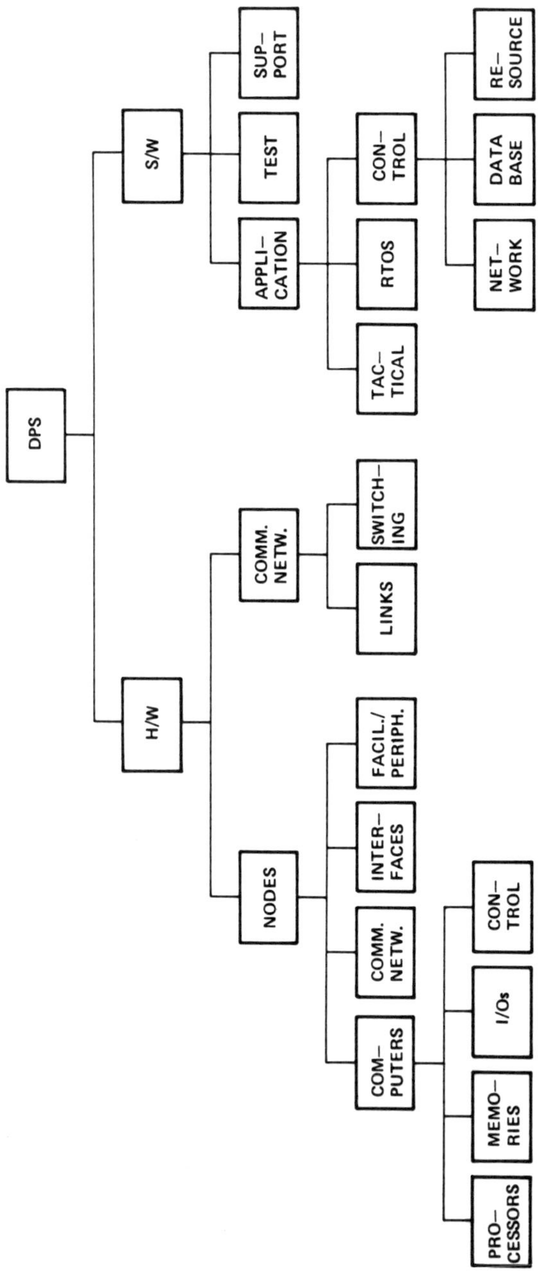

Figure 2.2-3. Payoff Tree General Structure

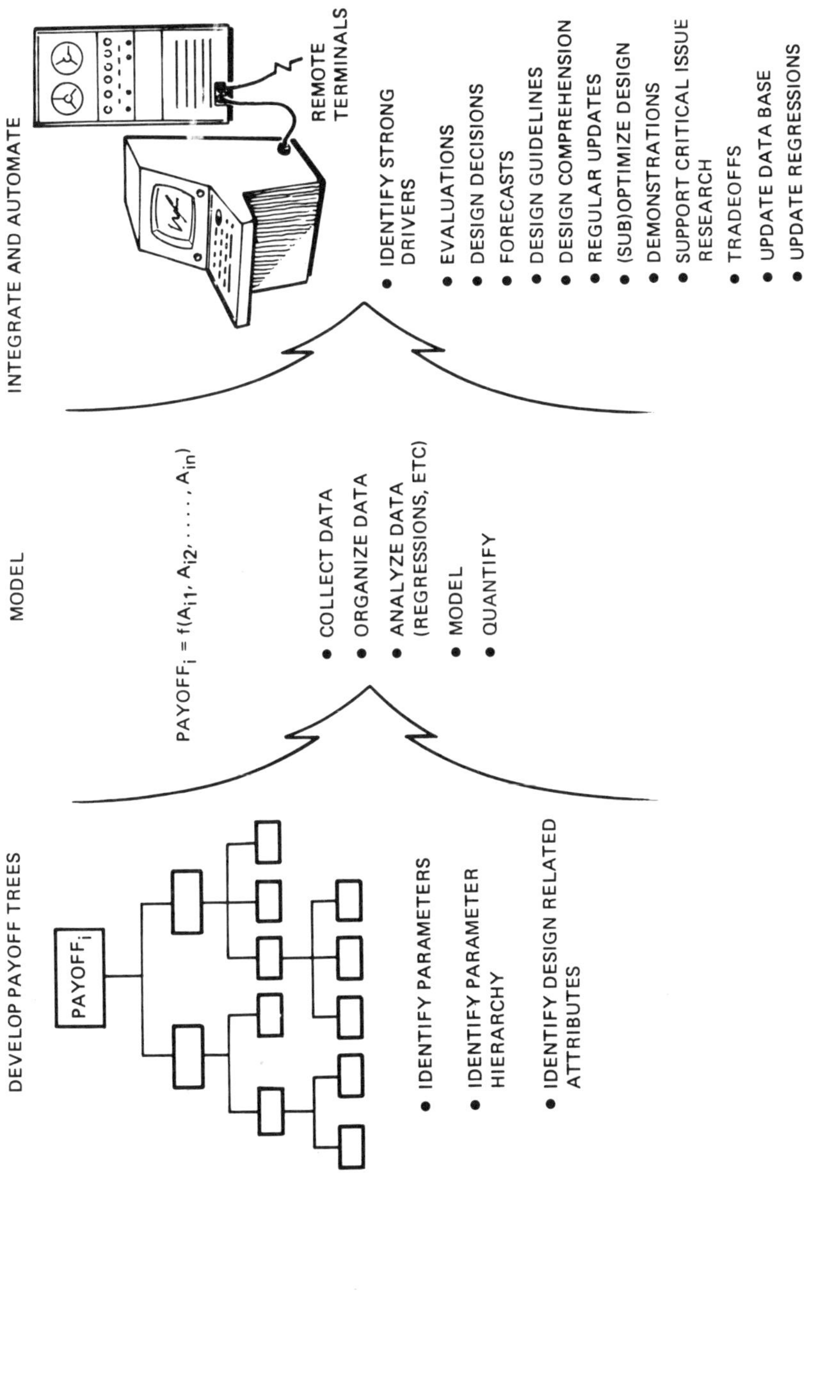

Figure 2.2-4. Payoff Development

both cases the methodology is the same (Figure 2.2-4). Whenever necessary and possible, the formulation includes the development of estimating relationships using regression analysis techniques applied to historical data. Forward extrapolations should be added to enable prediction of future trends to enhance the value of the design decisions. Finally, the resultant set of formulations should be implemented in an automated design facility to support the formulation of the objective functions for each design decision of the design process.

2.2.3 Payoff Measure Development

To illustrate the payoff measure approach and the concept of payoff "trees" we will discuss three candidate payoffs, reliability, fault tolerance and life cycle cost. Finally, we will discuss a data base which has been defined for use in building the analytic payoff models.

2.2.3.1 Reliability

2.2.3.1.1 Definition

Reliability of a system is commonly defined as "the probability of performing a specified function or mission under specified conditions for a specified time".

The above definition is simple enough, but, at levels above the part or subassembly level, especially for large, complex systems, it is potentially wrought with complications.

This definition makes reliability a system level payoff and for systems which are exposed to physical destruction, such as military ones, it is a major ingredient of the survivability payoff measure as shown in Figure 2.2-1. This figure also clearly indicates that failure rate, more precisely the apparent failure rate, and everything that goes into that (i.e., fault tolerance, fault intolerance, etc.) is the parameter that is common to both reliability and availability. Furthermore, if it were not for mission time, reliability and failure rate would be synonymous as they are often used.

In the following paragraphs some of the complexities contained in the words of the above reliability definition are explained.

Performing a Function or Mission

Since large, complex sytems may be able to carry out more than one type of mission (e.g., an aircraft may be used for a reconnaissance, bombing, intercept, or strafing mission), separate reliability models for each of these missions may be in order to make the problem more tractable.

Whereas ballistic missile defense (BMD) distributed data processing (DDP) systems are basically unimodal from a mission point of view, they are multimodal from a functional point of view. They must perform various system level functions such as search, detect, track, discriminate and intercept. Each of these functions may require different combinations

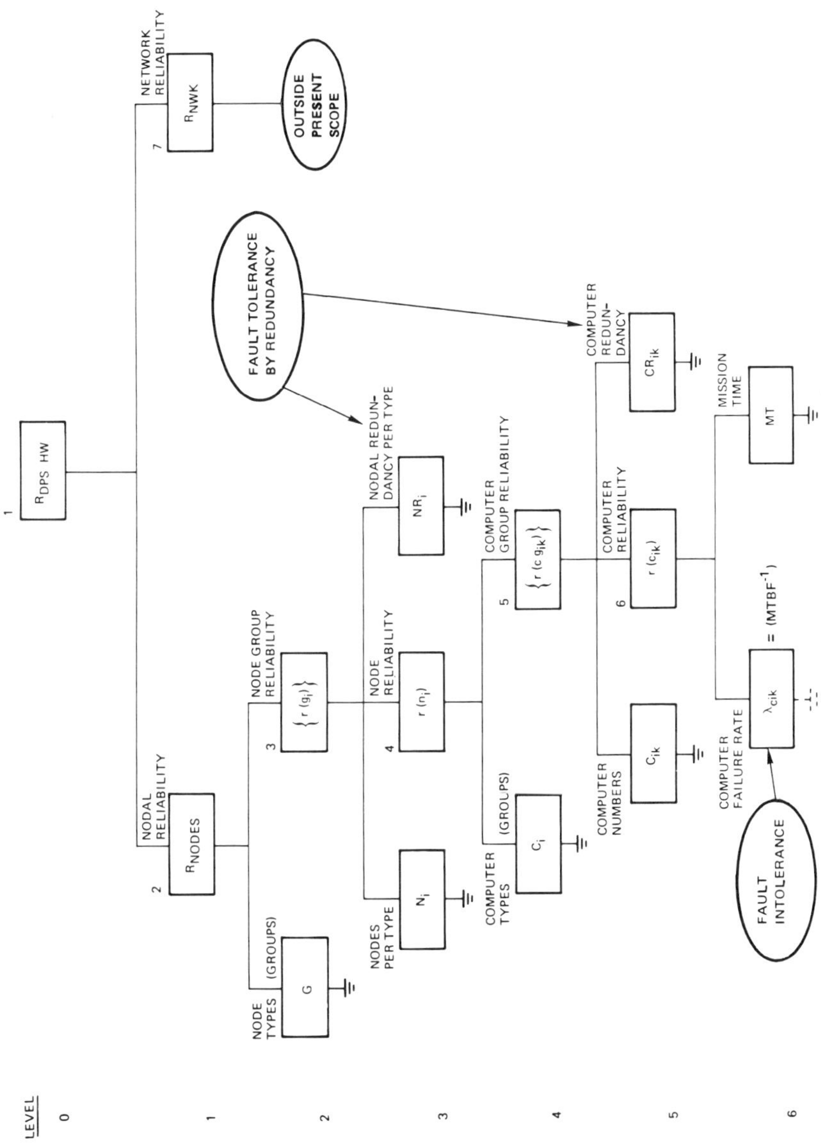

Figure 2.2-5. Reliability Payoff Tree

of system elements for different segments of the mission timeline, as a first-order reliability partitioning. A second-order partitioning could be made in accordance with mission time segments during which certain functions are in effect.

In any case, for each mission or function, the system's performance parameters and their allowable limits must be carefully defined, in other words, what constitutes performing a function (mission) must be made abundantly clear.

Under Specified Conditions

Reliability is a function of the conditions under which the system must perform its mission or function. That is, the stresses imposed on the system play an important role in the reliability that can be achieved. The stresses are environmental such as ambient temperature, humidity, vibration, shock, nuclear radiation, electromagnetic pulses (EMP), electronic countermeasures (ECM); internal such as power, voltage, current: and operational such as duty cycle.

Again, for large, complex systems different parts of the system may see entirely different stresses as well as at different time segments in the mission. For example, BMD DDP system components may be ground-based, airborne or space-based. Each of these environments poses different stress levels. Careful definition of the environmental and operational stress conditions is required for reliability evaluations.

In summary, reliability modeling must take into account that -

- multi-mission systems may see different environmental and operational stresses for different missions
- systems may consist of different segments which operate in different environments during the same mission
- systems or system segments may see different stresses during a given mission (for instance, satellite boost, orbit, reentry and recovery phases).

The "specified conditions" apply only to the hardware aspects since the software is indifferent to environmental and operational stresses.

For a Specified Time

Mission duration also poses problems in the reliability modeling of large, complex systems. Certain system elements may have mission time requirements much different from other ones. For example, a BMD system may have a satellite for early warning, which may have a mission time of a number of years while the ground-based terminal defense segment may have a mission time of a few minutes. Also, as pointed out earlier, a given segment may have time-varying internal and/or environmental stresses.

2.2.3.1.2 Reliability Payoff Tree

Figure 2.2-5 shows the decomposition of the data processing subsystem reliability payoff measure for a distributed data processing system.

In the following paragraphs each of the levels of decomposition is discussed starting at the network level (Level 1).

Level 1 - Network Level

DPS hardware reliability is determined by both the reliability of the nodal complex and that of the network connecting the nodes.

Level 2 - Node Group Level

As for survivability and availability the existence of different node types is recognized by treating nodes of the same type (operating capability) as a node group. The reliability of the nodal structure is a function of the reliabilities of the node groups, since each node group must be operable for the data processing system nodal structure to be sound.

Level 3 - Node Group Redundancy

The reliability of any node group depends on the degree of redundancy provided in that group as well as the reliability of the individual nodes.

Level 4 - Computer Group Level

The reliability of individual nodes in a given node group depends on the reliabilities of the serially dependent components in the node. Figure 2.2-5 shows only the computer components, however, the intercomputer network and the I/O devices for the node also need to be included at this level.

Level 5 - Computer Group Redundancy

This level is similar to level 3 except that it is for computer group reliability rather than node group reliability.

Level 6 - Computer Failure Rate

It is at this level where reliability deviates from availability and instead looks like the node failure branch of the survivability payoff measure. This level shows that computer reliability is a function of its computer failure rate* and the mission time (duration).

The inherent failure rate of computers (or any other component) refers to the fault intolerance of such components. Fault intolerance deals with failure prevention, fault tolerance with failure masking and is of crucial importance in the payoff hierarchy. Its relationship to reliability is shown in Figure 2.2-6.

Fault tolerance is a payoff measure in its own right and will be discussed next.

---

* Failure rate equals the inverse of mean time between failure (MTBF); i.e., $\lambda = 1/\text{MTBF}$.

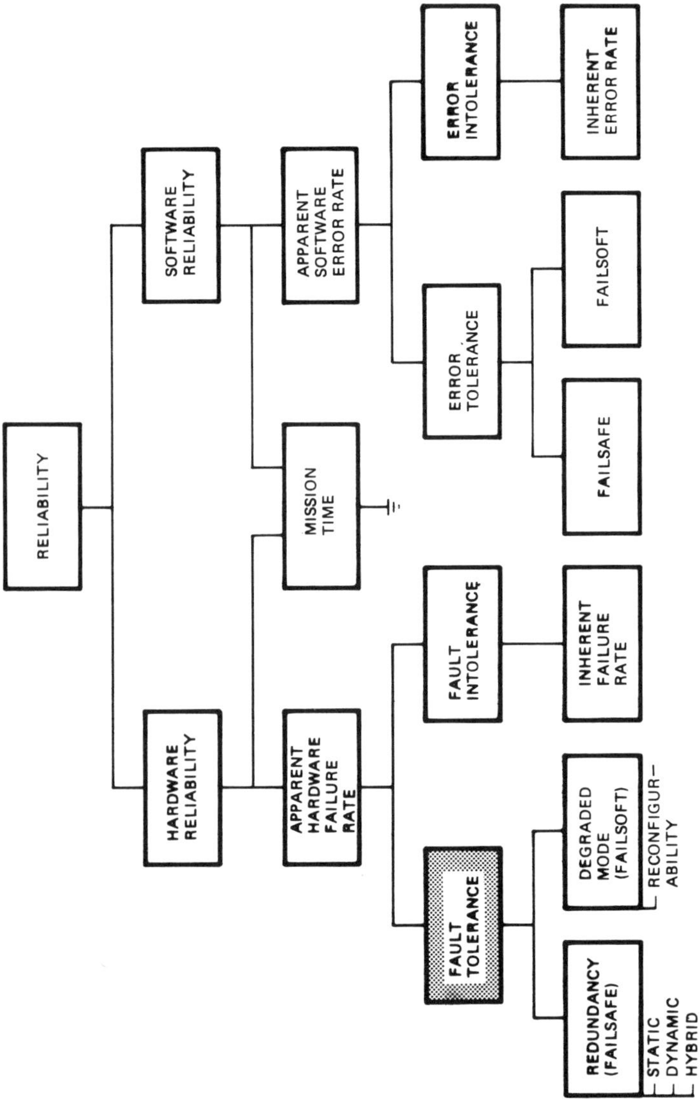

Figure 2.2-6. Fault Tolerance Relationship to Reliability

2.2.3.2 Fault Tolerance

2.2.3.2.1 Definition

The fundamental concepts and terminolofy of Fault Tolerance are under continuing scrunity [2-25]. However, for our discussion, fault tolerance may be defined as follows:

> "Fault tolerance of a data processing system is the capability of the data processing subsystem to overcome hardware failures and/or software errors without human intervention."

Fault tolerance has become such an important, but difficult, approach to improve reliability/availability that it has developed into a significant field of study. Because of its importance, complexity, and difficulty it has been given payoff measures status even though it is in reality a parameter of availability and reliability (and hence survivability). Whereas fault intolerance is an attempt to provide failure prevention, fault tolerance deals with failure resillience.

Fault-tolerant features are very design controllable and conveniently applied at the node and intranodal component levels. Fault tolerance interrelates strongly with the survivability, availability, reliability, form factor and cost payoffs and with fault intolerance. Therefore, it provides a large (but complex) spectrum of tradeoffs. Fault tolerance can be achieved by a broad scope of design options. By judicious consideration of fault tolerance design options, it is possible to achieve a DPS balanced with respect to survivability, availability, reliability, form factor and cost.

2.2.3.2.2 Discussion

Systems (or system components) whose maintenance is difficult (located in remote and/or hostile environments, e.g., in polar regions, rugged mountains, enemy territory, or ocean-based) or impossible (spacecraft unless serviceable by space shuttle), demands high availability and reliability. But even for maintainable systems it may become ineffecient to meet stringent system reliability/availability demands, through fault-intolerant components, as system size and complexity increase (a definite, if not natural, tendency) and as the consequences of failure become more traumatic. For instance, the U.S. Air Force decided that it could not hope to achieve undegraded operation for its space based computers for five years by relying exclusively on individual component fault intolerance and is using a "self-healing" spaceborne computer having a reliability of 0.95 for a five year mission duration (see Figure 2.2-7).

The answer appears to lie in fault-tolerant design as an adjunct to the use of highly fault-intolerant components. Whereas the application of fault intolerance is an attempt to prevent failures from occurring, fault-tolerant design strives to correct (heal) failures when they do occur.

Fault tolerance has basically two major aspects, i.e., reconfigurability and redundancy. These aspects will be discussed next.

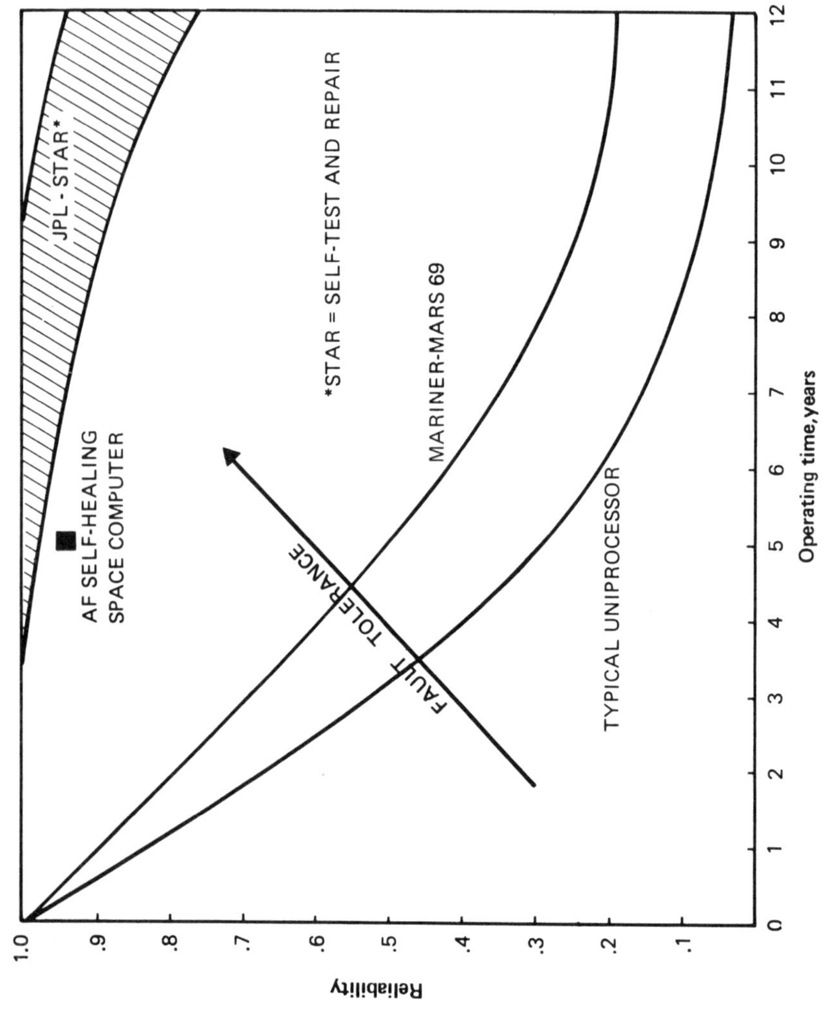

Figure 2.2-7. Fault Tolerance and Reliability

Reconfigurability

Reconfigurability is synonymous with fail-soft operation or graceful degradation, i.e., upon occurrence of a failure the system reconfigures itself so that catastrophic system failure is averted but system performance may be degraded. Reconfigurability does not need to involve redundant components when providing only partial fault tolerance - under graceful degradation.

Fault tolerance by redundancy, on the other hand, allows failures without performance degradation, i.e., fail-safe operation. Systems which exhibit effective operational "dependability" [2-25] must possess both fail-soft and fail-safe characteristics.

Redundancy

Redundancy provides fault-tolerance by adding duplicate components. Basically, two categories of redundancy implementation have been identified, i.e., static and dynamic redundancies. Static redundancy means that extra components are added on-line (powered) which share the load and whose outputs are compared and voted on. Dynamic redundancy means that extra components (spares) are added off-line (standby) which are switched in automatically to replace failed components. The third one, hybrid redundancy, is, of course, a combination of the basic categories.

Redundancy increases reliability/availability, but, by its nature, at the expense of cost, form factor (volume, weight, power) and simplicity.

Static Redundancy. Static redundancy techniques, often referred to as "fault-masking" or "parallel redundancy" employ multiple, identical components operating simultaneously in parallel/series configurations to protect against "failed-open" and "failed short" situations or in parallel-with-voting configurations to protect against failure-caused errors. This way the effects produced by faulty elements will be masked (or voted) out by properly functioning neighboring elements. Examples of static redundancy architectures are component quadding (at the part level) and multiple (usually triple) line voting schemes (at higher component levels), called NMR (N-modular redundancy, where: $N = 2n + 1$) which permit n module failures without system degradation. Static redundancy has advantages and disadvantages. If it is applied massively, i.e., everything is at least doubled, it is very expensive and increases the form factor (volume, weight, power) considerably. This can be improved by selectively applying static redundancy only to high failure rate and/or high risk components. Furthermore, for long mission durations (spaceborne elements) and/or high inherent component failure rates, the application of static redundancy becomes counter-productive. This is due to one of the disadvantages of static redundancy, i.e., all components are powered which involves higher failure rates than for unpowered standby components.

Typically, at the time beyond which the reliability of individual elements of the network is less than 0.5, the reliability of a static redundant network becomes less than that of an equivalent nonredundant network due to the permeating influence of faulty elements.

An advantage of static redundancy is that it is simple and introduces a minimum of the inherent unreliability introduced by the redundant design. This arises from the fact that static redundancy does not require fault detection, isolation and recovery devices and techniques, nor interruptions or delays of operation, as is the case with dynamic redundancy.

An important side feature of static redundancy, not mentioned in the literature, is that it can provide excess capacity when no or few failures have occurred (not unlikely for short mission times). This may permit the system to cope effectively with larger than expected loads.

Finally, the nature of multiprocessor computer architectures is such that they offer redundancy as an inherent property when task loading does not demand the use of all processors/memories of a multiprocessor configuration.

Dynamic Redundancy. Dynamic redundancy, also referred to as "standby sparing," consists of providing extra units which automatically replace defective ones. One of the advantages of dynamic over static redundancy is that only failed units are duplicated rather than all units, i.e. it is selective rather than massive. This more efficient use of redundant components is obtained at the expense of the need for additional features such as fault detection, isolation and recovery, which, in turn, pose unreliability problems of their own. Furthermore this causes interruptions and/or delays in operations during recovery. Another advantage is that the standby units are unpowered which, as a rule, means lower failure rates.

As Avizienis [2-27] points out, the application of dynamic redundancy to a computer architecture requires that design choices must be made in the functional design state, and their additional resources (computation and storage) accounted for. These choices include:

Modularization, i.e., define a modular computer architecture with emphasis on a minimal number of intermodule connections; consider functional modules versus partitioning into subcomputers. Rennels Experience indicates that the degree of subdivision into replaceable (spareable) modules is guided and limited by the following considerations:

1) Since reliability is strongly influenced by the weakest link in the critical chain, partitioning should be such that the resulting modules and their fault-tolerant designs produce modules possessing about the same module reliability.

2) Too fine a subdivision into replaceable modules may be ineffective due to the unreliability of the recovery and interconnect structures.

3) Computational primitives which are closely related should be placed in the same module to minimize interconnects and to enhance computational efficiency.

Fault Detection, i.e., select real-time fault-detection methods.

Recovery, i.e., select appropriate, real-time recovery procedures.

"Hard Core" Protection, i.e., protect those parts of the system which provide the fault detection and recovery capabilities and are required to function correctly before a recovery can take place.

Intermodule Communication, i.e., choose between communication by bus or individual module-to-module paths, a major tradeoff.

Hybrid Redundancy. Hybrid redundancy, provides fault tolerance by a combination of both static and dynamic redundancy.

An example of a hybrid-redundant computer system is the JPL-STAR (Jet Propulsion Laboratory Self-Test and Repair) computer [2-27] and the U.S. Air Force's self-healing spacecraft computer. Figure 2.2-7 demonstrates the dramatic effects on computer reliability of fault-tolerant design.

2.2.3.2.3 Software Aspects

So far only the hardware aspects of fault tolerance have been discussed. However, tolerance to software errors is of considerable importance since the production of error-intolerant software has reached only limited success. In addition, software can be, and is often, used to support or augment fault-tolerant design. The software aspect of fault tolerance awaits considerable research and analysis before it can be used effectively in the context of parametric modeling.

2.2.3.3 Life Cycle Cost

2.2.3.3.1 Definition

The data processing life cycle cost (LCC) is defined as follows:

> "The data processing subsystem (DPS) life cycle cost is the cumulative cost to design, develop, validate, operate and maintain the software and hardware of the DPS".

Hence, it is the cost associated with the data processing subsystem, including both hardware and software, starting with the allocation of the requirements to the DPS and ending with the removal from service. Figure 2.2-8 illustrates the four major phases of the life cycle cost and the next two lower levels for the development phase.

2.2.3.3.2 Hardware Aspects

Hardware costing is complex but reasonably straightforward. The major part of hardware costs is incurred in acquisition during the implementation aspect of the development phase (see Figure 2.2-8). For this reason this branch of the life cycle cost payoff has been further developed as illustrated in Figure 2.2-9. At the nodal level, the hardware consists of networked multiple computers, internally distributed computers with multiple processors and associated memories and I/O devices. The major cost drivers for each of the computer building blocks are listed under each of the boxes of the sixth level in Figure 2.2-9. The interrelations of these cost drivers lead to hardware tradeoffs. For example:

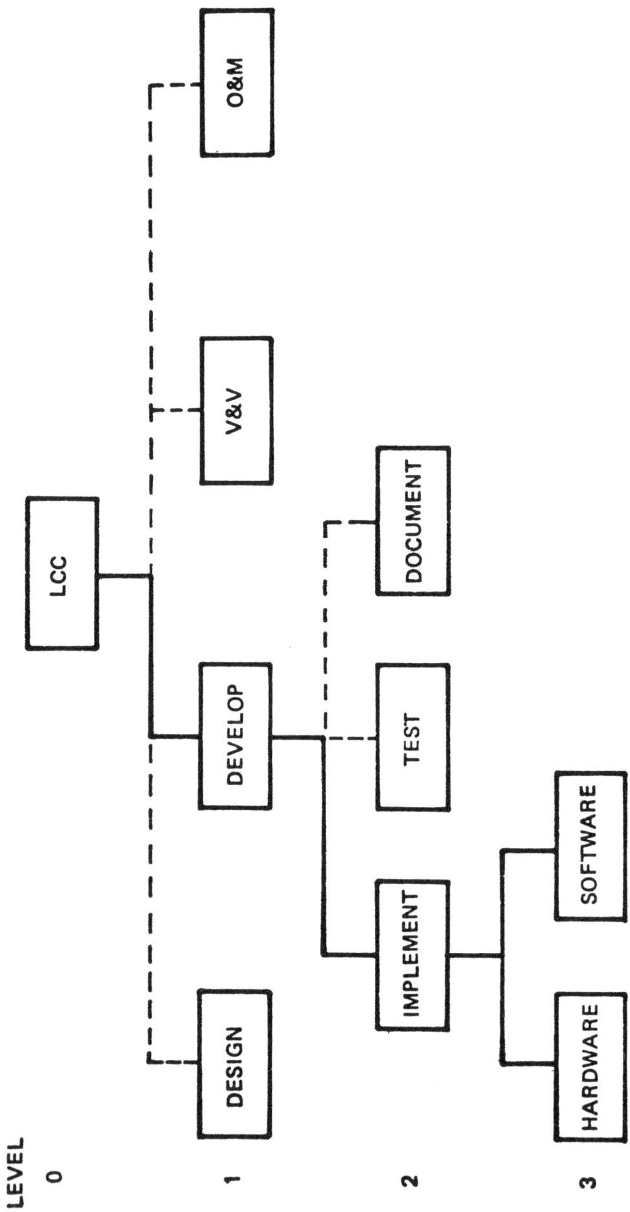

Figure 2.2-8. Major Components of Data Processing Life Cycle Cost

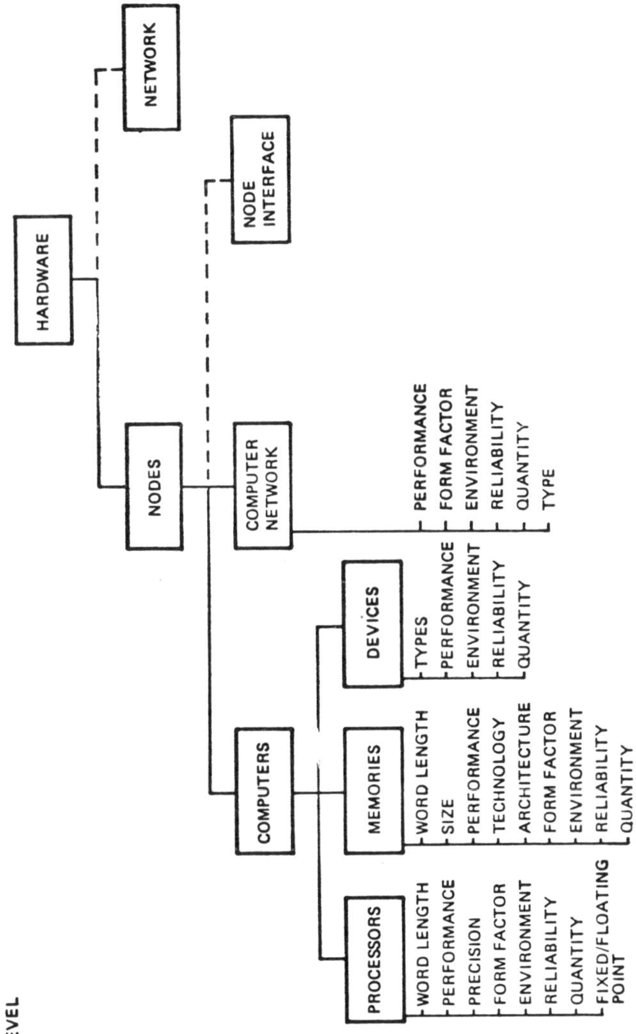

Figure 2.2-9. Hardware Acquisition Cost Decomposition

- Word length and precision relate to the design variable of accuracy.

- Performance is usually expressed in terms of the speed at which single instructions, instruction mixes or benchmark programs are executed and/or of memory access speed and cycle time.

- Form factor considerations of volume, weight and power are factors which can be critical for air- or spaceborne nodes.

- The environment in which the data processing subsystem must operate can have a significant impact on cost. Environments can range from benign to severe with cost ranging accordingly.

- Reliability involves the fault intolerance (inherent failure rate) of a component. Low failure rates can be obtained at a price but only up to a point. For very high reliability requirements redundancy is needed. If degraded performance is allowed dynamic reconfigurability will provide some degree of fail-soft behavior.

- Quantity refers to the number of a single component type needed, including redundant ones, to achieve a desired level of reliability (see reliability above) and system performance.

2.2.3.3.3 Software Aspects

Figure 2.2-10 [1-8] demonstrates the trend of the software contribution to the total data processing subsystem cost. This tendency is so strong that by 1985 the software cost is expected to run close to 90% of the total dp subsystem cost. This is in part a consequence of rapidly declining hardware cost, but to a greater extent due to increasing software (a labor-intensive product) cost. At the same time maintenance is taking a much larger bite (73% projected for 1985 versus 35% in 1955) out of the software cost dollar -- a message for the quality aspects of the data processing design problem.

Software cost modeling has been found to be elusive and the results of efforts to-date are sparse and limited in their usefulness. From a cursory survey nine models were identified, eight of which consider development costs only and one O&M costs only. None provide life cycle costing. Yet, O&M costs are estimated to cost the user up to many times the combined software and hardware acquisition costs.

Figure 2.2-11 illustrates the manner in which software decomposes for the purpose of cost estimation. The major components of the tactical software are shown to be:

- Distributed real-time control (DRTC) software which provides resource management capabilities in the

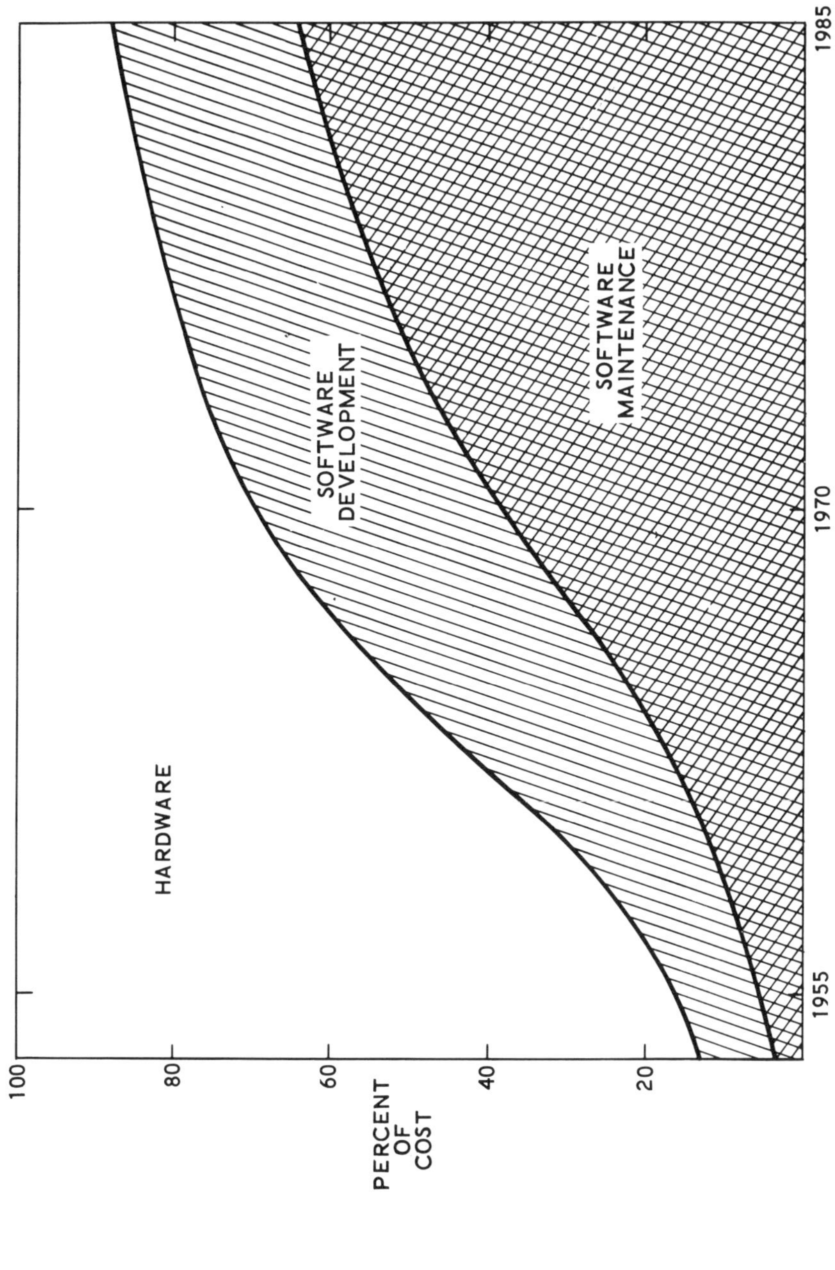

Figure 2.2-10. Hardware-Software Cost Trends

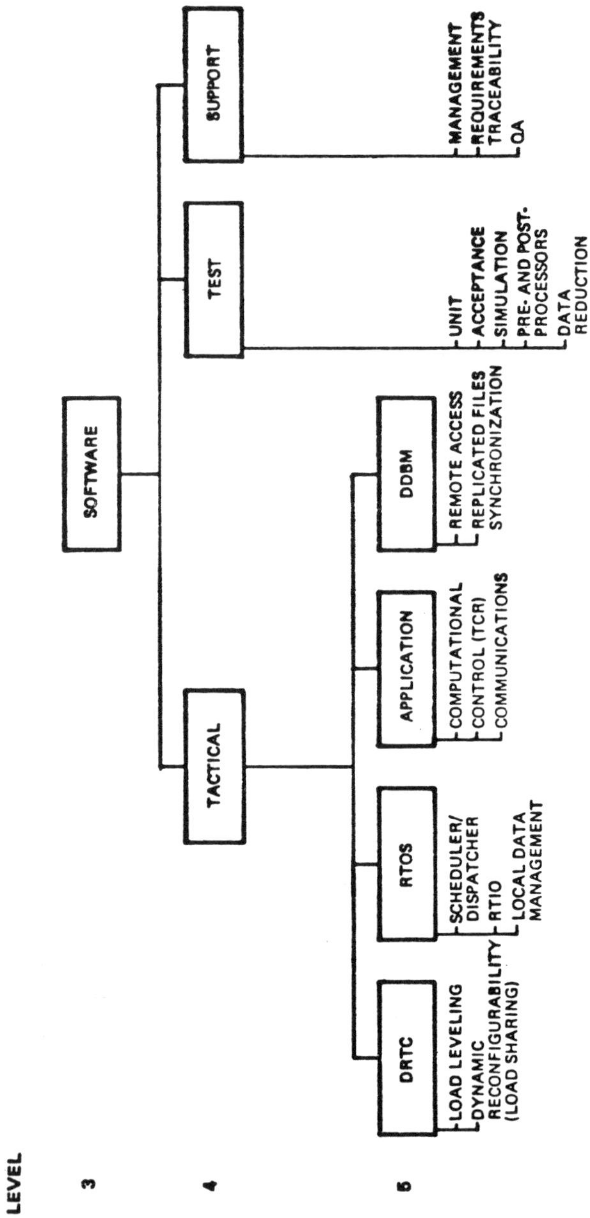

Figure 2.2-11. Software Acquisition Cost Decomposition

form of load leveling, load shedding, and dynamic reconfiguration.

- Real time operating system (RTOS) which provides scheduling, dispatching, input/output and local data management services.

- Application software which provides the user dependent services

- Distributed data base management (DDBM) software to support remote access of data files and synchronization of replicated files at various locations.

Even though software cost modeling is in its infancy, considerable consensus exists that a major software cost driver is the size of the program in terms of deliverable, executable, machine language instructions (DEMIs). A recent and promising cost model is discussed in [2-2]. Given the DEMIs and other information the model computes the cost in man-months for each of the software development phases. It requires a productivity (manmonths per DEMI) rate as input for each part of the software having different degrees of complexity (for instance, productivity can range from as good as 0.33 to 1 manmonth (mm) per 1000 DEMIs for personal software to as poor as 10-33 mm/1000 DEMIs for real-time deliverable software). Some of the other cost drivers considered by the model are the following:

- language order (from microcode to HOLS)
- development computer accessability; user turnaround (from batch to timeshare)
- computer experience
- adaptability to similar program
- requirements volatility
- speed requirement
- storage characteristics
- quality requirements
- applications experience

The model does not account for maintenance cost - like virtually all cost models - , however, Figure 2.2-12 provides an indication of how language level and program size affect maintenance cost.

2.2.4 Payoff Data Base Development and Use

In order to support the development of payoff models and estimating relationships and to make meaningful forecasts, data on the design-controllable and payoff-influential data processing subsystem parameters must be collected and organized. Regression analyses are then performed on the data to identify and establish estimating relationships and to carry out forecasts.

2.2.4.1 Data Collection and Matrix

Computer data were initially collected and organized in the form shown in Figure 2.2-13 which is an example taken from TRW's "Computer matrix" document [2-3]. The matrix consists of a large amount of hardware data which has been collected and organized into a multidimensional computer matrix. The matrix consists of data collected on specific items of data processing hardware (computers, processors, memories, etc.). Each item of hardware is a row entry, its characteristics are shown in columns to the extent known and applicable. Figure 2.2-13 depicts a single sheet of the matrix. For convenience, the sheet has been divided up into four parts (A, B, C and D).

For any data base to be useful, however, it must remain up to date and readily accessible. In the computer field, with its explosive and hard-to-predict growth rate and pattern, data freshness and up-to-dateness are difficult to maintain unless the data base is regularly updated.

2.2.4.2 Automation

To make the data base readily accessible and regression analyses manageable, automation was instituted at the Ballistic Missile Defense Advanced Technology Center (BMDATC) Advanced Research Center's (ARC) data processing facilities in Huntsville, Alabama. The data presently contained in the matrix (Figure 2.2-13) consists of 475 computing elements from 92 vendors obtained from 112 references and was transferred to the CDC 7600 and organized using the Requirements Engineering and Validation System (REVS) as a data base management tool. The data base was structured using REVS' Extended Requirements Statement Language (RSLXTND) capability which allows users to define their own language for interacting with a relational data base. The language entities defined are as follows:

1. Elements (the "nouns" of the language)
2. Attributes of the elements (the "adjectives")
3. Relationships between the elements (the "verbs")

Specific names of the entities are listed in [2-2] and are defined in [2-4]. Figure 2.2-14 illustrates the manner in which the computer elements relate to each other as well as to other data bases.

The data can be extracted using the Requirements Analysis and Data Extraction (RADX) program which is part of REVS. Examples of some query types possible with RADX are shown in Figure 2.2-15 through 2.2-17 (taken from [2-4]).

Data is entered and/or changed using the Requirements Statement Language (RSL), a component of REVS.

2.2.4.3 Analyses

The ability to quickly obtain the functional, physical, environmental, cost, etc., characteristics of a particular computing element or to

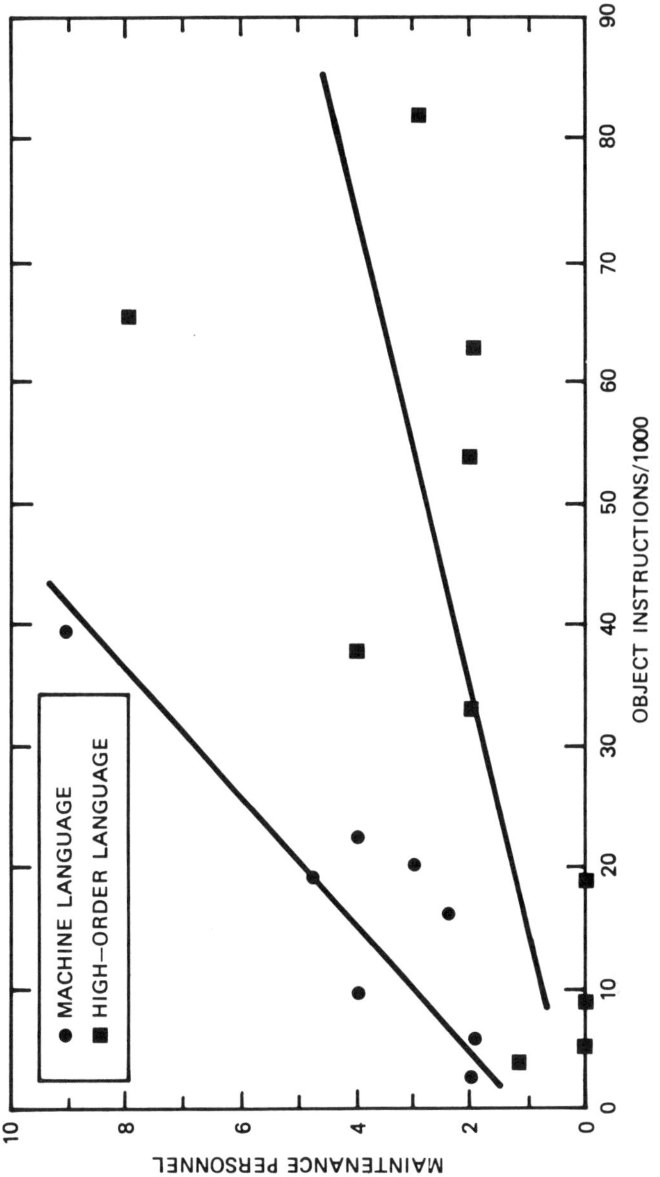

Figure 2.2-12. Effect of Language on Update and Maintenance Costs

DP H/W TECHNOLOGY MATRIX

PART A

MANUFACTURER, MODEL	APPLI-CATION	YEAR (STATUS)	CLASSIFI-CATION	WORD SIZE (BITS) DATA	WORD SIZE (BITS) INSTR.	PERFORMANCE INSTR. EXEC. TIME (μS) ADD	INSTR. EXEC. TIME (μS) MULT.	INSTR. EXEC. TIME (μS) DIVIDE	BENCHMARK NAME	BENCHMARK TIME (μS)	INSTR. MIX NAME	INSTR. MIX MIPS	MEMORY SIZE (WORDS) BASIC	SIZE (WORDS) MAX.	SPEED (μS) CYCLE	SPEED (μS) ACCESS
CARNEGIE MELLON UNIV.																
C.mmp	GP	1974	MULTI-MINI	16									1M	16M		
Cm*	GP		MULTI-MICRO													
CDC																
469		1973														
469R[2]		1970	μP?	16		2.4	10.4	30.4			T	.11	8K	16K	4.0	
479	GF	1974	μP?	18		2.0	7.0	11			T	.26	8K, 16K	32K	.4	
480(AN/AYK-14(V))	MIL.AIR	1977	μP (MODULAR)	16		4.0	5.0				T	.20	16K, 32K	512K	CORE: .9 SEMI: .4	
1604		1960														
3600		1963	GP													
5400B		1968		24		1.0	10	11			T	.21	8K	32K	1.0	
5600		1974		16		1.3	5.2	11			T	.29			1.0	
1700/5600		1974		16		2.6	8.6	12			T	.19	16K	262K	1.0	
6200(Cyber 72)	GF		LARGE MULTI	60									4K	128K		
6400(Cyber 73)	GF	1964	LARGE MULTI	60								.57	4K	128K		
6500(Cyber 73)	GF	1966	LARGE MULTI	60									4K	128K		
6600(Cyber 74)	GF	1964	LARGE MULTI	60								2.5	4K	128K	T.V	
6700(Cyber 74)	GF	1967	LARGE MULTI	60									4K	128K		
7600(Cyber 76)	GF	1968	LARGE MULTI	60					MATRIX FACT.	10 EL.: 600		13	SCM: 2K LCM: 64K	SCM: 64K LCM: 256K		
7700	GF, MIL	1971	LARGE MULTI	64								20	SCM: 2K LCM: 64K	SCM: 64K LCM: 542K		
AMPP(Cyber 176)	GF	1974	LARGE MULTI	16,24,32		.8	2.6	5.6			T	.50	16K	524K	.68	
MP60/5600		1969		32		2.6	8.6	12			T	.19	16K	262K	1.0	
FP																
AN/AYK-14	MIL	1976		16		.8	4.4	4.4			T	.44	16K, 32K	512K	.4	
AN/UYK-25(V)		1967		36		1.3	5.2	11			T	.29	4K	262K	1.0	
Cyber 18-20		1976	MINIC	16		1.8							32K	256K	.75	
Cyber 175		1974	LARGE MULTI	60									16K	256K		
STAR-100		1973	PIPELINE(VECTOR)	64					MATRIX FACT.	10 EL.: 500 100 EL.: 80nS		30				
STAR-100A			VERY LARGE									100				

DATE: APRIL 1978

SHEET 3 OF 27

Figure 2.2-13. Sample of Data Processing Hardware Matrix

DP H/W TECHNOLOGY MATRIX

PART B

MANUFACTURER, MODEL	TECHNOLOGY		INSTRUCTIONS			PHYSICAL					COST ($)	REFERENCES
	MEMORY	PROCESSOR	LENGTH (BITS)	NUMBER	SET	VOLUME (CU. FT)	WEIGHT (LBS)	POWER (W)	MTBF (KHRS)	ENVIRONMENTAL RUGGEDNESS		
CARNEGIE-MELLON UNIV.												
C.mmp	IC, CORE	IC										9, 43,56
Cm*												56
CDC												
469												7
469R[2]				42		.060	7	17	7			3
479	CORE, SEMICONDUCTOR			42		.026	24	90	5	MIL-E-5400		3, 10
480(AN/AYK-14(V))	CORE, SEMICONDUCTOR		48							MIL-E-5400, 16400, 4158		10, 11, 15
1604												
3600												7
5400B				64		1.34	75	290				3
5600									4			3
1700/5600						1.7	50	430	3			3, 15
6200(Cyber 72)												43
6400(Cyber 73)	CORE										735K	3, 43
6500(Cyber 73)												7, 43
6600(Cyber 74)	CORE										7.5M	7,8,17,43
6700(Cyber 74)												43
7600(Cyber 76)	CORE							100 KW			7.5M	3,7, 9,14,15, 17,43,42
7700	CORE							200 KW				3
AMPP(Cyber 176)						.87	48	450	2			3
MP60/5600				137		1.7	50	430	3			3
FP												
AN/AYK-14								500	2.5			3
AN/UYK-25(V)						1.7	80	430	4			3
Cyber 18-20	SEMICONDUCTOR		16, 32									12
Cyber 175												43
STAR-100												7,8,15,44,42
STAR-100A												15

DATE: APRIL 1978

SHEET 3 OF 27

Figure 2.2-13 Sample of Data Processing Hardware Matrix (Continued 1)

DP H/W TECHNOLOGY MATRIX

PART C

MANUFACTURER, MODEL	CPU ARCHITECTURE	I/O						SPECIAL FEATURES
		WORD SIZE (BITS)	NO. OF LINES	DMA	TRANSFER RATE (WORDS)	INTERRUPTS		
						LEVELS	VECTORED	
CARNEGIE-MELLON UNIV.								
C.mmp	16 PROCESSORS MAX.(DEC PDP-11/40) CROSSBAR, TIME-SHARED/COMMON BUS I/O,							
Cm*	MULTIPLE DEC LSI-11.							
CDC								
469								
469R[2]								
479		16		OPT.				
480(AN/AYK-14(V))	μPROCESSOR SLICE CHIPS, μ PROGRAMMABLE.	16	16					BUS EXTENDER.16- or 32-BIT EMULATION
1604								
3600								
5400B								
5600								
1700/5600								
6200(Cyber 72)	2 PROCESSORS, CROSSBAR, TIME-SHARED BUS		20					MAX. 160 I/O DEVICES.
6400(Cyber 73)	2 PROCESSORS, CROSSBAR, TIME-SHARED BUS		20					MAX. 160 I/O DEVICES.
6500(Cyber 73)	2 PROCESSORS, CROSSBAR, TIME-SHARED BUS		24					
6600(Cyber 74)	1 PROCESSOR, CROSSBAR, TIME-SHARED BUS	12	24					DISTR. COMPUTING, FUNCTIONAL PARALLELISM.
6700(Cyber 74)	2 PROCESSORS, CROSSBAR, TIME-SHARED BUS		24					
7600(Cyber 76)	1 PROCESSOR, CROSSBAR, TIME-SHARED BUS		15					DISTR. COMPUTING, FUNCTIONAL PARALLELISM.
7700								
AMPP(Cyber 176)								
MP60/5600								
FP								
AN/AYK-14								
AN/UYK-25(V)								
Cyber 18-20		16		YES		16		MICROPROGR. OPTION
Cyber 175	1 PROCESSOR, CROSSBAR, TIME-SHARED BUS		24					
STAR-100	ARITHMETIC PIPELINES							
STAR-100A								

DATE: APRIL 1978

SHEET 3 OF 27

Figure 2.2-13 Sample of Data Processing Hardware Matrix (Continued 2)

identify which computing elements satisfy particular sets of characteristics, i.e., in general, to make searches of the data base, is of great convenience to the designer. In addition, the easy analysis of the data in terms of possible interrelationships of characteristics, further support design with scatter diagrams, estimating relationships and forecasts. To this end a computer program was developed, called Computer Data Analysis Program (CODAP) which is described in [2-5]. The program extracts data from the data base, generates a matrix (Figure 2.2-18 shows the subset of computers having both cost and speed data), and regresses upon data as indicated by the user. The user can at present select from three types of regression techniques, i.e.,

- linear (linear: $y = ax + b$)
- log-log linear (power: $y = ax^b$)
- log-linear (exponential: $y = ab^x$)

The program calculates the coefficients a and b and generates scatter diagrams. The program, as well as the data base, is resident on the CDC 7600 at the BMDATC's ARC facility in Huntsville, Alabama and uses the routines of the International Mathematical and Statistical Library (IMSL) already present at that facility.

Figure 2.2-19 shows the log-log linear regression results for cost versus speed using the 40 data sets shown in Figure 2.2-18. The correlation is 0.716 compared to 0.626 for linear and 0.460 for log-linear. The correlation may improve when some of the presently erroneous and missing data have been corrected and included respectively. The 40 data points regressed upon, form a mixture of small, medium and large computers (see Figure 2.2-18). Earlier regressions were performed on medium and large machines only which resulted in better fits, again using power curves (see dashed curve in Figure 2.2-20 taken from Appendix IE: "Life Cycle Cost Development and Data Base" of [2-6]).

Results of analyses of the data base with respect to mean-time-between-failure (MTBF) are shown in Figure 2.2-21 (taken from Appendix 1B: "Availability Development and Data Base" of [2-6] and modified).

Early regression results for form factor (power, volume and weight) as well as forecasts and additional data concerning computing elements can be found extensively in [2-6]. When future major data base updates have been completed, all of these early regression results will be updated using the CODAP program.

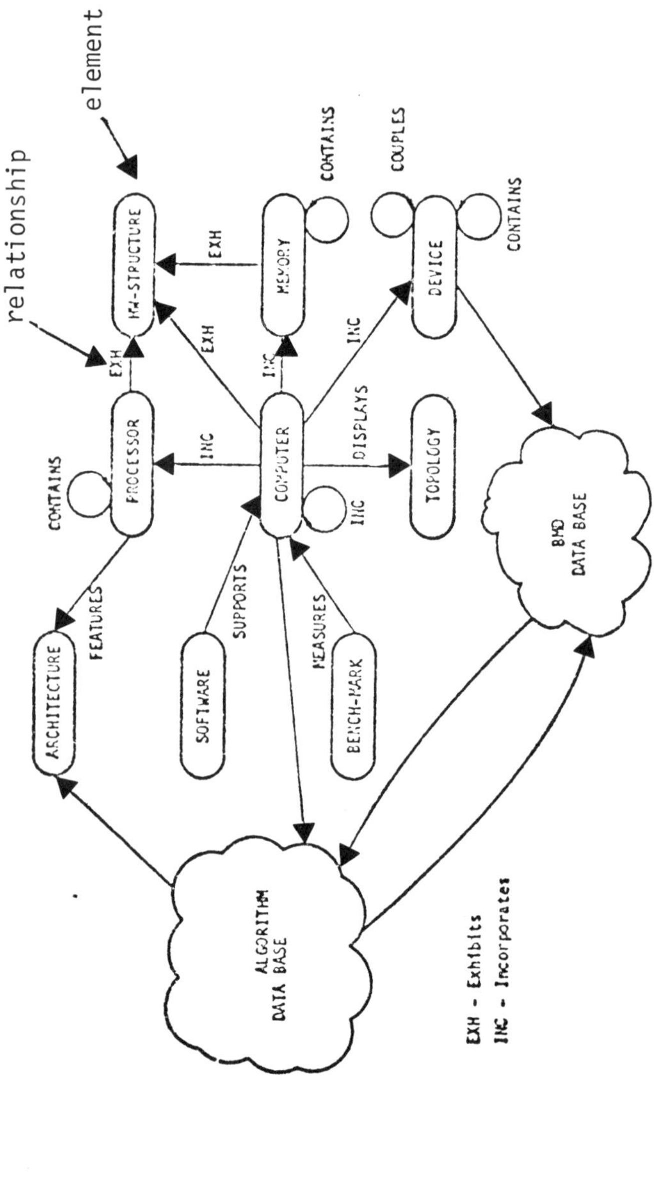

Figure 2.2-14. Element Types and Relations in Computer Data Base

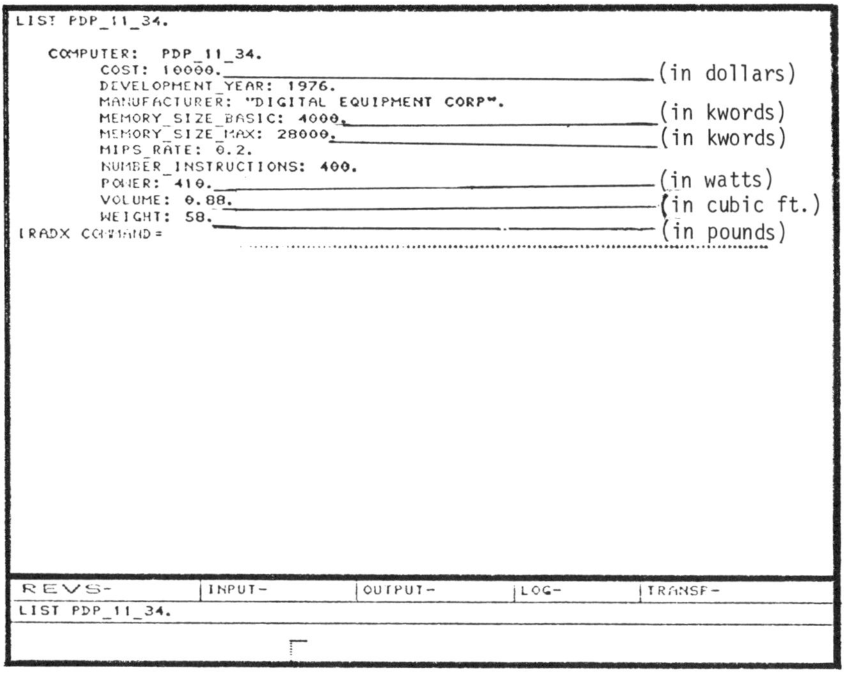

Note: Request for all available attribute information on PDP-11/34 computer.

Figure 2.2-15. Example 1 of Computer Data Base Query

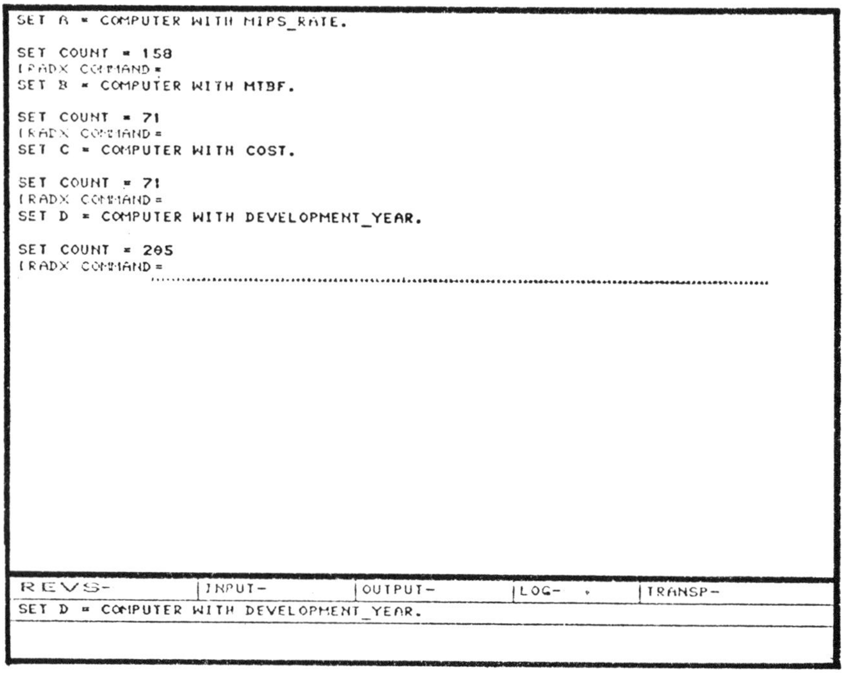

```
SET A = COMPUTER WITH MIPS_RATE.

SET COUNT = 158
[RADX COMMAND=
SET B = COMPUTER WITH MTBF.

SET COUNT = 71
[RADX COMMAND=
SET C = COMPUTER WITH COST.

SET COUNT = 71
[RADX COMMAND=
SET D = COMPUTER WITH DEVELOPMENT_YEAR.

SET COUNT = 205
[RADX COMMAND=

REVS-    |INPUT-    |OUTPUT-    |LOG-    |TRANSP-
SET D = COMPUTER WITH DEVELOPMENT_YEAR.
```

Note: Request for count of computer entries having:

a) Speed (MIPS) information
b) MTBF information
c) Cost information
d) Development year information

Figure 2.2-16. Example 2 of Computer Data Base Query

```
SET O = A WITH MIPS_RATE > 0.75.

SET COUNT = 20
IRADX COMMAND =
SET P = O WITH MIPS_RATE < 1.5.

SET COUNT = 5
IRADX COMMAND =
APPEND COMPUTER MIPS_RATE COST MANUFACTURER.

IRADX COMMAND =
LIST P.

   COMPUTER:  AN_UYK_30_F.
        MIPS_RATE: 0.8.
        MANUFACTURER: "HUGHES".
   COMPUTER:  ATMAC.
        MIPS_RATE: 1.4.
        COST: 35000.
        MANUFACTURER: "RADIO CORP OF AMERICA".
   COMPUTER:  B_6503.
        MIPS_RATE: 0.88.
        COST: 947000.
        MANUFACTURER: "BURROUGHS CORP".
   COMPUTER:  DECSYSTEM_10.
        MIPS_RATE: 1.0.
        COST: 420000.
        MANUFACTURER: "DIGITAL EQUIPMENT CORP".
   COMPUTER:  I_4PI_ASP.
        MIPS_RATE: 0.82.
        MANUFACTURER: "INTERNATIONAL BUSINESS MACHINES".
IRADX COMMAND =

REVS-          |INPUT-          |OUTPUT-          |LOG-          |TRANSP--
LIST P.
```

Note: Request for listing of all computers (and their model number, speed, cost and manufacturer attributes) having a speed of

$$0.75 \text{ MIPS} \le \text{Speed} < 1.5 \text{ MIPS}$$

Figure 2.2-17. Example 3 of Computer Data Base Query

MANUFACTURER	MODEL	MIPS	COST (K$)	POWER (W)	VOLUME (FEET)	WEIGHT (LB)	MTBF (YRS)
AMDAHL COMPUTER CORP	A_470V7	6.40	3500.0	------	----	-----	---
AMDAHL COMPUTER CORP	A_470V6	4.00	3000.0	------	----	-----	---
AMDAHL COMPUTER CORP	A_470V5	2.60	2400.0	------	----	-----	---
AUTONETICS	MR_P16	.03	5.0	4.	.0	.5	25.0
AUTONETICS	D216	.14	50.0	48.	.3	15.0	5.0
BURROUGHS CORP	B_6503	.88	947.0	------	----	-----	---
CRAY RESEARCH, INC	CRAY_1	30.00	4500.0	115.	477.0	******	---
CONTROL DATA CORP	C_6400	* .57	735.0	------	----	-----	---
CONTROL DATA CORP	C_6600	* 2.50	7500.0	------	----	-----	---
CONTROL DATA CORP	C_7600	13.00	7500.0	100000.	----	-----	---
DATA GENERAL CORP	ECLIPSE_C_330	.45	180.0	------	----	-----	---
DIGITAL EQUIPMENT CO	DECSYSTEM_20	.40	310.0	------	----	-----	---
DIGITAL EQUIPMENT CO	DECSYSTEM_10	1.00	420.0	------	----	-----	---
DIGITAL EQUIPMENT CO	VAX_11_780	.70	87.0	------	----	-----	---
DIGITAL EQUIPMENT CO	PDP_11_34	.20	10.0	410.	.9	58.0	---
DIGITAL EQUIPMENT CO	PDP_11_70	.40	72.5	------	----	-----	---
HARRIS	H_5R	.26	95.0	1800.	6.3	230.0	---
HEWLETT-PACKARD	H_3000_SERIES_II	.28	220.0	------	----	-----	---
INTERNATIONAL BUSINE	I_4PI_ML_1	.38	30.0	72.	34.0	18.0	5.0
INTERNATIONAL BUSINE	I_370_148	.45	840.0	------	----	-----	---
INTERNATIONAL BUSINE	I_370_138	.21	515.0	------	----	-----	---
INTERNATIONAL BUSINE	I_360_75	.65	1345.0	------	----	-----	---
INTERNATIONAL BUSINE	I_360_65	.59	432.0	------	----	-----	---
INTERNATIONAL BUSINE	I_360_50	.17	397.0	------	----	-----	---
INTERNATIONAL BUSINE	I_360_44_HS	.28	420.0	------	----	-----	---
INTERNATIONAL BUSINE	I_360_44_HAS	.19	390.0	------	----	-----	---
RADIO CORP OF AMERIC	SUMC	.20	200.0	30.	.5	16.0	---
RADIO CORP OF AMERIC	R_70_55	.31	451.0	------	----	-----	---
RADIO CORP OF AMERIC	R_6	.30	510.0	------	----	-----	---
RADIO CORP OF AMERIC	ATMAC	1.40	35.0	9.	.7	30.0	25.0
RAYTHEON	RP_16	.28	30.0	110.	----	16.0	6.0
ROLM	AN_UYK_19	.30	25.0	200.	.6	40.0	---
TELEDYNE	TDY43	.27	40.0	300.	----	34.0	4.2
TEXAS INSTRUMENTS	TI_2520	.18	50.0	90.	.3	16.0	2.2
TEXAS INSTRUMENTS	TI_2540	.29	100.0	300.	1.1	60.0	1.0
UNIVAC DIV	AN_UYK_7	.18	500.0	2500.	10.4	500.0	---
UNIVAC DIV	AN_UYK_10	.15	120.0	2300.	11.9	410.0	---
XEROX DATA SYSTEM	SIGMA_5	.37	500.0	------	----	-----	---
XEROX DATA SYSTEM	SIGMA_7A	.40	640.0	------	----	-----	---
XEROX DATA SYSTEM	SIGMA_7	.41	700.0	------	----	-----	---

*erroneous data

Figure 2.2-18. Sample Computer Matrix - MIPS/COST Subset (40 data points)

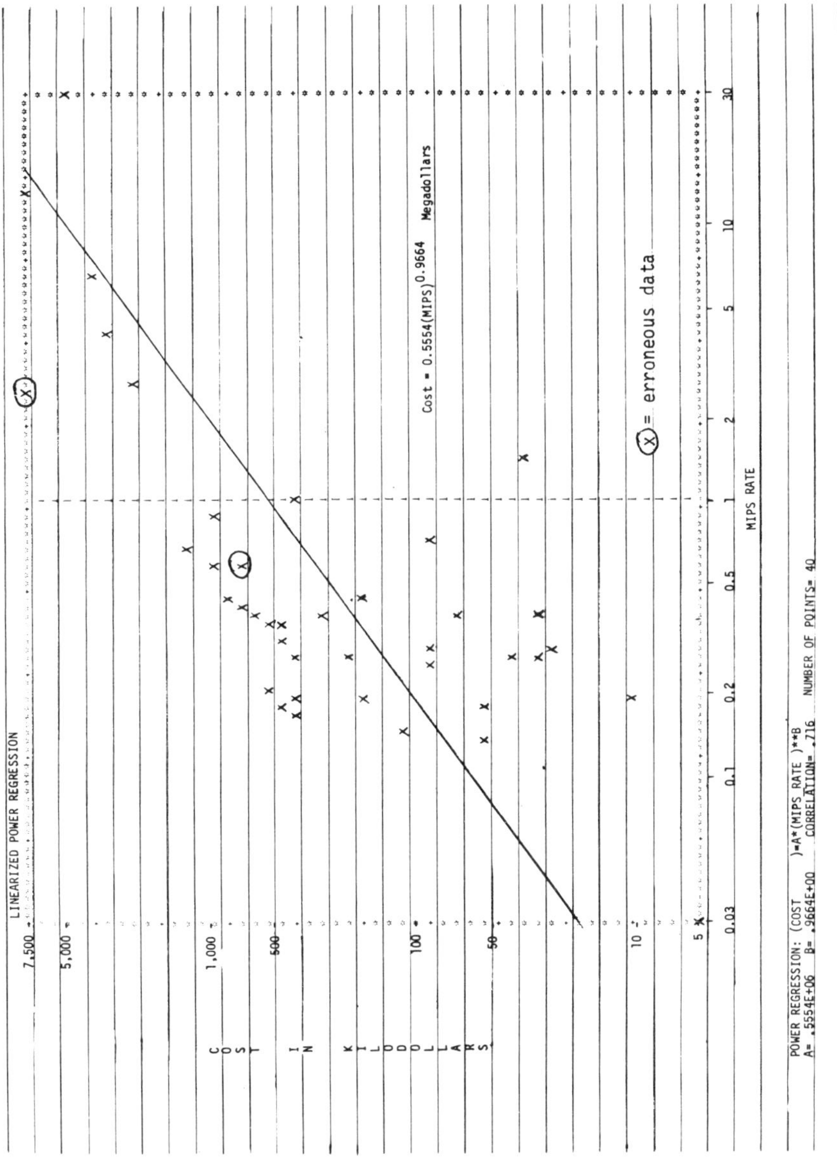

Figure 2.2-19. Sample Log-Log Linear Regression Analysis of Data of Figure 2.2-18.

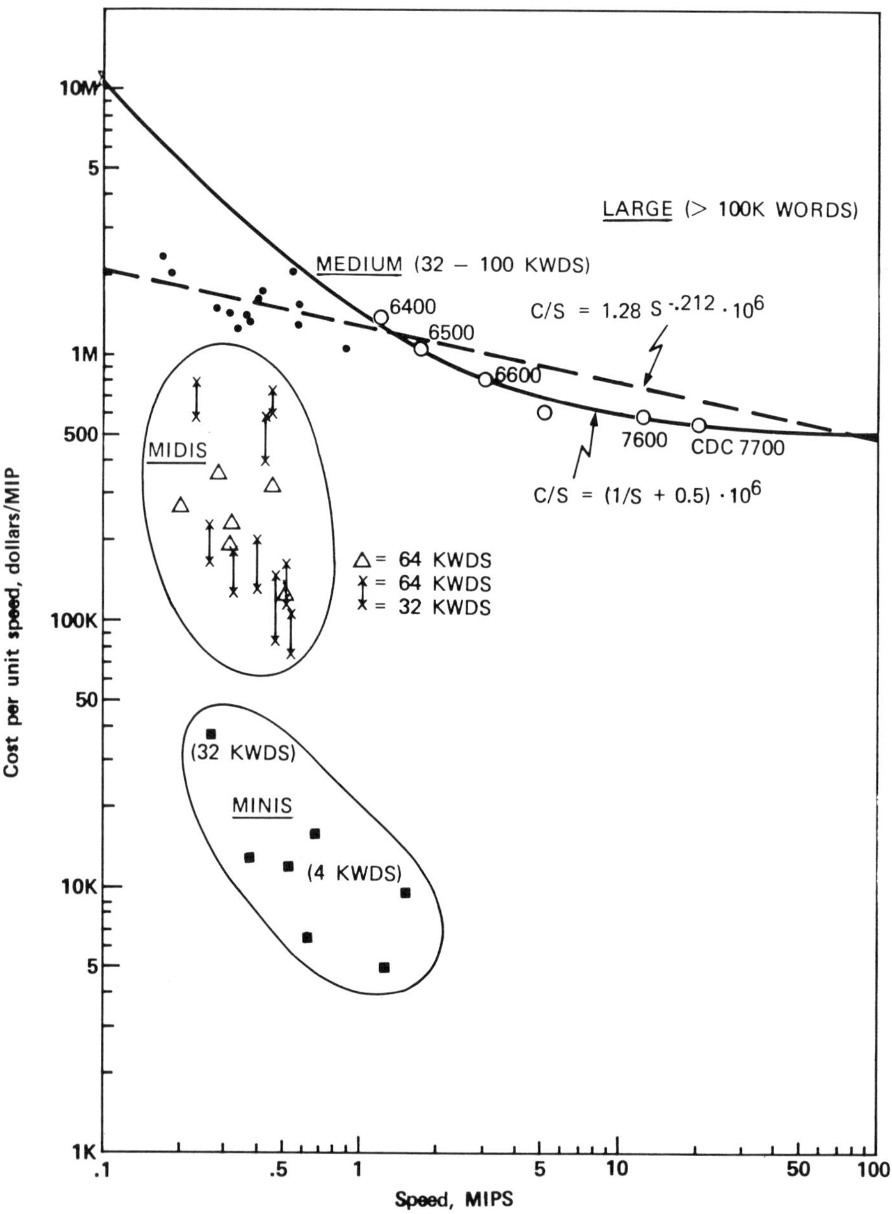

Figure 2.2-20. Computer Cost Data

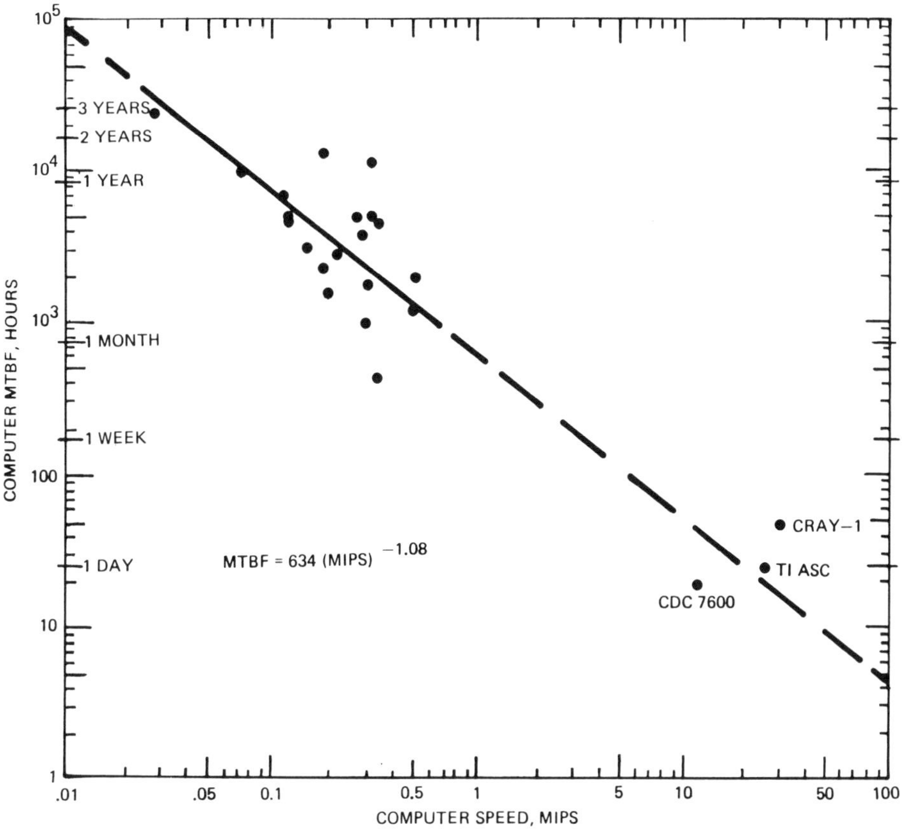

Figure 2.2-21. Computer MTBF as a Function of Speed

2.3 PARTITIONING/ALLOCATION

2.3.1 Introduction

The development of hardware and software requirements for modules of a distributed system is accomplished through a systematic decomposition and assignment of data processing subsystem requirements. That decomposition process is referred to as partitioning of requirements. The assignment process is referred to as allocation. In both steps, partitioning and allocation must address both functional processing requirements and the data which is shared between processing requirements.

In the past, for centralized systems, the hardware was usually preselected during the system engineering activity based on preliminary estimates of the applications resource requirements and operating system overhead costs. All too often these preliminary estimates changed due to such factors as: changing requirements, algorithm development uncertainties, or algorithm effectiveness variations. This hardware selection approach simplified the design process to that of only software -- i.e., fitting the problem into a fixed solution space.

With distributed processing systems the design process is complicated -- the hardware design/selection process can now be traded off against the software design. The natural process structure of the applications can and should strongly influence the hardware structure. The accurate definition of the natural process structure and its associated data interaction are of absolute necessity to the success of the partitioning/allocation step.

If the problem representation is biased or inaccurate - then the partitioning/allocation results will also be biased or inaccurate; e.g., if we inadvertently develop a serial representation of the problem then we will have no recourse other then to develop serial implementations.

The partitioning and allocation steps are two distinct but inter-related activities. The partitioning activity emphasizes the natural problem structure with little dependence on hardware implementation constraints. However, the allocation activity emphasizes hardware implementation constraints and technology state-of-the-art. Due to this distinction in emphasis, a single partitioning of functions and data may be used in developing several candidate system allocations - for example one allocation may be based on off-the-shelf hardware while a second is based on semi-custom hardware using state-of-the-art chips.

Results of the partitioning activity will produce a hardware implementation independent, directed graph representation of the problem with explicit representations of concurrency and parallelism; e.g., concurrent logic flow (CLF) diagram (Figure 2.3-1). Each node on the graph represents a processing step and node-to-node communications as distinct messages on a data flow graph (DFG) (Figure 2.3-2). No implications of data base structure are imposed. Later the partitioning of data will be based on the natural node-to-node communications traffic, as a minimum, each message representing a uniquely maintained data entity.

Results of the allocation activity will produce an assignment of the processing nodes and data entities to physical hardware. As a result such hardware considerations as throughput, storage and bandwidth limitations will be incorporated.

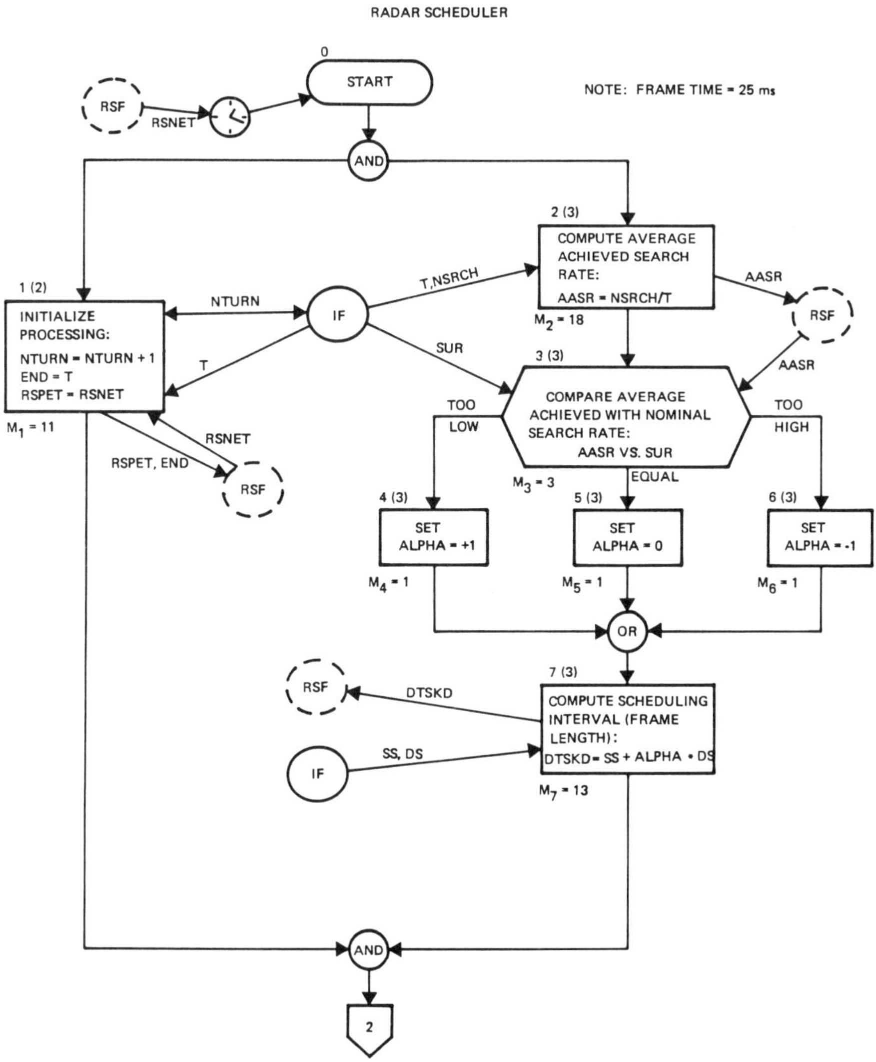

Figure 2.3-1. Example Detailed Concurrent Logic Flow (CLF)

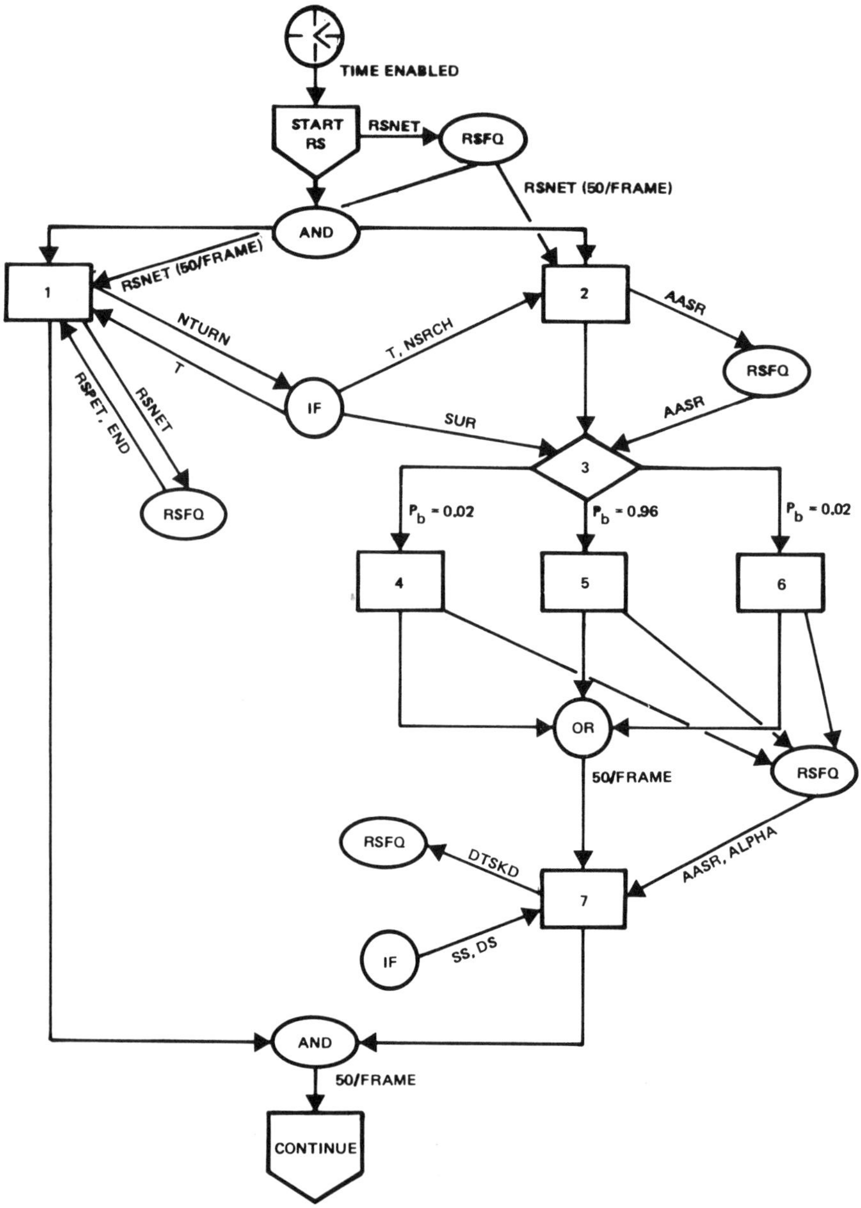

Figure 2.3-2. Example DFG for Radar Scheduler (RS) CLF

2.3.2 Definition of Natural Problem Structure

Key to the development of the natural problem structure is the ability to define and explicitly represent the problems inherent concurrency and parallelism. In addition, the problem elements (i.e., both operational requirements and associated data) must be defined in terms of those key parameters upon which the partitioning and allocation will be based. The problem representation is one research area which can be supported by contemporary requirements engineering techniques, such as those discussed by Ramamoorthy and Ho [2-7]. Kung's discussion [2-31] of parallel algorithms and matching architectures addresses many principles which apply to the system problem structure.

Although most requirements engineering techniques documented currently are based on centralized data processing implementation approaches, they do provide a foundation which can be extended to distributed data processing. Of those requirements engineering methodologies most well known, the TRW methodology 2-8 and support tools (SREM are felt to be most readily applicable to distributed data processing).

Because of their emphasis on centralized data processing applications the current methodologies have not had to support two features key to the design of distributed data processing.

- Shared data representation: The access, flow and location of data shared between processing entities now becomes a critical design consideration
- Traceability for recursive decomposition: The requirements will now be decomposed to support multiple levels of design; each level will be a decomposition of the prior level and include additional requirements for control.

In addition, many languages which support the development of requirements data bases and the evaluation tools which support the data base analysis, support only static consistency analysis of the requirements. However, none are structured to support dynamic and/or quantitative analysis such as that which is necessary to support message traffic analysis and throughput loading.

2.3.3 Partitioning/Allocation Guidelines

In general, we find that in both steps, the objectives are idential; that is, the exploitation of the system level payoffs (Reference Section 2.2) through **conscientious** partitioning and allocation of processing requirements and data. Since the emphasis of the partitioning and allocation steps are quite different, it is only natural that the guidelines and factors which drive these two steps also differ.

2.3.3.1 Partitioning

Current work in the area of partitioning has concentrated on the three system payoff objectives of performance (via concurrency), reliability (via reduced complexity) and growth (via information hiding*) [2-28, 2-29]. This work provides a valuable foundation from which to start to develop the necessary rules and techniques for partitioning. However, they are limited in their scope and for the most part are not directed at the distributed data processing design problem. For example, guidelines for improving reliability concentrate on improving the system's intolerance to fault and therefore do not address aspects of fault tolerance through function and data redundancy.

2.3.3.1.1 Functional Processing Partitioning Guidelines

As an illustration, we provide a set of sixteen applications partitioning guidelines for the payoffs of performance, reliability (by fault intolerance) and growth (Figure 2.3-3). These guidelines could be weighted as to their importance to the partitioning of application functional requirements at each level of the design process. The guidelines are developed based on considerations of the inherent problem structure (such as data flow and usage, processing and data manipulation characteristics, sensitivity to change in threat, etc.) rather than implementation considerations such as HW and SW technology limitations. There are several payoffs for which partitioning rules/criteria have not been developed directly; e.g., cost, deployability, form factor, survivability and fault tolerance. However, partitioning rules and criteria developed around performance, reliability and growth do have second order effects on the other payoffs.

The partitioning guidelines should be derived from an analysis of the parametric payoff models. The models provide the foundation for identifying the key design factors which have the strongest (positive or negative) influence on the payoffs. These factors then can be used as the basis for establishing the partitioning guidelines. For example, the processing response requirement which might be budgeted a high priority function(Figure 2.3-3, Guideline #1) could be strongly influenced (weighting factor 0.7) by communications bandwidth, computational throughput, and degree of multitasking associated with a node design. Therefore, partitioning the applications into modules which separate those alphas having extremely tight response requirements (with correspondingly high throughput requirements, Guideline #14) allows the designer the choice of allocating the modules to different computers within the node to reduce the potential competition for computational resources and increased execution wait delays due to such competition. We acknowledge that the designer must trade off the benefits of reduced execution delays with increased communication delays which result from functional allocation across computers. The same consideration is addressed at the HW/SW design level in which the decision to implement the module in HW is highly influenced (weighting factor 1.0) by its response and throughput requirements.

---

* Information hiding isolates (in a single module) a requirement which has a high probability of change.

DESIGN OBJECTIVE				DESIGN LEVEL WEIGHTING ($0 \leq w \leq 1.0$)		
Performance	Reliability	Growth	APPLICATIONS PROCESSING PARTITIONING GUIDELINES	Node Design	Computer Design	HW-SW Design
X			1. Partition processes with different response requirements(e.g., execution priorities).	.7		1.0
X			2. Partition processes with similar resource profile timelines.	1.0		
X			3. Partition processes which have different computational structure (e.g., highly arithmetic vs. highly logic).	.7	.6	.5
X			4. Partition processes which operate on disjoint data sets (e.g., all objects in track, all objects within range R).	.5		
X	X		5. Partition processes to minimize number of module types, not necessarily number of modules.		.6	.8
X	X		6. Partition processes into modules of equivalent resource characteristics (e.g., operations, storage).	1.0	.8	
		X	7. Partition processes with different sensitivity to threat (i.e., external data stimuli).	.3	.5	.8
	X	X	8. Partition processes into modules to reduce the number and complexity of their interfaces.	.5	.7	.8
	X	X	9. Partition processes which operate on different classes of data, (e.g., initial track returns, precommit track returns).	.5	.9	
		X	10. Partition processes which require different hardware and/or software technology implementation (e.g., modules implemented in HOL versus microcode).	.5	.7	.9
		X	11. Partition processes which perform external interface functions (e.g., radar interface translation, network interface) into independent modules.	.9		
		X	12. Partition processes which perform data manipulation and data management from those which perform data translation (e.g., data message unpacking from message processing).		.8	.5
		X	13. Partition processes which perform control functions (e.g., sensor control, interceptor control).	.4	.6	
X			14. Partition processes which have a large data rate/throughput requirement (indicative of parallel processing potential).	1.0		
	X	X	15. Partition processes which operate on different data states (e.g., valid, invalid, radar return).	.7	1.0	
X			16. Partition processes with extremely high I/O bandwidth requirements (enablement messages).	.9		

Figure 2.3-3. Applications Processing Partitioning Guidelines

2.3.3.1.2 Data Base Partitioning Guidelines

A similar partitioning problem occurs with the data base. During the problem definition phase, data access and flows will be defined between processing functions. The data access and flows will define the flow of control data (enablement messages) and global data (shared) between all processing functions. The logical grouping of data is referred to as data partitioning, and initially is viewed as messages which are determined by the natural reading (input) and writing (output) of data by the processing functions. In cases where multiple processing functions read and/or write the same data the largest common data group will become the natural partition (Figure 2.3-4). In the example (Figure 2.3-4), the data groups of each processing function contain partial overlap, and the common data can be denoted as a subset and a unique data partition from that data which is unique to a single processing function. In the example only one data group (indicated by cross-hatching) is common to all three processing functions (i, j, k), and would become a unique data group shared by all three functions. Three other data groups (indicated by shading) are shared by two functions; either i-j, j-k, or i-k, and would also become unique data groupings. This approach to partitioning data into groups based on function usage of the data will improve the ease with which the data base designer can check for dead lock potential, and implement dead-lock prevention techniques. In addition, this approach will tend to result in large numbers of data groupings which adds to the complexity of the data allocation and structuring problems of the data base designer. Further partitioning the logical data groups into modules, offers a similar means of reducing the dimensionality of the design problem as that associated with the applications partitioning.

This research in the area of partitioning data has also been based on the payoff considerations of performance, reliability and growth. At the node design level, the driving data partitioning considerations are directed at reducing intercomputer communications of remote file access, insuring reliability requirements are met through replication of data (when necessary), and distributing the data management overhead across computers (Reference Guidelines #1, 4 and 9). At the computer and HW/SW levels, the driving considerations are reducing access response times of local data modules and reducing the impact of growth (Reference Guidelines #7 and 8). These consideration are reflected in the nine example data base partitioning guidelines (Figure 2.3-5). As with function partitioning we acknowledge that different guidelines will have different emphasis at different levels of design, this emphasis might also be denoted by weighting coefficients.

2.3.3.2 Allocation

The assignment of functions and data assumes the number (not inter-connection) of physical resources has been pre-determined. Such an assumption is reasonable and in many cases may be dictated by available hardware or by procurement constraints. For most of the DDP architecture configurations which we expect to encounter the number of physical resources - N will be far less than the number of partitioned functions (M_1) and data (M_2) to be allocated,

$$N \ll M_1 \text{ or } M_2$$

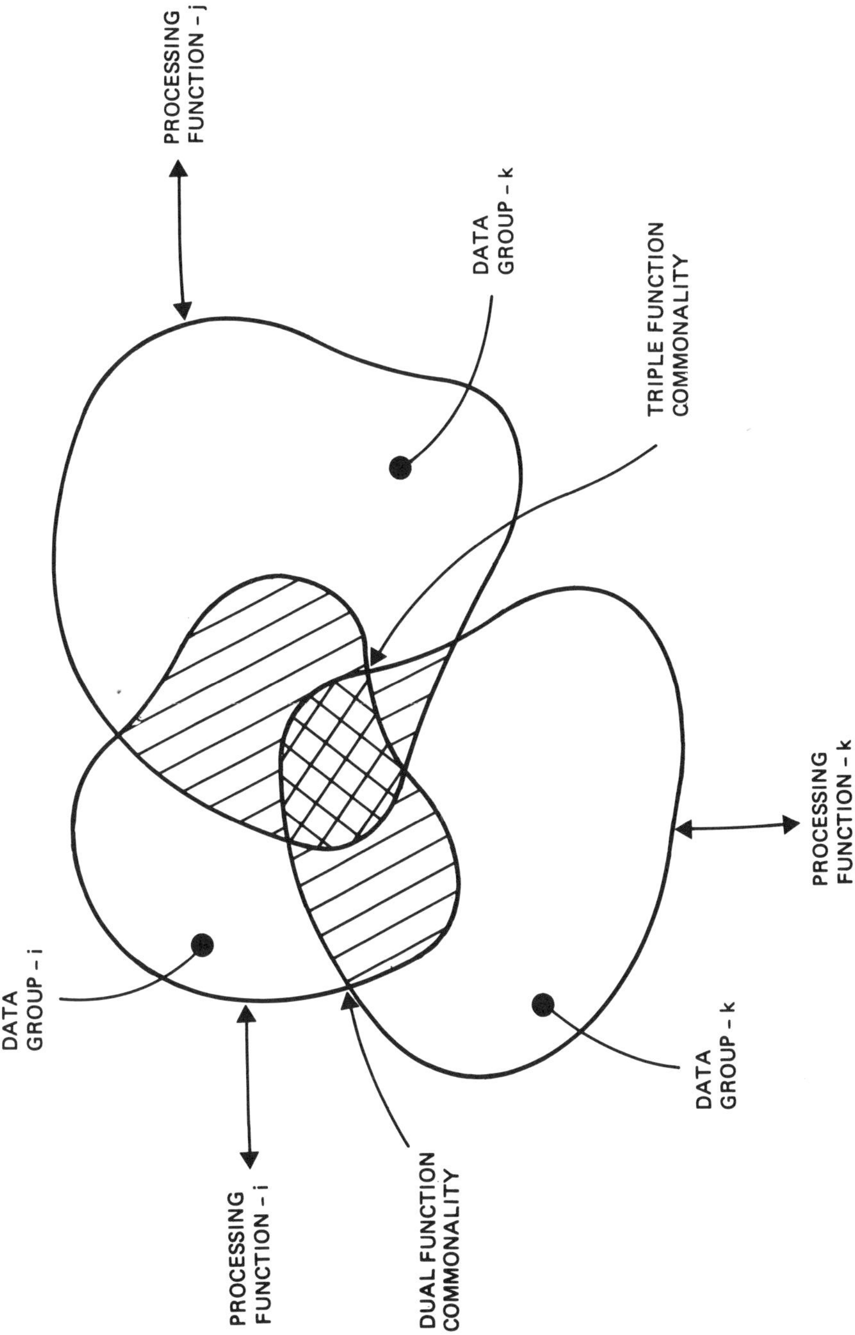

Figure 2.3-4. Natural Partitioning By Data Usage.

DESIGN OBJECTIVES				DESIGN LEVEL WEIGHTING ($0 \leq w \leq 1.0$)		
Performance	Reliability	Growth	DATA BASE PARTITIONING GUIDELINES	Node Design	Computer Design	HW-SW Design
X	X		1. Partition data into modules with approximately similar resource requirements (e.g., storage, communications, data base; access/update frequency).	1.0		
		X	2. Partition data with highly dynamic (over time) storage profiles.	.7	.4	.8
		X	3. Partition data whose storage and/or alpha access characteristics are highly sensitive to threat permutations (e.g., tactics, sophistication).	.8	.8	
X	X	X	4. Partition data to minimize the number and complexity of alpha access and update interfaces of each data module (ideally one data module per alpha).	1.0	.9	
		X	5. Partition data to minimize the need for file replication for performance reasons; i.e., access response.	.8		
X			6. Partition data with unique data access/update requirements (e.g., global sort, associative search, other).		.5	.5
X			7. Partition data with IPC and system status from global shared data.	.5	1.0	1.0
X			8. Partition data having extreme access response timing requirements.		1.0	1.0
	X		9. Partition data having a critical value to the application into separate modules for potential replication (e.g., global object state file, status tables, other).	1.0	.5	

Figure 2.3-5. Data Partitioning Guidelines

By structuring the functions and data to identify their interdependencies, the allocation problem can be formulated as an optimization problem whose objective is to assign the functions and data in a manner which "minimizes" their collective interdependency. The optimization problem then has a potential dimensionality of:

$$N^{M_1+M_2}$$

This states that the problem complexity (or number of potential assignment combinations) increases exponentially with the number of resources (N; i.e., processors, computers, or computing centers) in the network, and exponentially with the number of partitioned functions (M_1) and data (M_2) to be allocated.

There are two techniques for reducing the inherent combinations of the allocation problem. The first involves simplification of the problem formulation, such as decomposing the problem into separate subproblems which collectively yield the same results as the initial problem formulation. One such decomposition could involve separating the function allocation from the allocation of data. This would simplify the original problem from one of

$$N^{M_1+M_2}$$

possible combinations, to one involving

$$N^{M_1} + N^{M_2}$$

possible assignment combinations; a reduction of $(M_1+M_2)/(M_1M_2)$. The second technique uses constraints to bound and direct the enumeration process. These constraints will typically restrict the location, size, timing or redundancy of the function and data assignment across resources.

2.3.3.2.1 Determination of Resource Dimension

The natural problem structure should be used to bound the architecture dimensionality. The architecture dimensionality is defined as the number (not organization or type) of physical resources upon which the applications and data modules are to be mapped. The dimensionality is based on an analysis of the concurrencies/parallelisms inherent in the applications and system structure.

The architecture dimensionality can be visualized differently depending on the level of design. At the subsystem level of design, the architecture can be visualized in two dimensions: one representing the number of physically distributed node types, and the second representing the number of copies of each node type. Subsystem architectures will preferably contain a small number of node types (≅3-5 types) from which large network subsystems (≅20 - 50 nodes) can be created. The architecture dimension at the subsystem level will be driven primarily by structural characteristics of the system and requirements such as survivability or external interfaces. Considerations of the natural problem structure will have very little impact on the architecture dimension at the subsystem level of design. The external interfaces of the data processing subsystem will typically include data sources such as sensor subsystems, principal command center, or user terminals, and data sinks such as interceptors, interceptor farms, or forward command posts. The location of these centers and their interface requirements will be the major factor in establishing the number of node types within the subsystem architecture. Considerations such as survivability, cost, technology limitations, and node form factor* constraints will influence the degree of replication (number of copies) of each node type.

As the design progresses through the lower levels (e.g., node and computer system levels), the natural problem structure becomes a more significant influence on the architecture dimension. As the influence of the problem structure becomes more significant, architecture dimensionality can be visualized as a cube (Figure 2.3-6), with the three axes representing three dimensions of potential concurrency/parallelism within the problem structure. Given the problem representation as a logic flow diagram, the logic-length dimension of the architecture will represent the number of discrete stages which can be concurrently executed along any logic branch of the applications. Exploitations of logic-length concurrency will lead to vector architectures [2-9] such as data flow machines. The logic-width dimension of the architecture represents both the number of discrete processing steps which can be concurrently executed on a single instance of data, and the number of processing threads which can be executed concurrently. Exploitation of logic-width concurrency could lead to multiprocessors, such as the research vehicles of Carnegie Mellon University [2-10]. Finally, the data-width dimension represents the degree of replication of the basic architecture structure defined by logic length and width dimensions, and therefore the number of data instances which can be executed in parallel. Exploitation of data-width concurrency could also lead to parallel or associative architecture configurations such as the PEPE [2-11] or STARAN [2-12].

The higher the degree of **concurrency, the higher the degree of potential architectural dimensionality. The degree of architecture dimensionality** will affect both the performance and reliability/fault tolerance of the architecture. Increasing the dimension along any of the three axes will improve the performance throughput (data processed per unit time) of the architecture. Concurrency along the logic length path will typically lead to much poorer loading characteristics than logic width distribution. Increasing the architecture's logic-width dimension will also reduce the processing response time of a single data instance. The reliability is inherently decreased by increasing the architecture's dimension along either the logic length or logic width axes. However, increasing the architecture's data-width dimension will permit increased reliability through redundancy. Finally, increasing the dimension along any of the three axes will serve to improve the growth potential of the architecture through increased modularity. However, control complexity can become a significant issue with architectures based on logic (width and/or length) concurrency because of the multiple instruction streams. For architectures based on logic concurrency, control can be simplified if the data and control interactions between the multiple control streams can be minimized.

For distributed architectures with multiple levels of distribution, no single algorithm for determining the architecture dimensionality can be

---

* "form factor" requirements include size, weight, and power.

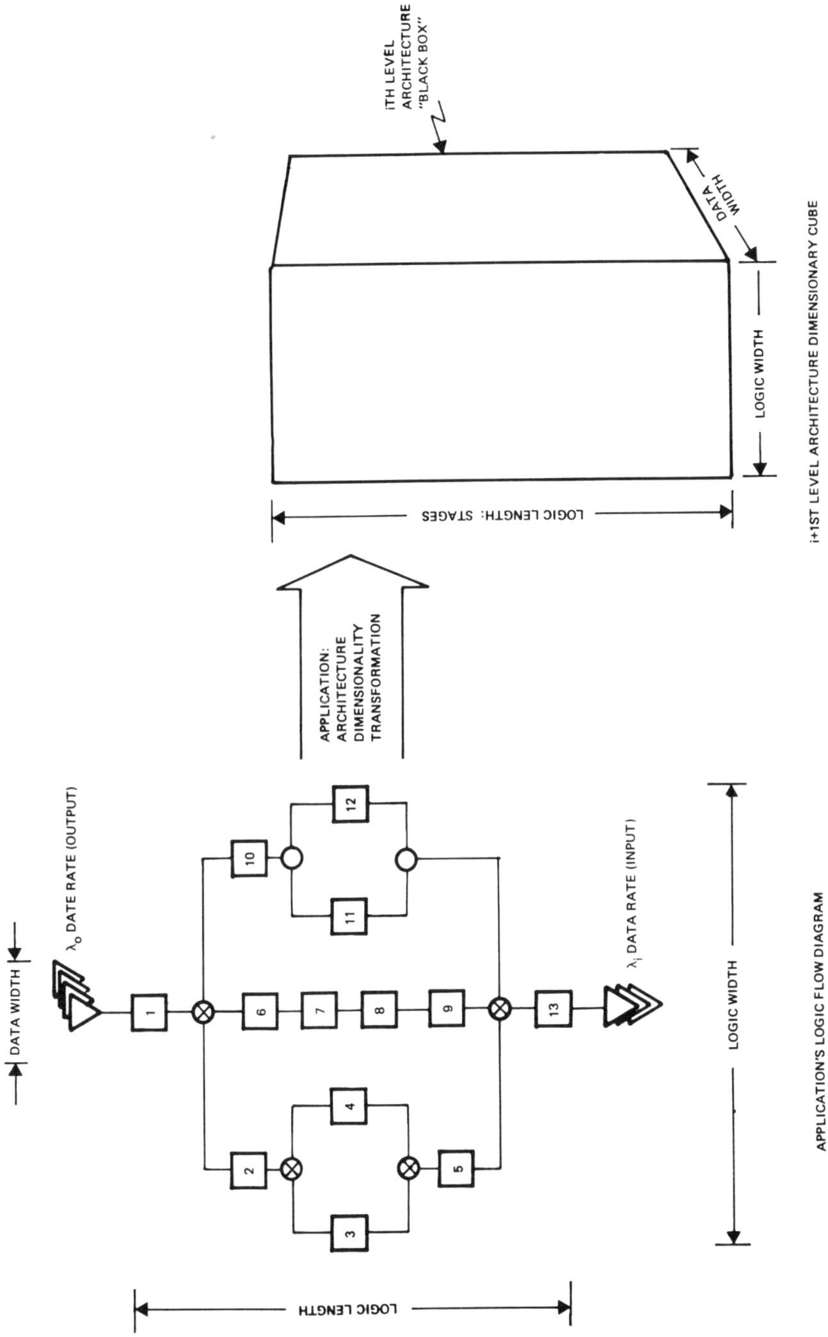

Figure 2.3-6. Concept of Architecture Dimensionality-Node and Computer Levels

applied at every level of design. Instead, several factors (Figure 2.3-7) must be considered collectively to determine the preferred architecture dimensionality at each level. These factors vary from design level to design level. One approach to determining a preferred architecture dimensionality for the node design level is outlined in Figure 2.3-8. The approach first considers the architecture dimension which results from using prespecified (e.g., off-the-shelf) components (substeps 1.1-1.3). One approach to obtaining this dimension could be based on the summation of all resources represented in the application's logic-flow diagram, divided by the throughput available with the prespecified off-the-shelf components. The quotient would approximate the lower bound* on the dimensionality. A second approach may be based on dividing the total application resource requirements by the largest module's resource requirement. Both of these dimensions assume commonality of computing resources. A third approach may be used when both sizing estimates and port-to-port times have been provided (substeps 1.4 and 1.5). This approach will define a lower bound on the number of computing components required to meet the worst-case critical-path port-to-port response requirements. Many algorithms associated with multiprocessor scheduling can be used to support this step; for example, Fernandez and Bussell [2-13] provide a good comparison of techniques for finding the lower bounds on the number of identical computational resources.

In addition, architecture dimensionalities may be determined purely on the basis of the applications structure (substeps 1.6-1.8). The structural considerations of the applications can provide additional architecture dimensionalities, one representing only the number of stages along the maximum-length logic path (substep 1.6), a second representing only the maximum number of concurrently executable modules (logic width) at any one stage of the logic length (substep 1.7), and a third representing the maximum concurrency (logic-length by logic-width) within the application's logic (substep 1.8). A substantial amount of attention has focused on pipeline and vector architectures as cost-effective means of applying concepts of concurrency to improve performance and reliability of computer systems[2-9,2-14].The fundamental problems which plague the designers of such architectures are well known, namely: (1) pipeline configuration bottlenecks, (2) sequencing strategy, (3) storage conflicts, and (4) applications-architecture suitability. These same issues will plague the designer at higher levels of design when the architecture is based on the exploitation of the application's inherent logic concurrencies.

To illustrate a heuristic approach for determining architecture dimensionality based on the applications structure, a hypothetical logic flow diagram has been postulated (Figure 2.3-9). Given the applications logic flow consisting of 10 computational entities (i.e., ξ_1 through ξ_{10}), which have been partitioned into 7 applications modules, we could determine the maximum architecture dimensionality (substep 1.8) by first creating a process interaction graph. The interaction graph illustrates the maximum number of stages within the applications (i.e., the longest path through the applications logic), and the maximum width within any single stage. For the example, the maximum logic length, P_1, P_2, P_3, P_6 P_7 is 5 stages, and the maximum logic width, P_3, P_4, P_5, is 3.

* Approximate in that neither the control overhead nor the requirements compatibility of each module to the off-the-shelf components is considered.

ARCHITECTURE DESIGN LEVEL	FACTORS AFFECTING ARCHITECTURE DIMENSIONALITY
1. SUBSYSTEM LEVEL	• EXTERNAL DPS INTERFACES (INPUT/OUTPUT) - LOCATION - INTERFACE REQUIREMENTS: COMPLEXITY, DATA RATES • NODE FORM FACTOR (POWER, SIZE, WEIGHT) CONSTRAINTS • LOGIC INTERFACE REQUIREMENTS • OPERATIONAL REQUIREMENTS - SURVIVABILITY - COST - PERFORMANCE: CRITICAL RESPONSE • COMMUNICATIONS TECHNOLOGY CONSTRAINTS
2. NODE LEVEL	• LOGIC STRUCTURE - LOGIC LENGTH - LOGIC WIDTH - DATA WIDTH: RATE - LOGIC BRANCH PROBABILITY - LOGIC INTERFACE: PROBABILITY • OPERATIONAL REQUIREMENTS - PERFORMANCE: THROUGHPUT & RESPONSE - RELIABILITY/AVAILABILITY - COST • ARCHITECTURE FORM FACTOR CONSTRAINTS • COMMUNICATIONS TECHNOLOGY CONSTRAINTS • HARDWARE AVAILABILITY
3. COMPUTER SYSTEM LEVEL	• LOGIC STRUCTURE - LOGIC LENGTH - LOGIC WIDTH - DATA WIDTH - LOGIC BRANCH PROBABILITY - LOGIC INTERFACE: PROBABILITY • OPERATIONAL REQUIREMENTS - PERFORMANCE: THROUGHPUT & RESPONSE - RELIABILITY/AVAILABILITY - GROWTH - COST • HARDWARE AVAILABILITY
4. SW/HW LEVEL	• HW/SW AVAILABILITY • ALGORITHM PARALLELISMS • OPERATIONAL REQUIREMENTS - PERFORMANCE: THROUGHPUT & RESPONSE - RELIABILITY/AVAILABILITY - COST

Figure 2.3-7. Factors Affecting Architecture Dimensionality

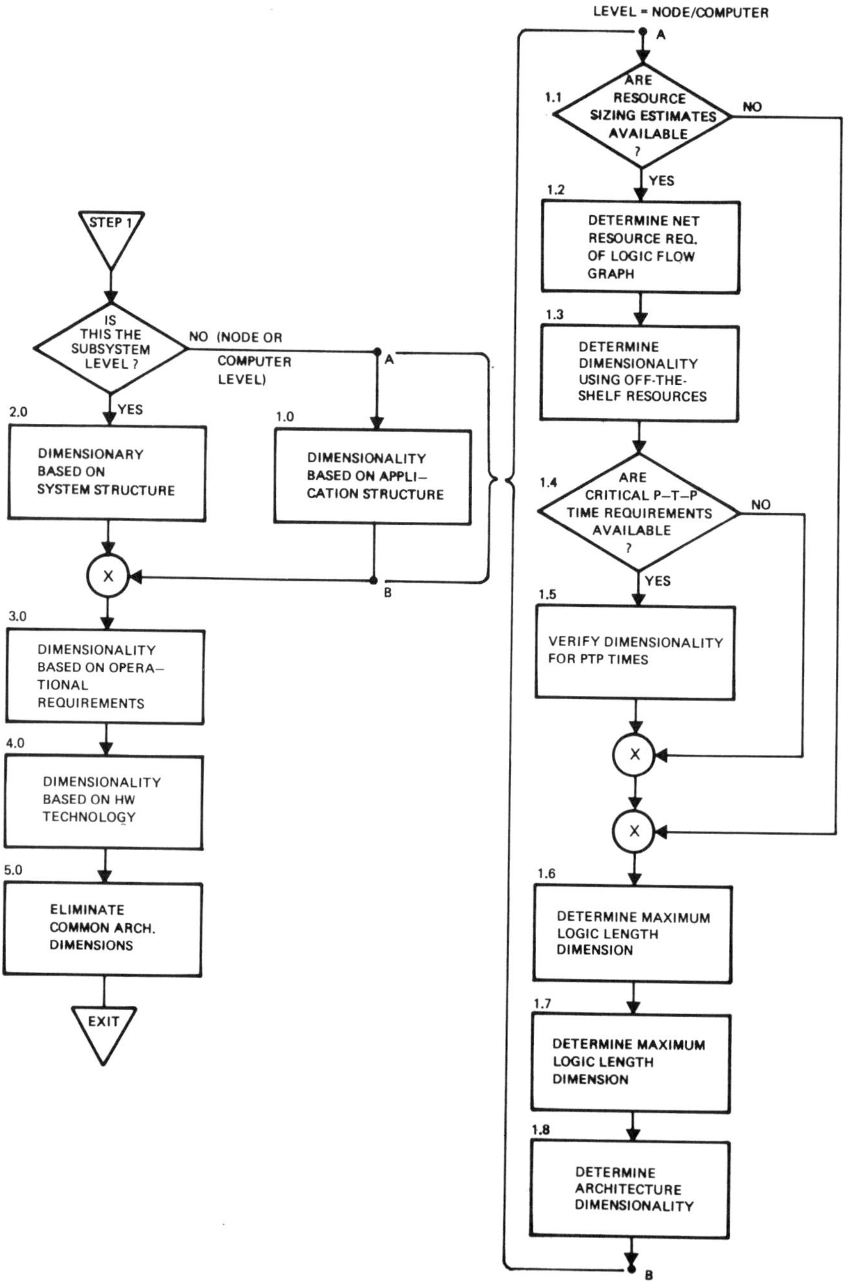

Figure 2.3-8. A Baseline Approach to Architecture Dimensionality

Together they would represent a 5x3 architecture dimensionality, consisting of 7 discrete processing components. This architecture then represents an upper bound on the logic concurrency which can be exploited. Analyzing a timeline of the utilization of each processing component can indicate the availability of each component to support reduction in the architecture dimensionality (to 5 stages) without loss of maximum concurrency.

An alternative dimension could be based on only the maximum logic length (5), or on only the maximum logic width (3). Typically, larger architecture dimensionalities will be designated if performance throughput or response requirements become stressing. The notion of maximum concurrency is not necessarily always the preferred objective, and should be traded against increased control complexity overhead costs availability/reliability and other payoffs. Similarly the axis along which architecture currency is based can have a significant effect on the overhead costs incurred in controlling the architecture.

2.3.3.2.2 Module Assignment Across Computing Components

Once the architecture dimensionality is defined, the requirement and data modules are mapped across computing components, which are treated as black boxes. The mapping can be performed in two distinct but tightly coupled steps: (1) the assignment of partitioned requirements modules, and (2) the mapping of data modules. The mapping step as we have seen (Section 2.3.3.2) is a combinatoric problem in nature; i.e.,

$$N = n^m,$$

where the total number of possible assignments of m modules to n computing resources is N. This inherently combinatoric mapping problem exists at each level of the design process. At the subsystem level, the problem becomes one of assigning abstract requirements and data modules to geographically distributed black-box node types. At the node design level, the problem becomes one of assigning requirements and data modules across black-box computer systems within a node. At the computer system design level, the assignment is across black-box processors within a computer. At the hardware/software design level, the assignment is to hardware and software within each processor.

Four related problems, multiprocessor scheduling, circuit-board layout, chip design, and distributed data base design, can all be formulated as combinatoric assignment problems. Multiprocessor scheduling typically considers multiple tasks to be assigned without preemption to meet some global performance-oriented objective. The assignment typically includes performance-oriented constraints on the assignment, such as minimum execution times, maximum throughput, or maximum utilization efficiency. The circuit-board layout and chip design problem is a static design problem in which the objective and constraints are time invariant. The data base design problem is probably the closest to that of the distributed system design problem. However, all four are far less complex than the design problem the distributed systems designer must face. In addition, the problem formulation of each of these design problems, and the assignment solution technique employed, are usually quite specialized and not versatile enough to support other formulations of the same problem, and certainly not the design problem of distributed systems.

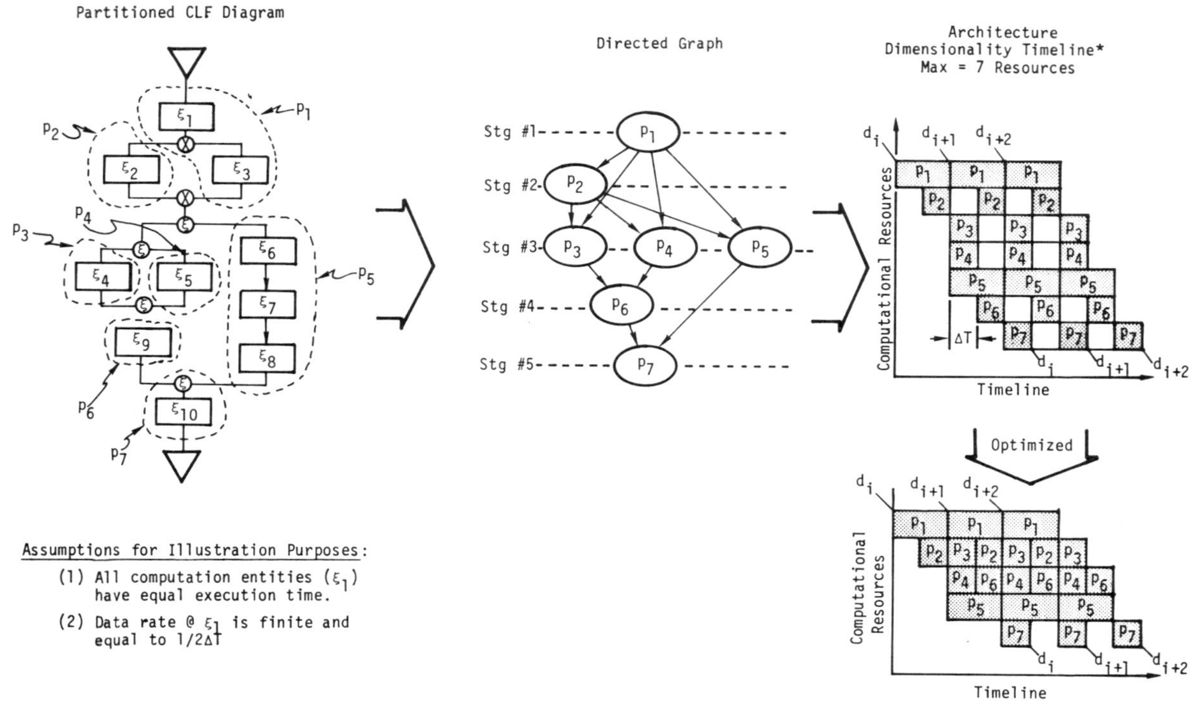

Figure 2.3-9. Determination of Architecture Dimensionality - Applications Logic Based

THE GENERAL ASSIGNMENT PROBLEM. Examining formulations of these four types of problems provides some insight into a general formulation of the assignment problem for distributed system design. Of greatest interest is the distributed data base design problem[2-15] and its solution approaches. The basic problem addressed is the assignment of data files across a network of user applications. Typically, these models are formulated around minimizing a performance objective such as data accessibility[2-16,17] or communication and storage costs [2-18,19]. In each case, the objective function is formulated as an integer variable, often determined from a weighted summation of several factors. Often these factors are dynamic (time variant) over the operation of the system; for that reason, optimum allocations can be produced only for selected time slices of the system's operational timeline. In most cases, optimum allocation of files for a time slice of the system's operational life can produce suboptimal allocations for other points in the timeline. An alternative approach is to define a single objective function as an integral of several critical timeframes of the system's operation. The resultant file allocation would be suboptimal for any one time frame, but closer to a global optimum. Still another approach would be to perform several file allocations (one for each critical time period), compare the resultant allocations, and manually synthesize a final allocation based on the composite results of multiple allocations.

One such approach is embodied in a tool developed by TRW to support the complex mapping step [2-30]. The tool, referred to as the allocation model, is based on a heuristic branch-and-bound algorithm. The model has the ability to handle design constraints and its general utility across multiple levels of design. The model (computer program DDPALOC) is operational on the TRW TSS (CDC 6600) and has been used successfully for several testcase problems. This model has proved to be quite satisfactory for small to medium-sized problems. For large problems, however, the user must accept suboptimal solutions because of the computation times. The current model is based on module coupling, which is defined as integer variables derived from weighted summation of multiple factors (see Figure 2.3-10). The coupling factors have proven to be a principal concern of the allocation step at the network and nodal design levels. However, at the computer and hardware/software design levels, the allocation criteria became more dependent on the internal characteristics of the modules.

The dynamic nature of most operational environments causes the coupling and internal factors, on which the allocation model is based, to vary over the engagement. This problem can be approached in two ways. The first is to repetitively use the current static allocation model at critical periods of the engagement. The second is to extend the model to accommodate the dynamics of the allocation factors over time. The second approach would require an extensive effort on the user's part to develop continuous time functions of the allocation factors in addition to substantially increased run times of the program. The allocation that would result would be no more accurate than the functions developed to represent the allocation factors. We prefer to keep the model simple and place the burden of synthesizing the multiple allocations produced over the engagement on the designer.

CONSTRAINTS. The design environment which we face will involve considerations of constraints on the (data and requirement) module assignments. The constraints complicate the design problem, but also simplify the combinatorics of the assignment process.

Physical constraints. A variety of constraints on the physical structure of distributed processing system must be anticipated in the mapping step. At the network design level, physical node locations will be identified or constrained. In airborne systems, weight volume, and power ceilings may be imposed on DPS elements. Availability, reliability, and survivability requirements; port-to-port response times; and processing accuracy will be specified. A summary of typical allocation constraints to be anticipated is tabulated in Figure 2.3-11, categorized as timing, location, size and redundancy constraints. Response time constraints will tend to be expressed in terms of allowable separation distances between modules, as determined by estimated communication delays. Modeling the communication delays imposed by distance, particularly for ground-based and space-based systems, requires that the physical locations of the black-box resources be defined. Since these points will be mobile in some cases, it may be necessary to define position on a worst-case or time-relative basis.

System engineering constraints. System engineering constraints include a number of limitations on the data processing components' (node, computer, processor) size and location; for example, number of components, on a fixed or minimum/maximum basis; node locations, e.g., to force co-location of data processing nodes with other system elements, or to avoid vulnerable locations or attack points; component capacities in cases where form factors (size, weight, power) are significant considerations; communication path routing, bandwidth or data volume on specific communication paths (i.e., ground-to-space pathes) may restrict connectivity (i.e., limits on the number of points with which a node may directly communicate).

MODULE MAPPING. An approach to module mapping is illustrated in Figure 2.3-12. During the mapping of the applications modules (substeps 2.1-2.4), the effects of data interactions and sharing between applications modules are not considered explicitly. Instead, the effects of shared data are considered indirectly as coupling factors between applications modules. For example, if module i writes data into a data module and that data is read by module j, then that data interaction will be modeled as a message between the two applications modules and included as a factor in their coupling relationship.

Following the mapping of applications modules, the shared data modules will be mapped across resources (substep 2.9). Current allocation models proposed by Chu [2-19], Levin and Morgan [2-17], and Mahmoud [2-18] are considered adequate for these steps and can be applied several times at key points along the system's operational timeline. The final allocation of the data would then be determined by collective analysis of all mappings. In cases where a single file is observed to migrate around the architecture, the designer may choose to locate the file at a single point in the architecture or replicate the file at several points and pay the additional overhead for managing replicated copies.

REDUNDANCY REQUIREMENTS. The derivation of the physical architecture structure must provide redundant capacity for survivability, graceful degradation, reliability/fault tolerance, and availability. At the network design level, the survivability requirement is a primary factor and is principally satisfied at this level. The other redundancy requirements may be satisfied either by additional nodes (hardware, software, and data), or by redundant elements or capacity within nodes. In general, it is more

DESIGN LEVEL	ALLOCATION PHASE: TYPICAL MODULE MAPPING FACTORS	
	Coupling	Internal
Subsystem	• Data Flow (peak, average): - Frequency (msgs/sec) - Msg size (wds) - Msg type (control/ status, data base, IPC) - Msg transmission response time requirement - Relative time and duration of peak msg flow for each msg type, a. control/status msgs b. DDB msgs c. IPC msgs • Module Interface Complexity: - # msg types - # distinct interfaces (threads) - external interfaces (e.g., sensors, C^3) for data source - interface sensitivity to change in requirements/ performance - criticality of interface to system operation	• Survivability of module • Processing response requirement • Relative module resource requirements: - computation - storage • Data load on module
Node	• Data Flow (peak, average) (see Subsystem design level) • Module Interface Complexity (see Subsystem design level)	• Equivalent Instruction counts (equiv. ADDS) • Storage (wds) - global data (shared) - load module • Processing response requirement
Computer	• Global Data Access: - Global data reads - Global data writes	• Type of Computational Operations (FLT.PT, Logical, etc.) • P-T-P Response Budget(sec) • Resource Requirement Profile (MIPS vs. TIME) • Type Data Manipulation Operations (search, sort, etc.) • Accuracy/Precision (differences)
Processor	• Module Interface Complexity (see Subsystem design level)	• Instruction Counts • P-T-P Response Budget • Type of Computational Operations (see above, Computer level) • Type of Data Manipulation Operations (see above, Computer level) • Storage (wds): Data Base

Figure 2.3-10. Key Criteria & Parameters for Partition & Allocation Phases

MAJOR DESIGN LEVEL	CONSTRAINT DESCRIPTION
	LOCATION
NETWORK	• REQUIRE COLOCATION OF SPECIFIED DP ELEMENTS WITH SYSTEM COMPONENT • SPECIFY REQUIRED AND CANDIDATE NODE LOCATIONS (PARAMETERIZE COUPLING ON DISTANCE) • SEPARATE DP ELEMENTS TO SATISFY SURVIVABILITY - SEPARATION OF CLASSES OF ELEMENTS PER NODE ASSIGNMENTS - SPECIFY BOUNDS ON NUMBER OF SELECTED NODE LOCATIONS - REDUNDANCY
	SIZE
ALL	• NODE COMPONENT CAPACITY (BOUNDS) - WEIGHT, VOLUME, THROUGHPUT, STORAGE, POWER, MESSAGE TRAFFIC
DPS	• COMMUNICATION BANDWIDTH OR DATA VOLUME LIMITS, PATH ROUTING
	TIMING
ALL	• CONSTRAIN SEPARATION OF STRONGLY COUPLED PROCESSES WHERE "C" IS MEASURED IN TERMS OF SEVERITY OF TIME RESPONSE REQUIREMENTS (DISTANCE-DEPENDENT PER COMMUNICATION DELAYS)
ALL	• THREADS WITH CRITICAL TIMING SHOULD NOT BE DISTRIBUTED
	REDUNDANCY
NETWORK, NODE	• SPECIFY REDUNDANT ELEMENTS IN DECOMPOSITION, ENFORCE DISTRIBUTION (SEPARATION) IN ALLOCATION: ESTABLISH INTERCONNECTIONS IN PHYSICAL DESIGN PHASE -- FOR SURVIVABILITY
COMPUTER	• RELIABILITY (COMPUTER LEVEL) DESIGNED AFTER ALLOCATION, BUT ALLOCATION MODEL MUST INCLUDE SIZE AND TIMING FACTORS TO ACCOMMODATE RELIABILITY-REDUNDANCY

Figure 2.3-11. Classes of Allocation Constraints

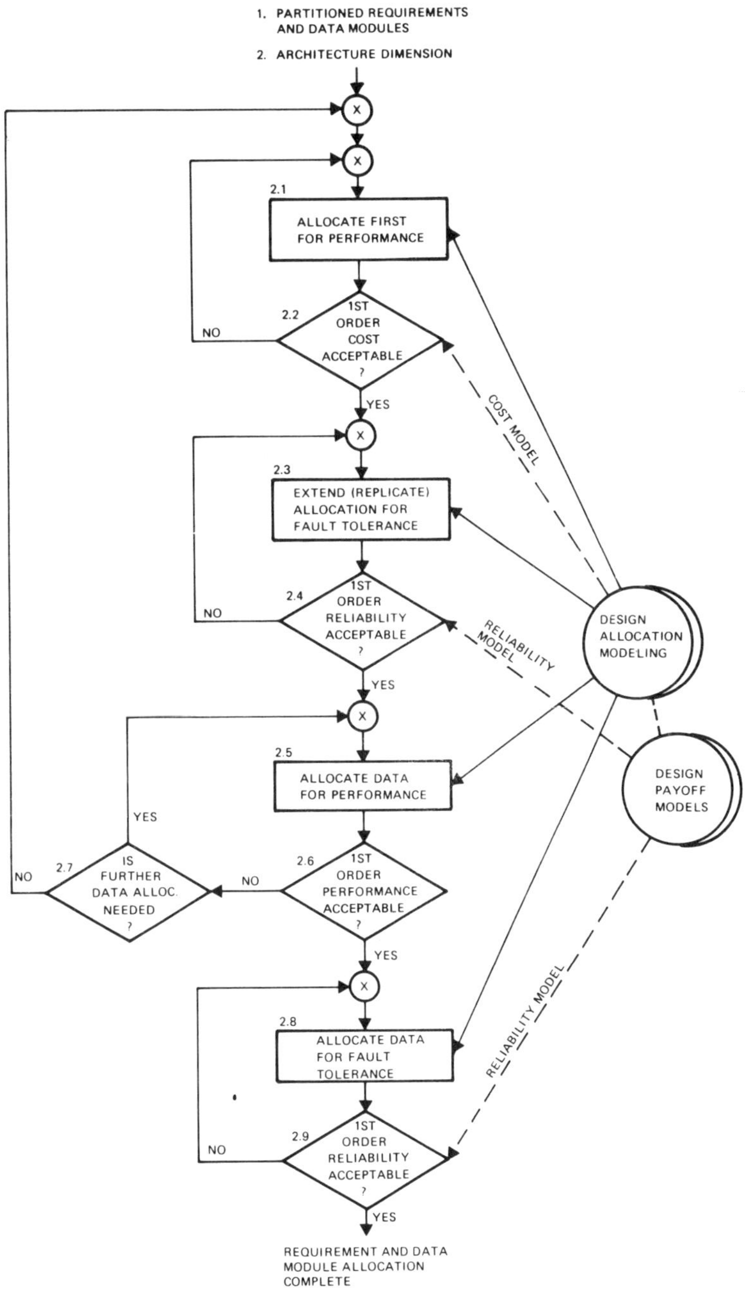

Figure 2.3-12. Macro Step 2: A Baseline Approach to Module Mapping

cost-effective to provide redundancy within nodes because of the facility and communication costs associated with extra nodes.

The designer must explicitly specify the applications, data modules, and resource redundancy required for survivability. This means that when an element is defined in the analysis phase, its redundant counterparts will also be included. These elements must be identified early to support the mapping process and also for consideration of resource requirements (i.e., throughput, storage and communication) necessary to maintain the redundant elements. The redundancy required in support of reliability and availability is a function of the physical design, since it is based on the provision of additional physical components, components that are introduced during the architecture dimensionality step.

Because of the complexity of the objective function formulated around functional and performance requirements, one approach to simplification is to decompose the objectives into several subobjectives. For example, the objective functions would first be formulated around performance/cost. The mapping which results could then be evaluated for reliability and adjusted (if necessary) to meet reliability requirements. Such adjustments could involve either reducing the architecture's serial dimensionality or replicating key modules to improve the fault-tolerance aspects of the architecture. For such a multiple-pass mapping approach, each pass would be constrained to meet performance requirements of throughput and critical port-to-port response. The assignment objective function would typically include such considerations as:

- Minimize message traffic
- Minimize number of resource-to-resource interfaces
- Maximize common resource (throughput) requirements across "black-box" resources
- Minimize communication bandwidth
- Equalize communication loading over network topology
- Equalize resource requirements (throughput and storage) over the network.

For each module mapping, the resulting black-box computing and logical communications requirements would be evaluated with respect to key payoff considerations; e.g., cost, reliability.

DATA ALLOCATION. One data allocation approach could be to first map the shared data modules to ensure that performance (data access response) is met (substeps 2.5-2.7). This would include the decision to replicate files if necessary from a performance response viewpoint. This mapping would be based on the application modules' use of the data.

In most cases, data will be placed at the user location (application module which performs the read) to improve access response. In the event that more than one application module reads the data, the data could be assigned to the user with the most critical data access time budget as determined during the analysis phase. After the assignment, the delays associated with remote access of the assigned data modules could be analyzed, and if their respective time budgets could not be met through remote access the data could be replicated for performance and placed local to the applications module. Only in the event that data access response budgets cannot be satisfied through data module replication would the initial assignment of applications modules be revised (substep 2.7).

Following the data assignment, the result could be analyzed for its inherent reliability; i.e., the question is posed: Are the replicated data modules (for performance) adequate to satisfy the fault tolerance (redundancy) for reliability? If not (substep 2.9), the data modules could be further replicated for reliability. At this point a distinction would be made between data replicated for performance and data replicated for reliability. This would be necessary to permit different data base synchronization protocols to be used.

The data allocation problem is perhaps the most emphasized of the distributed design process. Several models of the "file assignment" problem have been developed over the years; many of the initial models were based on optimizing a cost function which considers the factors of communications traffic due to file access/update and file storage cost. The early models of Chu[2-19],Whitney[2-20]and Casey[2-21]emphasized the file assignment problem in query processing systems; i.e., systems in which the file access/update pattern was assumed to originate at the processing nodes within the network rather than being generated by programs which were not assigned a priori to processing nodes. Morgan and Levin [2-16] addressed the program/data file relationship, and formulated a model which integrated the program and data file assignment problem within a computer network.

Most problem formulations will involve a combination of preassigned programs and data, and a complex set of constraint considerations. Typical constraints will include access response requirements, communication bandwidth, processor storage, processor message handling (overhead), and processor throughput. Many other constraints can evolve when security or fault tolerance become design considerations.

2.4 PERFORMANCE MODELING

2.4.1 Introduction

There exists a wide range of techniques for performance modeling of distributed systems (Figure 2.4-1) with varying degrees of modeling detail, model development cost, and performance result confidence. Starting with "rules-of-thumb", very little detail of the specific problem is required to apply such models. Instead, they are based on experience with similar problems. Such performance rules as, (1) 90:10 rule for data base access [2-22], (2) 100 MLI (processor overhead) per message; or (3) utilization thresholds for contention oriented bus protocols, often will guide the early design decisions of a distributed system before details of the applications have been developed. At the opposite end of the spectrum, processor benchmarking requires "applications-like" code to be available.

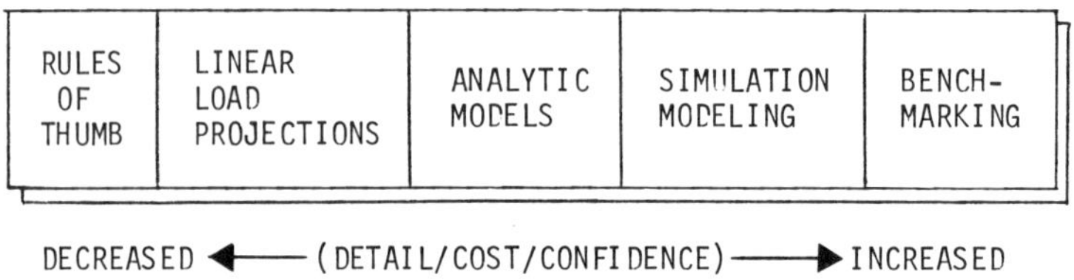

Figure 2.4-1. Performance Modeling Spectrum

In this section three of the most emphasized performance modeling techniques are examined - analytic modeling, simulation and benchmarking.

2.4.1.1 Analytic Contention Modelling Introduction

A characteristic of distributed data processing systems is that various system components may interact in ways that are unlike and unknown in systems containing a single processor.

One such important type of processor interaction is the contention of two or more processors in a multiprocessor system for the use of a limited number of shared resources. The term resource is used here to denote any type of device which may be accessed by any of the processors of the system. Banks of memory, I/O channels, special computational devices, are all typical types of data processing resources which could be simultaneously accessed by more than one processor. Assuming that a mechanism exists for choosing the first among the contending processors to receive use of the device, there remains the fact that other processors will be forced to wait for the use of that device and, in effect, suffer some loss of processor performance as a result of the increased response time associated with such shared devices.

Analytical models are intended to provide a low-cost steady state snapshot of this contention phenomenon. The analysis often relies on the techniques of queueing theory for the formal approach and initial results, but also uses statistics derived through simulations when the theoretical models are not appropriate. The analysis is founded on an attempt to understand the behavior of a system of several processors contending for the use of several devices of a single type (e.g., memory) to extending these results to systems containing collections of dissimilar devices (e.g., memory, I/O bus, special devices, etc.).

Analytic contention modeling provides a snapshot performance picture of the system and is therefore designed to be used in multiple passes for any complex architecture utilizing several classes of devices. Each pass addresses the contention resulting from a single class of shared resources for a single period of the overall operational timeline of the system.

2.4.1.2 Simulation Modelling Introduction

When a time-varying threat model is applied to a DDP architecture, it is virtually impossible to state with any confidence that all requirements are being met unless a computer simulation is used. A timeslice hand analysis is not accurate enough since queue buildup, wait times and time-dependent computer utilizations cannot be adequately predicted.

Thus, proposed DDP architectures are examined during Step 11 (synthesis phase, see Figure 2.2-1) by simulation and trace software packages. The simulation package uses as an input driver the threat timing model developed in Step 1 in the elaboration phase (see Figure 2.2-1A). Some of the important outputs of the simulator are CPU utilizations, task utilizations, queue wait times, queue lengths, task run times, and threat execution times. It is feasible to optimize key parameters of the DDP design; e.g., the allocation of tasks to computers, the number of computers, the speed of the computers, frame sizes, and frame offsets.

The trace package provides the wait, run, start and end times of each task for each stimulus type. Several important thread times are also accumulated for each return and for groups of returns. Both tools may be used for both analyses of the candidate architectures and for design of improved architectures.

2.4.1.3 Benchmarking Introduction

Benchmarking is a calibration mechanism for processor performance as opposed to a prediction mechanism for system performance such as analytic centention modeling and simulation. Benchmarks permit estimation of a processor's performance in a dedicated, standalone, best case environment.

The benchmark test cases are selected as being representative of the applications code to be developed. The benchmark test cases may be based on such commercial baselines as the Whetstone or it may be a selected subset of the applications code. The benchmark tests must be carefully controlled when used to compare machines across different vendors or across different product lines within a single vendor. Benchmark performance can often be misleading because of the performance biases which result from variations in compiler efficiencies, native instruction sets, and pure hardware performance. For example, it is possible for one machine to provide a higher MIPS (Millions of Instructions Per Second) rating but execute a benchmark slower than a second machine due to differences in native instruction set and/or differences in compiler efficiency.

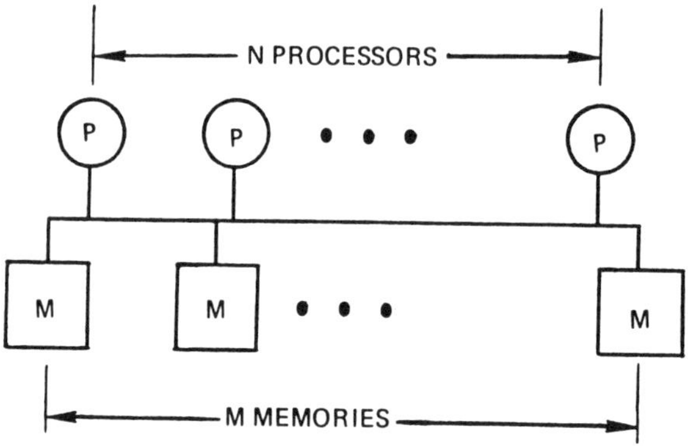

Figure 2.4-2. General System Configuration

2.4.2 Contention Modeling

A commonly proposed technique for achieving throughput improvements in advanced computer architectures is to take advantage of inherent software concurrencies through the use of multiple processors. Theoretically, such systems are rated as having throughputs equivalent to the sum of the throughputs of the component processors. In implementing such systems, however, the effective system throughput is invariably less than the theoretic potential described above. A major* reason for this performance loss is that the several processors will interfere with each other's normal sequence of operations.

One typical mode of interprocessor interference is the situation in which the several processors contend with each other for the use of a limited number of shared resources. This contention phenomenon may occur in a variety of situations. Figure 2.4-2 is a simple schematic depicting one such situation in which N processors have common access through some sort of switching device or high speed bus to M memory banks. We assume that the data bus or switching device does not interfere with the processors' access to the memories, that is all N processors could be making simultaneous use of this device. What remains then is the processor interference at the memories themselves. In general this will consist of two or more processors making simultaneous access requests of a particular memory unit, only one will be selected (at random) for access, and the other processors will be forced to queue up and wait for their turn to receive service at the memory bank.

---

* We also acknowledge the degradation effects of control and communications handling overhead in distributed systems which usually exceed that of contention.

It is this necessity of making processors spend additional time in waiting which causes the reduction in the total effective system throughput. A similar interference effect will occur when other types of resources, such as special computational devices (e.g., processor's floating point unit or limited bandwidth data channels), are used in a shared manner by several processors.

Analytic models for contention analyses can provide quick-look performance comparisons between multiple candidate architectures. The relative performance comparisons would permit zeroth-order cost-performance tradeoffs between architectures. Such a model would not be intended to provide verification of an architectural design, instead simulation modeling would be preferred.

Formulation of the contention model must include: (1) stating assumptions necessary to define the system; (2) choosing a mathematical approach for system modeling that encompasses these assumptions, and (3) solving the resulting equations to yield specific analytic results. The results would yield steady-state performance predictions of the system at a key (e.g., peak load) time slice of the system's operation. Analytic models must be used recursively to develop a performance indication of the system's dynamic behavior. The model formulation is the major step - the selection of the mathematical solution approach and the solution itself, though important, are secondary. If the formulation is based upon inaccurate assumptions of the behavior of the system or its input data profile the solutions will be in error regardless of its mathematical correctness. The model formulation can significantly complicate the mathematical solution technique, and possibly result in the formulation of an unsolvable problem. To illustrate this we discuss two model formulations, an elementary and an advanced.

2.4.2.1 Elementary Model

The elementary contention model is presented because it serves as a useful preparation for understanding the more advanced model, but also because it is meaningful in its own right as well as being simpler to use than the advanced mode.

We begin by stating the basic system assumptions. We assume a system architecture very similar to that shown in Figure 2.4-2 except that the resource type is not restricted to memory banks but may be quite general. There are then three basic assumptions:

1) T_r, resource cycle time, is a constant for all of the identical resource units,

2) All processors access each of the resource units with equal likelihood, and

3) All processors spend the same average amount of time, (T_p), following access of a resource device, in performing internal computations before making another access attempt.

With these as a set of system definitions it is possible to use the techniques of queueing theory to develop a mathematical description for a number of relevant system parameters. The most important single parameter, however, is the unit response time, defined as being the time from the original processor access attempt at a specific resource device to the point at which the processor is finished with the device. Clearly this response time includes any time spent by the processor in waiting as well as the actual resource cycle time, T_r. A formula for this response time is available in terms of the parameters previously defined but it is more useful to define a new parameter:

$$f = \frac{T_r}{T_p + T_r}$$

Where:

f represents the fraction of time each processor would normally spend engaged in resource accesses if there were no interference from other processors.

Since f is a dimensionless quantity it is preferable to use it in general formulas where the scaling effects of particular system cycle times would otherwise confuse matters. We have then, for R, the effective (degraded) resource cycle time:

$$R = \frac{1}{2}\left\{(2 + \frac{N}{M} - \frac{1}{f}) + \sqrt{(2 + \frac{N}{M} - \frac{1}{f})^2 + 2\left[2(\frac{1}{f} - 1) - \frac{N}{M}(1 + \frac{1}{M})\right]}\right\}$$

Where:

N represents the number of processors accessing the M memory banks.

This fairly simple formula may be used to determine various other system parameters derivable from the resource response time. These will be treated separately in the section on system throughput.

2.4.2.2 Advanced Model

While the respone time formula for the elementary model was straightforward and convenient to use it represents a situation that is too limited in scope to be applicable to anything but the simplest of situations. By altering one of the fundamental system assumptions we make the model somewhat more general in its applicability. The second assumption, when altered, will read as follows:

2') Each processor will access the jth resource unit with probability a_j, $\left(\sum_{j=1}^{M} a_j = 1\right)$

This allows the modeling of situations in which the processors may all behave identically but may reference the units, say memory banks, in some sort of preferential manner. The technique for solving such a problem becomes quite involved, and we can merely state the final results in terms of the parameters defined to this point. We have for R_j, the response time of the jth resource unit:

$$R_j = \frac{2 - a_j\left(\dfrac{fN}{1 - f + f\sum_k a_k R_k}\right)\left(1 + \sum_k a_k R_k\right)}{2\left[1 - a_j\left(\dfrac{fN}{1 - f + f\sum_k a_k R_k}\right)\right]}, \quad 1 \le j \le M.$$

These represent a system of M non-linear equations in the unknowns R_j. Unlike the formula resulting from the elementary model these cannot be solved explicitly, instead numerical techniques must be applied to obtain the desired results.

We illustrate the use of this more advanced model by hypothesizing a situation in which three processors are connected to three physically identical memory banks. The processors are assigned the execution of identical code so that all will spend the same fraction of their time in memory access activities. The data base, however, is not uniformly distributed among the memory banks. Memory bank 1 will receive 50% of the memory accesses, memory bank 2 will receive 35% of the processor data requests, while memory 3 will be accessed in only 15% of the requests. Clearly memory 1 will be the most congested and memory 3 will be the least, but by using the above formulas we may obtain more quantitative values for the different memory response times.

By assigning a_1, a_2, and a_3 the values of 0.50, 0.35, and 0.15 respectively and solving the above set of equations for a variety of values of f we obtain the data graphically presented in Figure 2.4-3. Plotted on this same graph are the results of using the same input parameters in a detailed digital simulation; a much more expensive and time consuming procedure than solving the equations of the analytic model. It is noteworthy though that the analytic and simulation results largely agree in their values for the degraded response times.

Although the given formulas make reference only to the increased resource response times it is a relatively simple matter to derive other system parameters as is described in the next section.

2.4.2.3 System Throughput

Although the degree to which processor contention effects processing response time are considered important performance indicators, the general figure of merit most often desired is the system's throughput. In this section the relationship between extended response times and degraded computational throughput will be described with specific examples given to illustrate the concept involved. To keep the discussion simple, the systems addressed will be restricted to those covered by the elementary model, extensions to the more advanced scheme are straighforward.

The obvious place to begin is to provide a definition for computer throughput. If we define an operational cycle as being the time between consecutive processor references to the shared resource device and k is the average number of instructions executed during such a cycle then we propose the following definition of processor throughput Θ :

$$\Theta = \frac{k}{T_p + T_r}$$

where T_p and T_r are as defined previously. This gives a value for Θ in instructions per second. Using this as the fundamental definition we then define the system effectiveness, $\mathcal{E}$, as the portion of a processor's throughput not lost to contention effects. In terms of previous parameters this gives

$$\mathcal{E} = \frac{\Theta'}{\Theta} = \frac{T_p + T_r}{T_p + R}$$

where Θ' refers to the effective throughput of a processor in the presence of other similar processors, and R is the resulting resource response time. If we use the definition of f, the fraction of time spent in resource accesses, we obtain

$$\mathcal{E} = \frac{1}{1 + f(R - 1)}$$

If we define the system degradation, $\mathcal{E}$, as the portion of original throughput lost to contention we have

$$\delta = 1 - \mathcal{E} = \frac{f(R - 1)}{1 + f(R - 1)}$$

Figure 2.4-4 presents the effects of contention on system throughput for a three processor system coupled to a variety of memory configurations. As the number of memories is increased and the data base kept uniformly distributed the likelihood of memory conflicts is reduced. The result is reflected in the graphs: For a given memory access frequency the loss due to contention declines with increases in the numbers of memories.

The above result is hardly surprising, as the case described was very simple. More complex situations often present behavior that is not so easily predicted. **A summary description of two more complex configurations is provided.**

We seek to determine the necessary excess throughput capacity required to exactly compensate for contention effects in replacing a single high speed processor coupled to three high speed memories with N identical processors of lower speed. In Case I we replace the processor but retain the high speed memories. In Figure 2.4-5 are presented the effects of using different numbers of slower processors. Two facts are noteworthy in this case. First of all, the required excess throughput capability is quite modest, typically less than an additional 5% of processor power is required. Second, the trend indicates that less additional processor power is required as the number of processors increases. The simplest way of seeing this is to observe that as the number of processors will be slower thereby spending proportionately less of their time in memory accesses and thus decreasing the likelihood of a memory conflict.

In Case II not only is the high speed processor replaced but the individual memories are also replaced with slower units. However, the ratio of cycle times of the replacement memories to replacement processors is maintained to be the same as in the original equipment (presumably if one is saving money by replacing expensive processors then more money is saved by replacing expensive with cheaper memories). Figure 2.4-6 depicts the required excess throughput capacity for Case II for different numbers of replacement processors. Here the results are strikingly different from before. First, the required additional capacity is much greater than before, as much as 30% or higher is typical. Secondly, the trend of growth is reversed: The more processors used, the greater the required excess capacity. This is understandable when one notes that since each processor retains the same memory access frequency as the original processor, the addition of more, albeit slower, processors, can only lead to increases in number of processor conflicts over memory.

2.4.2.4 Contention Analysis of Complex Architectures

Most of the prior discussion has been based on very simple architectures with only a single pair of resources causing contention; for example processor-memory, or processor-I/O. Unfortunately, the architectures which we more realistically anticipate facing will be composed of many types of resources which interact to produce many contributing elements of contention for the overall architecture.

The development of complex models which handle such multiple resource architectures can be extremely difficult and costly. Once they are developed they tend to become very limited in their scope of application. We have chosen to approach the problem differently. We have chosen to investigate the potential of using one basic model in an iterative, nested fashion to evaluate those complex architectures. The method of application of the model is currently under investigation.

We recognize that the extension of our model to evaluate complex architectures will result in inaccuracies in the performance results. However, these inaccuracies must be investigated over several architecture configurations to determine potential inherent model biases. Can these biases be predicted? Since the main purpose of this model is to support the definition of candidate architecture designs based on first-order cost-performance tradeoffs, we feel the inaccuracies are not major problems if they are consistent across architectures or can be predicted and backed out of our performance measurements.

One initial concept for iterative application of the model involves nesting the performance results of a sequence of successive performance measurements. Consider an example architecture (Figure 2.4-7) which contains six classes of resources which interact. The nesting approach applies a sequence of six consecutive contention analyses of the architecture starting with the resources directly interfacing the processors. In this case that

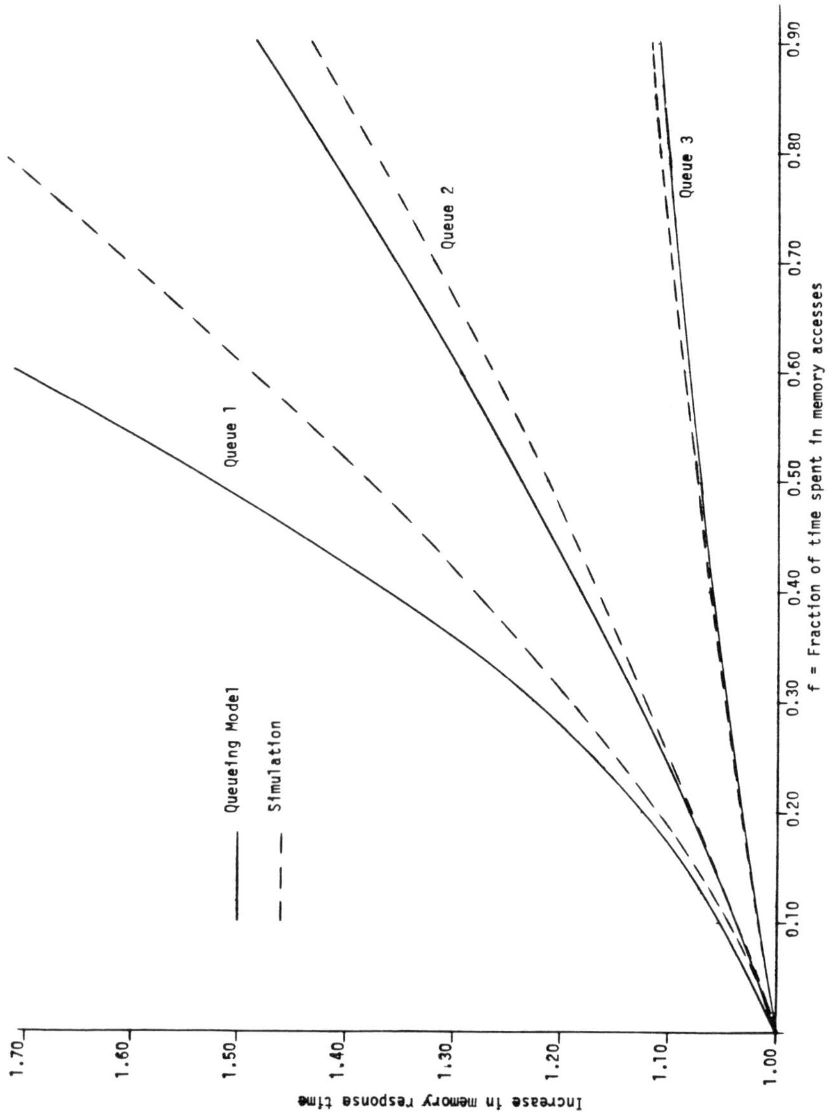

Figure 2.4-3. Memory Response Times

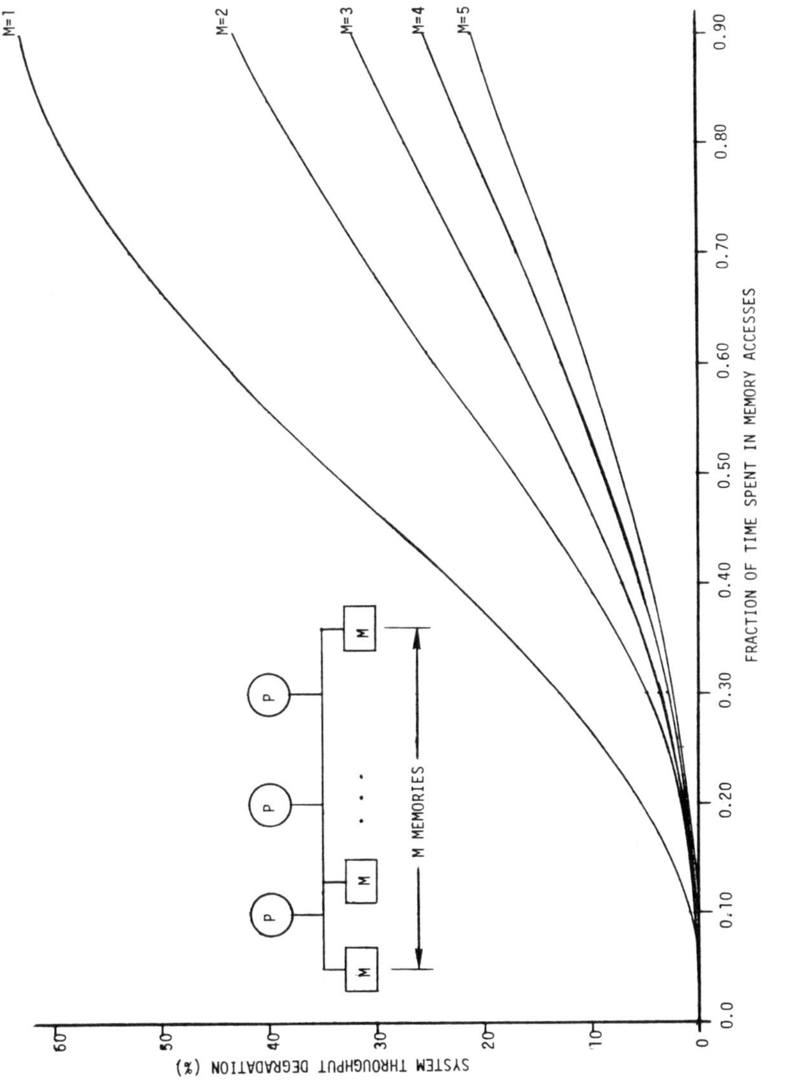

Figure 2.4-4. Throughput Degradation

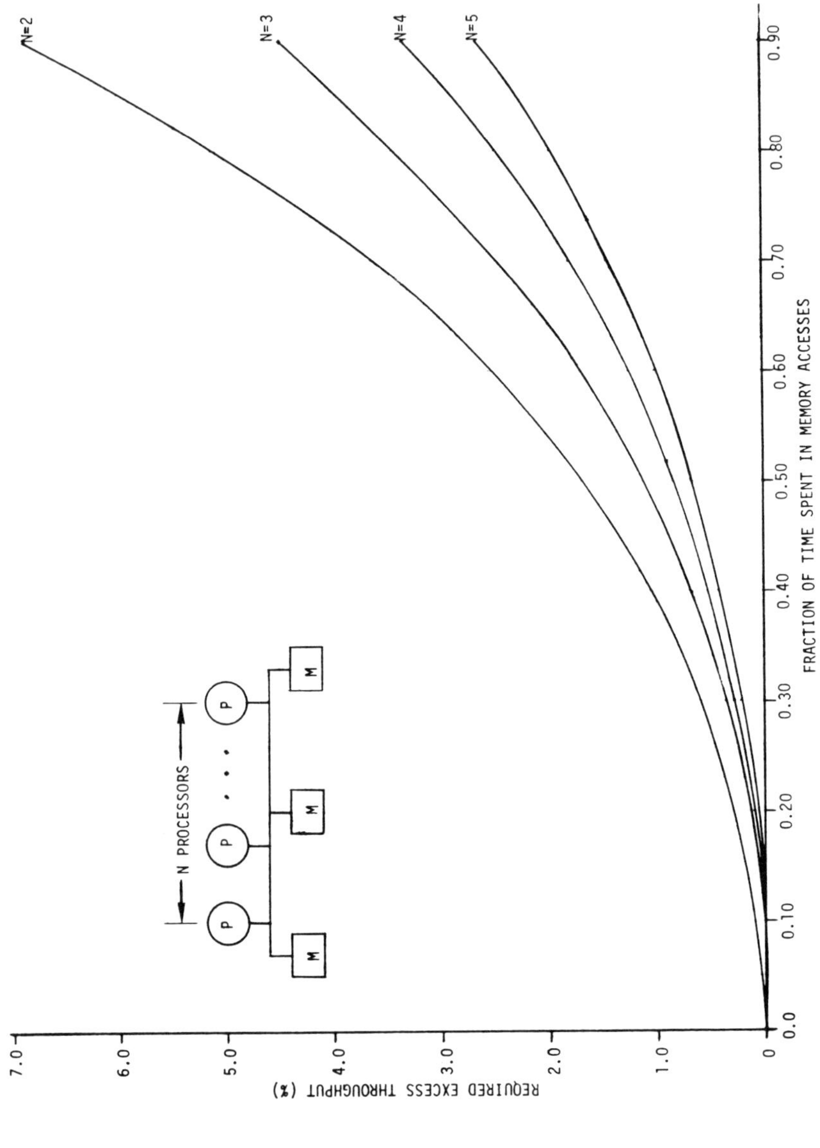

Figure 2.4-5. Case I: Slow Processors - Fast Memory

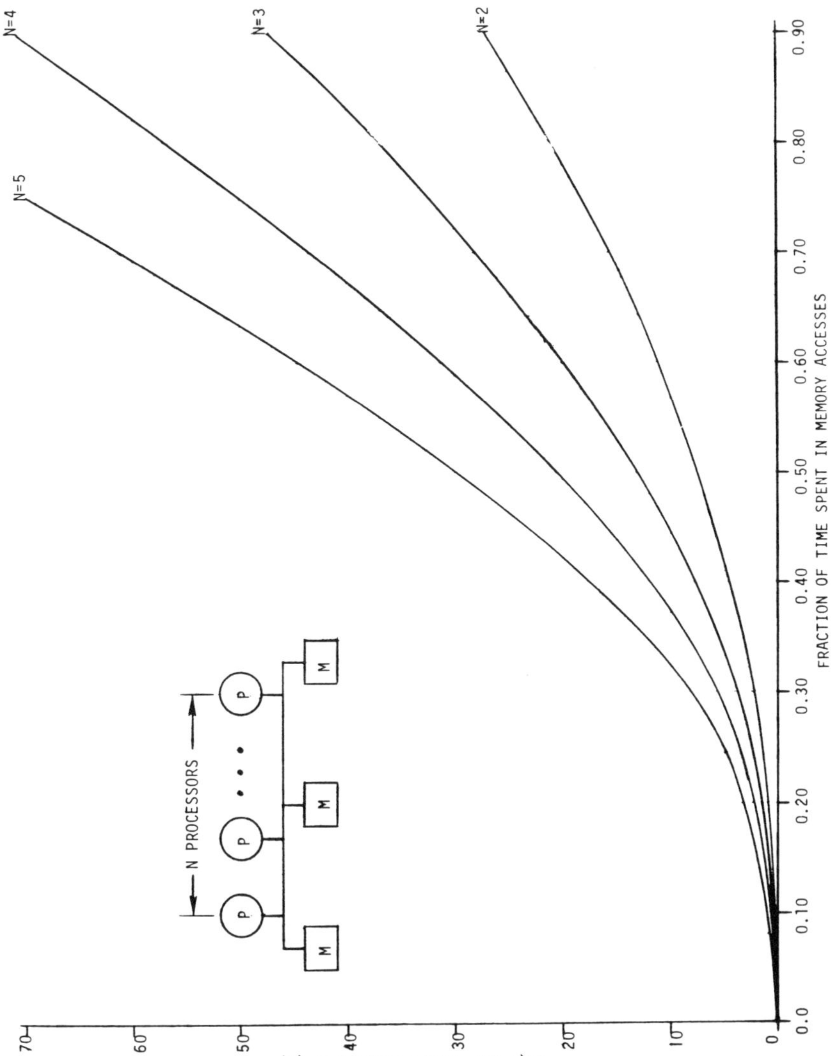

Figure 2.4-6. Case II: Slow Processors - Slow Memory

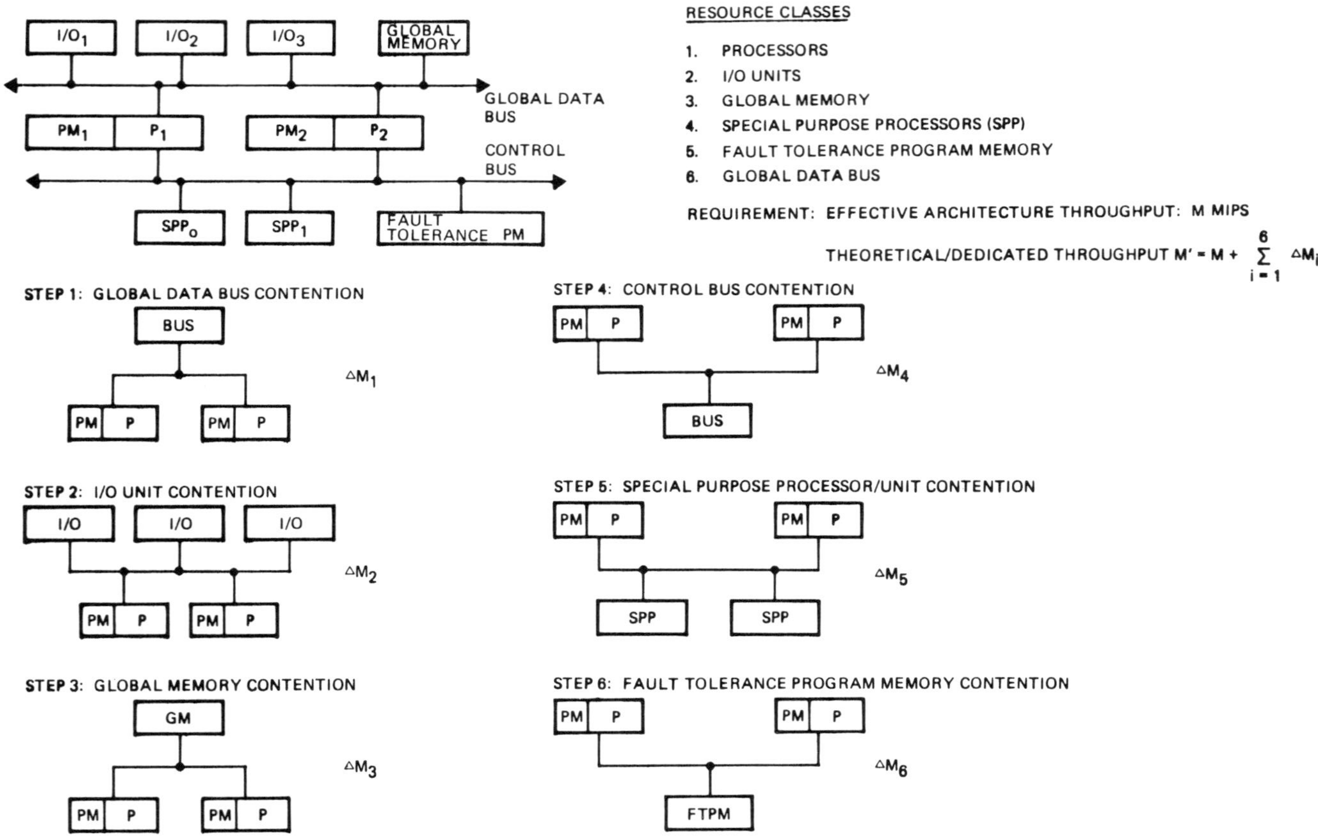

Figure 2.4-7. Contention Modeling Approach - Complex Architecture

would be the control and data buses. However, in most instances contention due to the control bus would be negligible. The contention due to the multiple processors sharing the data bus (Step #1) would be anticipated to cause some performance degradation. The model would permit the design to trade off bus bandwidth with processor throughput and number of processors to achieve some degraded but acceptable performance which would be considered the effective (theoretical throughput minus degradation) throughput of the processors. Using the effective throughput of the processors determined in Step #1, we would examine the further contention due to the input/output units of the architectures. In this step (Step #2) the number of processors are held constant and only the number of I/O units and their throughput relative to the processor throughput are traded off. This step would then produce a degradation component which would decrease the effective throughput of the processors.

The result following this procedure of nesting is a final effective throughput for the architecture of,

$$MIPS_{eff} = mips_i + \alpha_{error}$$

where $mips_i$ = effective throughput due to the ith resource interaction; or

$$mips = f\,(mips_{i-1})$$

$$mips_{i-1} = f\,(mips_{i-2})$$

$$\vdots$$

and, α_{error} = unknown inaccuracy between the apparent effective throughput as indicated by the contention model and the actual effective throughput of our architecture.

If α_{error} is a predictable bias in the value of $MIPS_{eff}$ for any architecture, or is a predictable quantity then its effects can be subtracted in the cost-performance tradeoffs of multiple architecture configurations. The validity of the α_{error} bias assumption, or its predictability must still be determined.

2.4.3 Simulation Modeling

Discrete event simulation modeling can provide a dynamic performance profile of a distributed processing system to support system design and/or validation. The model is based on functional models of the system's hardware components (e.g., processors, network), applications programs, real time control and data flow. The functional models are usually flexible and can be upgraded to include actual algorithms and in the final stage may include actual applications code.

The description of the functional models are often based on both architecture requirements and the resultant characteristics of the architecture design (Figure 2.4-8) to be developed. For example, an architecture requirement could specify that the network be based on a 1 MWPS bus, while the bus protocol could be an open design decision. The simulation could be used as a design/analysis vehicle from which to evaluate bus protocol options. The simulation would provide a means of

SIMULATION MODELS	TYPICAL MODEL DESCRIPTORS
HARDWARE	• PROCESSOR THROUGHPUT • BUS BANDWIDTH • MEMORY ACCESS TIME • PROCESSOR I/O BANDWIDTH • NETWORK TOPOLOGY
SOFTWARE	• TASK INSTRUCTION SIZE • TASK DATA INPUT/OUTPUT • ENABLEMENT/EXECUTION CRITERIA • LOGIC BRANCH CONDITIONS • TASK INSTRUCTION MIXES
DATA FLOW	• FILE DEFINITION • FILE LOCATION • FILE ACCESS/UPDATE TASK INTERFACES • READ/WRITE RECORD SIZE • FILE ACCESS/UPDATE COST
CONTROL	• TASK/PROGRAM SCHEDULER ALGORITHM • RESOURCE MANAGEMENT ALGORITHMS - GLOBAL LOAD BALANCING/SHEDDING - DYNAMIC FAILURE RECONFIGURATION • COMMUNICATIONS PROTOCOL • CONTROL ENABLEMENT/EXECUTION CRITERIA • CONTROL TASK COST INSTRUCTION COUNT

Figure 2.4-8. Typical Functional Model Simulation Descriptors

evaluating the sensitivity of such performance indicators as bus utilization, buffer sizing, and message transmission delays to various protocol options.

One of the drawbacks of discrete-event simulation is often the storage requirements necessary for maintaining the dynamic run-time event tables, pointers and system states. In addition, discrete event simulation as an evaluation tool for distributed system design, results in exponential increases in simulation run-time and storage requirements as the dimension and fidelity of the simulated system increase. Because of the complexity and cost of discrete event simulation, many simulation languages (e.g., TRW's SALSIM, GPSS, SIMSCRIPT) employ dynamic memory management on the Host machine as a means of reducing the storage requirements. More recently, the use of a distributed network of machines executing together as the simulation Host [2-23] have offered potential of reducing the simulation run-time. However, the use of a distributed Host approach to simulation requires solution to a critical issue, synchronization of the distributed Host processor clocks, and there are many synchronization techniques which have been studied [2-24].

To illustrate the utility of discrete event simulation, a discussion of discrete event simulation developed for performance evaluation of a distributed system architecture is provided.

2.4.3.1 <u>Discrete Event Simulation Operation</u>

The DDP system simulator is a discrete-event functional simulator capable of modeling a network of computer hardware facilities. The simulator utilizes TRW's Systems Analysis Language for Simulation (SALSIM) to handle the general functions required for a simulation management and statistics gathering and recording. The simulation is operational on the CDC 6500 timeshare system.

SALSIM is the name given to a collection of subroutines coded in FORTRAN intended to facilitate the programming of simulation applications. As with all discrete event-oriented simulation languages, SALSIM has the facility to handle the following three functions automatically:

- event timing and scheduling
- list processing
- dynamic memory allocation

The simulator models are often written in a higher order language. For TRW's SALSIM the language is FORTRAN with the calls to SALSIM subroutines imbedded in the code making for a very comprehensible code. An advantage of using SALSIM is the elimination of the size constraints on queues by taking advantage of the dynamic memory allocation capability of SALSIM. Thus, instead of defining queues as arrays with fixed maximum sizes, queues can expand and contract in length during the simulation.

To build the simulation, simplifications are often made such as:

- Hardware/software errors, and associated error recovery models are not considered.

- Communications is assumed to occur at infinite bandwidth; neither the communications processing nor resultant data rates are considered. Enablement messages are defined, and a data flow is identified, however.

- The processing internal to each applications model is sequential and yields a linear (not probabilistic) cost as a function of data processed. Each enablement message causes some processing, and spawns another enablement message.

Basically the model simulates several items termed "tasks" which gain control of or occupy certain entities called "facilities" for a specific period of time. A facility represents any computer hardware device which executes a task, i.e., a set of code or any part of a computer program.

Associated with each task is a parameter called instance. An instance is a unit of measure used in a particular task to determine the amount of processing time that particular execution of that task will require. The definition of an instance is dependent upon the function of the task. For example, if a task's function is to compute the sum of a variable number of addends, then the task's run time is a function of the number of addends and the number of instances for this task is the number of addends at each execution of the task. The number of instances associated with a task may change each time the task executes.

The tasks in a simulation interface with one another. When a particular task is completed it may cause one or more other tasks to execute. All of the tasks are assigned priorities to determine the order of execution when two or more tasks wish to use the same facility at the same time. The processing delays due to these scheduling conflicts, and the efficiency of the system in terms of throughput and percent utilization of the facilities are some of the parameters which can be analyzed.

Figure 2.4-9 gives an overview of the simulator. The three components of the simulator -- the operating system model, the application program model, and the hardware model -- are discussed below.

Operating System Model

The model of the operating system consists of routines which handle the dispatching of tasks, preempting and restarting tasks, and data management. These routines include the logic necessary to determine the priority of tasks, the status of the various hardware facilities such as memories and CPUs, and time order of all activities. There are simplifying assumptions from a real operating system, of course, but the following capabilities are available:

- Tasks may run on any number of CPUs but may run on only one at a time.

- When a task is scheduled to run, it will run on the first available CPU on which it is allowed to run .

- Tasks may be time enable or data enabled. Time enabled tasks run at a specific time and may or may not be periodic whereas data enabled tasks run when triggered by another task.

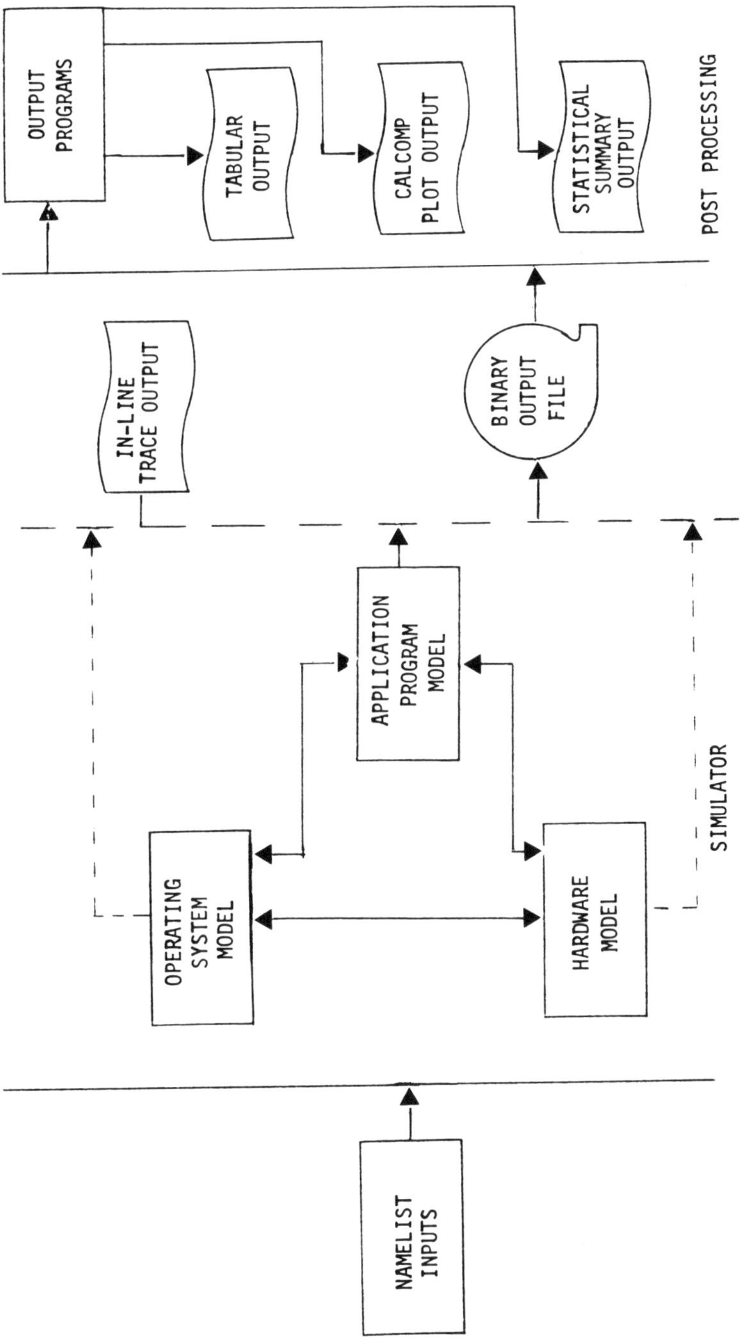

Figure 2.4-9. Simulator Overview

- Tasks are prioritized with zero priority tasks (those with highest priority) being tasks which can interrupt other tasks.
- Zero priority tasks may only run on one CPU.
- An interrupted task will always restart on the same CPU on which it was preempted.
- There is an operating system overhead. This is an input value for each application task. It is modeled as a percent multiplier to the basic cost of running each task.
- There is a startup cost (cost of loading the task) which is also an input value.

When a particular task has executed and another task must execute next, the first task is said to enable the second task. A task may enable itself. There are two types of tasks: data-enabled tasks and time-enabled tasks.

When a task has executed and another task is to be performed immediately afterwards, the second task is said to be data enabled and is placed in the correct queue for the facility in which it will execute. This queued task should execute as soon as its enabling task finishes execution unless the queued task is delayed due to a higher priority task in the same facility.

When a task executes and another task is to be performed at a specific time afterwards, the second task is said to be time enabled and is placed in the correct queue for the facility in which it will execute. This queued task will execute at the specified time unless the queued task is delayed by a task already executing or by a higher priority time enabled task in the same facility. Time-enabled tasks have priority over data-enabled tasks. If the specific time at which a time-enabled task is to execute is not dependent upon the execution time of any other task, then it may be treated as an exogenous event .

SALSIM considers events (tasks) to be of two types: endogenous and exogenous. Endogenous events are those events which are scheduled internally by the simulator. This corresponds to one task enabling another. Exogenous events are events caused from outside the simulated system, i.e., independent of what is going on in the simulation.

If the similar has a task "X" to model which is to be scheduled to execute every 10 seconds regardless of what other tasks may be doing, then that task "X" is treated as an exogenous event. An exogenous event is scheduled by placing it on the SALSIM input file. An entry on this file for task "X" would be necessary for each 10 second internal at which it is supposed to execute. A special SALSIM routine, EXOG, reads this file and insures that the events are enabled at the correct times in the simulation.

Hardware Model

When a task is executed, there are four parameters which determine the amount of simulation time the task will require. These parameters are:

1) the processing rate of the facility in which the task executes (instructions per unit time)

2) the number of instances the task must process

3) the task overhead - the number of instructions the task must execute independent of the number of instances it must process

4) the number of instructions the task must perform in processing each instance.

An instruction can be considered as the basic computing unit of which the tasks are composed. It may be a line of code, a basic operation such as addition, a state change of a flip-flop, or an entire subroutine. Its definition must be consistent with the definitions of task instances and facility rates.

The hardware model consists of the MIP ratings or speed of the CPUs and the number of instructions executed in running each task. There are input values -- a MIP rating for each CPU and instruction counts for each task. The following equation is used in calculating the run time as each task execures:

$$\text{RUN TIME} = \text{CET} * (\ 1.+\text{OSOH}) + \text{CLOAD/MIP RATING OF CPU}$$

where

$$\text{CET} = [K_0 + \sum_{1=1}^{20} K_I * \text{COUNT(I)}]/\text{MIP RATING OF CPU}$$

Here CET is the code execution time, OSOH is the percent operating system overhead, and OLOAD is the cost for loading a task. The two latter values are input for each task. The K_I are instruction counts input for each task. The COUNT(1) are determined inside each task and represent such timing concerns as the number of instances being processed, the number of items in various queues, the number of objects in the system, the number of track pulses, etc. The units of CET are dependent upon the units of the four parameters. The interpretation of these parameters is left to the user.

With each task is associated an instance limit. The instance limit is the maximum number of instances that the task can handle at each execution. If the number of instances scheduled is larger than this limit, then the task is scheduled to execute again immediately following its current execution with the extra instances as its instance count. If the instance limit is set to zero, then there is no limit to the number of instances which can be processed at each task execution.

Application Program Model

The application program model consists of the actual tasks that are being run on the hardware. Each task comprises a separate subroutine of the simulator. When a task "executes", this subroutine is called by the simulator's operating system.

Associated with each task is a parameter called instances. An instance is a unit of measure used in a particular task to determine the amount of processing time that particular execution of that task will require. The definition of an instance is dependent upon the function of the task. For example, if a task's function is to compute the sum of a variable number of addends, then the task's run time is a function of the number of addends and the number of instances for this task is the number of addends at each execution of the task. The number of instances associated with a task may change each time the task executes.

2.4.3.2 Inputs

Because of the need for simulation flexibility to support architecture design, the simulation is table drive. Some of the more important input constants are the following:

CPUNUM - number of CPU's (facilities) to be modeled (maximum of 25).
CPUSPD - speed of each facility in MIPS(array of size 25).
TSKNUM - number of application program tasks modeled.

NTABC, NTABTU, NTABQW, NTABRT, NTABO - table numbers for statistical output; considered hardwarired

ITRACE - flag controlling calling of subroutine TRACE which is called by all application program tasks modeled (0-don't call, 1-call)

FLAG(1)- flag controlling debug printing in subroutine ELIST where branching to every other routine takes place. (0-no print, 1-print)

FLAG(2)- not used

FLAG(3)- not used

FLAG(4)- not used

TSKATT - number of task attribures; fixed
TRIRATE- trilateration rate in seconds per pulse
RATEIS - interceptor search rate in seconds per pulse
TIRATE - track initiate rate in seconds per pulse
TRRATE - track rate in seconds per pulse
MTRATE - maintenance track rate in seconds per pulse
VRATE - verify rate in seconds per pulse
SRATE - search rate in pulses per second
XPROC - processor to be modeled
NPPOC - total number of processors
SPPE - search pulses per enablement of task RS (Radar Scheduler); SRATE/PRS
PRS - period of RS in seconds
DSP - duration of sector processing in seconds
DTA - duration of target area processing in seconds

DMONO - duration of monostatic engagement processing in seconds
DIT - duration of task IT (Interceptor Tracking) in seconds

The second set of namelist inputs defines the tasks to be modeled and the variables input for each task are defined as follows:

NAME - alphanumeric name of task, fixed since it must agree with the internatlly coded name. The names used for the tasks modeled are given below:

RADAR	- Radar Interface (initialization task)
ACQ	- Acquisition
FP	- Farm Processing
HMONO, HTA, HTRI	- routines used for internal logic, consider all their data fixed.
IC	- Interceptor Control
IP	- Intercept Planning
SIT	- Interceptor Track
MIT	- Cooperative Interceptor Track
MOOT	- Monostatic Object Track
MOT	- Cooperative Object Track
RRA	- Radar Returns Assimilation
RS	- Radar Scheduler
SDISC	- Sector Discrimination
SOT	- Sector Object Track
TADISC	- Target Area Discrimination
TAOT	- Target Area Object Track
TAPH	- Target Area Processing Handover
TIC	- Trilateration Interceptor Control
TIT	- Trilateration Interceptor Track
TOT	- Trilateration Object Track

OPUARRAY - array of length 5, CPU numbers on which this task may run; maximum of five numbers.

LOOP - priority of task, highest priority is zero, zero priority tasks may interrupt other priority tasks and can only run on one facility.

MAXINT - maximum number of instances which can be processed per enablement. Extra instances remain in the queue. If set to zero, implies no limit, i.e., all instances in queue are processed.

SUBNUM - subroutine number, fixed and must remain in current order.

ENBFLG - enablement flag (0-data enable, 1-time enabled).

PERIOD - period of task in seconds; zero for data enabled tasks

OSOH - operating system overhead as a fractional multiplier

CLOAD	- instruction count for loading task
COEFO	- instructions executed regardless of pulse type
COEF	- array of 19, instructions executed dependent upon pulse type
IDO	- object identification number
OTYPE	- object type (1-RV)
NSITE	- radar object is seen by
IPP	- radar closest to impact point of this object
IENTER	- time this object enters NSITE's field of view in seconds
ILEAVE	- time this object leaves NSITE's field of view in seconds

2.4.3.3 Outputs

SALSIM provides a package of statistical routines that are used to generate most of the output data. The statistics are gathered in the simulator such that it is not necessary to save or dump on tape large volumes of data to be statistically analyzed by a post-processor. A time interval is specified as input for each statistic and this interval is used to calculate the statistic as the simulation run is in progress. The post-processor then has only minimal formatting to perform. Typical outputs include:

- Resource (e.g., CPU) vs. time (Figure 2.4-10)
- Facility (e.g., CPU) queue wait time vs. time (Figure 2.4-11)
- Task queue length (min, max) (Figure 2.4-12)

Several levels of debug or trace information are also available which can be turned on and off over various time periods during the simulation to obtain detailed data if necessary.

2.4.4 Benchmark Performance Evaluation

Benchmarking provides a vehicle for performance calibration of a single processor which may be the building block of a distributed architecture. Results of the benchmark are often used to initialize analytic models for contention analyses and hardware models for simulation. Since the performance of a processor can vary significantly depending on the type of application and its instruction mix, benchmarking provides a method of predicting the performance of an architecture.

Several factors can effect the accuracy of the benchmark results and the resulting ability to predict the overall distributed system's performance. These factors include:

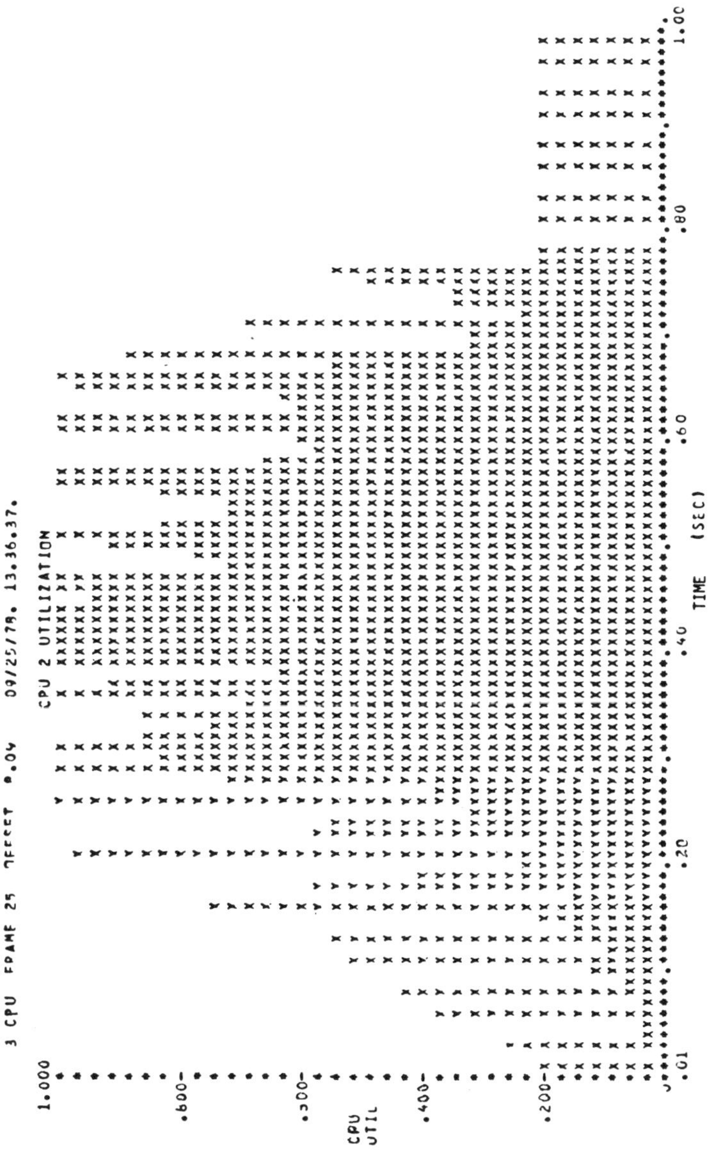

Figure 2.4-10. CPU 2 Utilization

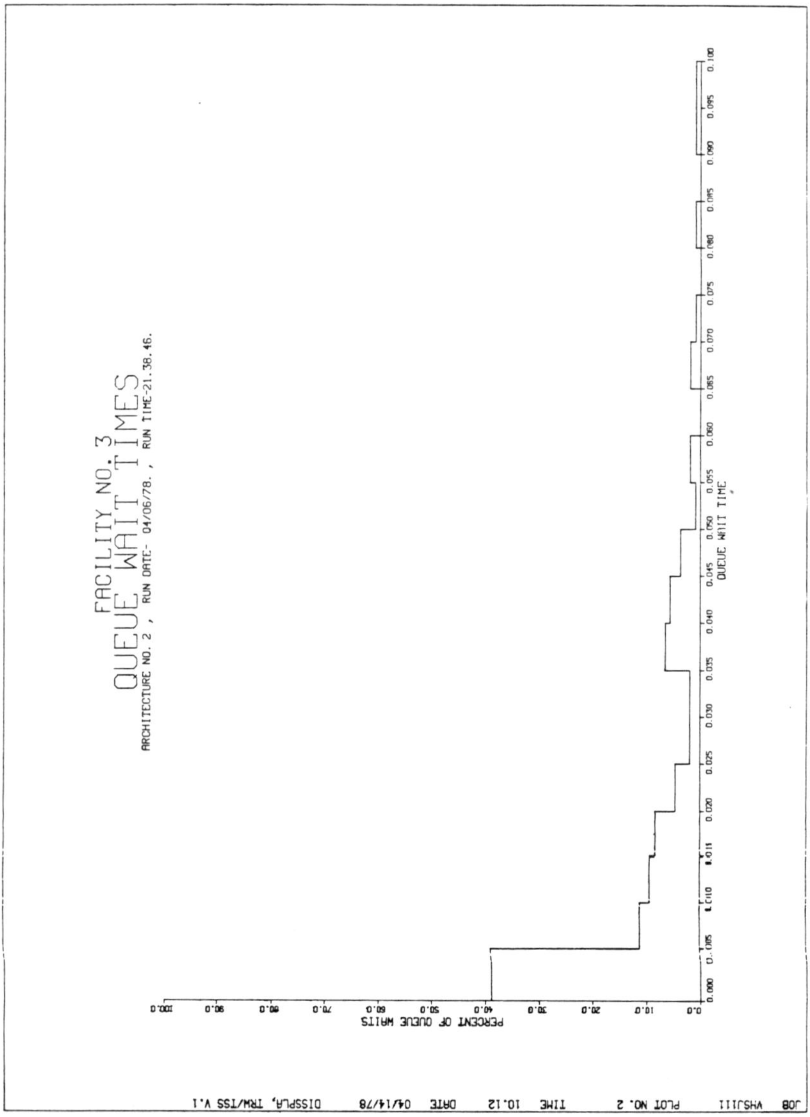

Figure 2.4-11. Facility No. 3 Queue Wait Times

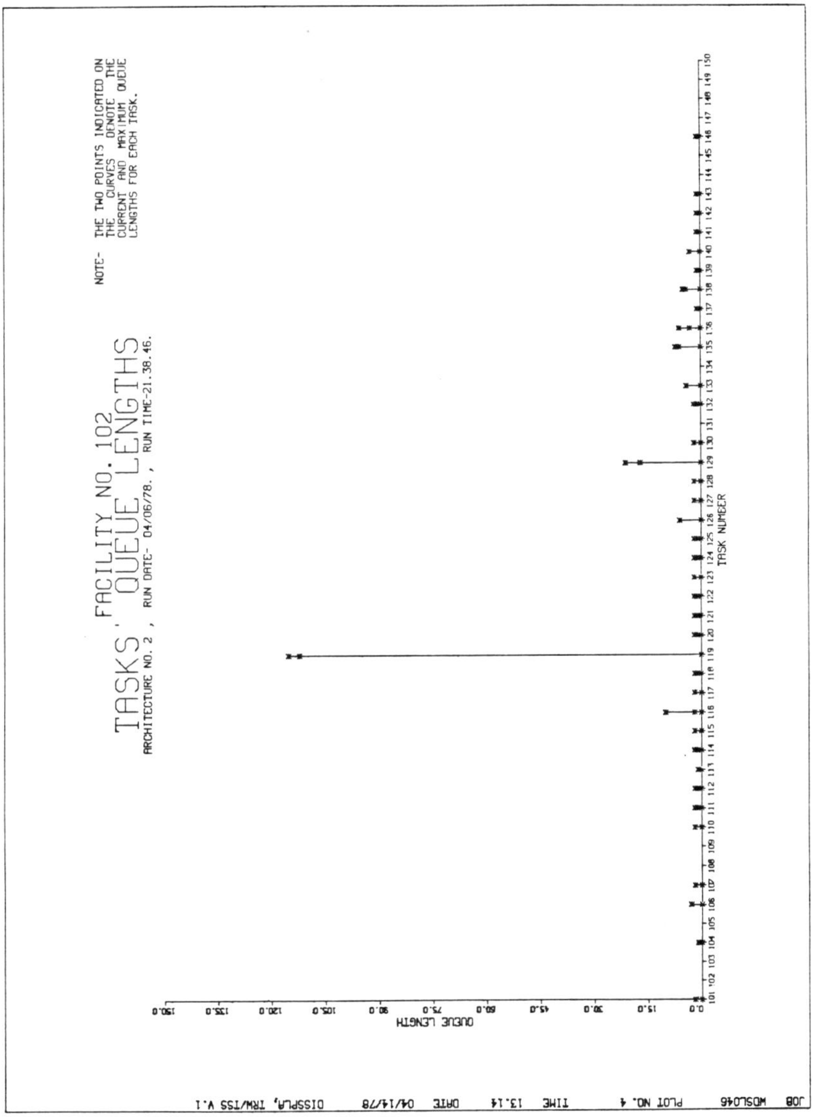

Figure 2.4-12. Facility No. 102, Tasks' Queue Lengths

- Test Case Selection: The benchmark must be large enough to be representative of the application, but small enough to be controlled and analyzable. Representativeness of the benchmark instruction mix, and its ability to predict the timing and processor overhead cost of handling external I/O are critical for extrapolation of the system's performance.

- Compiler Efficiency: The code optimization techniques such as strength reduction, folding and dead code elimination reduce the size and complexity of generated object code. Different vendors and vendor versions can often employ vastly different compiler optimization techniques which can lead to differing object code representations of the same HOL (e.g., FORTRAN) benchmark.

- Assembler Instruction Set: The instruction set complexity such as using three-operand instructions will result in compression of executable code and can improve performance. This characteristic could lead to inaccurate computer speed comparisons (MIPS) based on assembly language execution rates.

- Program Storage Word Size: The instruction length and instruction fetch approach will affect performance of the processor. Most contemporary architectures employ sophisticated schemes for instruction fetching and decoding to minimize the impact on the instruction execution cycle. Such techniques include multi-word fetches, instruction prefetch, and instruction stack machines.

- Processor Native Instruction Set: The fundamental processor object code (native instructions) may invoke hardware or firmware control of the processor. The sophistication of these invoked operations permit the execution of several arithmetic operations without additional memory fetch overhead.

- Hardware Implementation Technology: The circuit and memory technology, and the degree of HW customization will drive the raw speed of the processor. For example, the use of special/custom ships (e.g., TRW 16x16 multiply) will have major effects on the instruction execution speeds.

- Hardware Architecture Control Approaches: The use of internal processor concurrency will substantially enhance the effective processor speed. All supercomputers employ internal concurrency within and among functional units to increase performance. The FPS-120B array processor strives for concurrent execution of add and multiply functional units, each of which is a multi-stage unit.

- Internal Processor Interconnect Approach: The physical architecture interface between program and data memory, I/O channels and the processor will also effect processor contention and overhead. The internal memory bandwidth, I/O bandwidth and internal bus protocols can have a marked effect on the effective performance of a processor when operating in a distributed network of multiple processors.

All of these factors can have varying effects on the apparent benchmark performance results. Different vendors tend to exploit different factors to achieve high performance. For example, many of the supercomputer manufacturers (e.g., CDC 7600/7700, CRAY, SDC/BURROUGHS PEPE) emphasized the processor architecture as a basis for performance, while other vendors tended to develop sophisticated compilers with multipass optimization schemes for generating extremely efficient object code.

The true performance measurement is the actual speed with which a processor can execute the benchmark code. The use of a metric, such as machine language instructions per second (MIPS), can easily lead to a gross misrepresentation of a processor's relative throughput potential. This can be seen (Figure 2.4-13) by plotting the results of a candidate series of benchmarks for two different commercial computers, a P-E 3242 and a VAX 11/780 (with Floating Point Accelerator). The three benchmarks represented had various degrees of arithmetic operations ranging from 89% to 55%. In all three benchmark instances the arithmetic code contained heavy percentages of ADD/SUBTRACT (39-45%) and MULTIPLY (40-59%) operations.

The performance ratios of the P-E 3242 and VAX 11/780 have been plotted for pure speed in execution time (seconds) and computed MIPS. For all benchmark cases the P-E yields superior performance. However, relative superiority of the P-E for this benchmark series appears to range from **a mere 3% (89% arithmetic) to a respectable 27% (55% arithmetic) when correctly comparing execution times. However, if we use computed MIPS,**

with $$\text{MIPS} = \frac{\text{total MLI executed}}{\text{execution time}}$$

then the P-E advantage misleadingly appears much more superior, ranging between 50 and 67% better than the VAX. This is due to biases caused by such differences as compiler efficiency, internal processor architecture and processor native instruction set.

Finally, in considering the networked processor performance, the additional impact of processor message handling must be factored. Depending on the internal computer architecture, the processor cost of handling message traffic will vary. Special benchmarks can be developed, or operating system execution costs of handling message traffic may be predicted and used to reduce the processor timeline available to the applications code.

The projection of a processor's performance potential in a networked environment must consider the net effect of both the dedicated processor speed and also the processor cost implications of message handling.

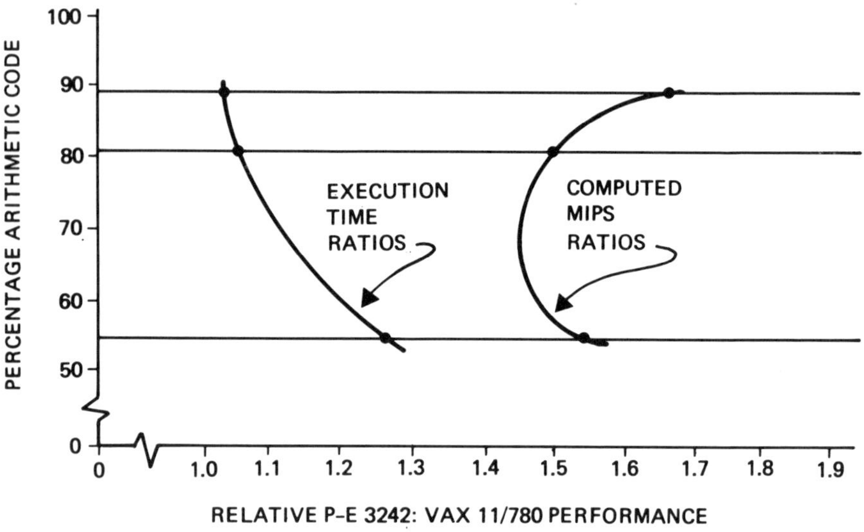

Figure 2.4-13. Potential Performance Misrepresentations

2.5 REFERENCES

[2-0] Phase III Distributed Processing Architecture Design (DPAD) Program, Vol. III: Revised Baseline Design Approach, Contract No. DASG 60-79-C-0039, Report No. 35010-79-A005, BMDATC, P.O. Box 1500, Huntsville, Al. 35807.

[2-1] "Advanced Data Processing Concepts, Volume I, Final Report", TRW DSSG and Dynetics, Inc., Huntsville, Alabama, 15 November, 1978.

[2-2] "Payoff Material for DDP Third Quarterly Report, IDL 2.2-1", TRW IOC 78.6923.10-65 (DDP 30451-78-044) from H. Agneessens to M. P. Mariani, 2 October 1978.

[2-3] "Computer Matrix", TRW IOC 78.6923.10-035 (DDP 30451-78-015; ADPC 78.6923.12-029), from H. Agneessens to M. P. Mariani and R. Turn, 9 May 1978.

[2-4] "Advanced Data Processing Technology, Fourth Quarterly Report, Advanced Data Processing Concepts", TRW DSSG, Huntsville, Alabama, 16 October 1978.

[2-5] "Computer Data Analysis Program - CODAP", TRW IOC 30451-79-001, from S. Katz to M. P. Mariani, 16 January 1979.

[2-6] "Distributed Data Processing (DDP) Technology Program, Volume 2 - Research Appendices", TRW DSSG and Burroughs Corporation, 31 December 1977.

[2-7] Ramamoorthy, C. V., and H. H. So, "Software Requirements and Specifications: Status and Perspectives", Tutorial: Software Methodology, IEEE Cat. No. EHO 140-0, pp. 43-164.

[2-8] Alford, M. W., "A Requirement's Engineering Methodology for Real-Time Processing Requirements", IEEE Trans. Software Engineering, Vol. SE-3, No. 1, January 1977, pp. 60-69.

[2-9] Ramamoorthy, C. V. and H. F. Li, "Pipeline Architecture", Computing Surveys, Vol. 9, No. 1, March 1977, pp. 61-102.

[2-10] Siewiorek, D. P. et al., "A Case Study of C.mmp, C*, and C.vmp: Part 1 - Experience with Fault Tolerance in Multiprocessor Systems", Proc. IEEE, Vol. 66, No. 10, Oct. 1978, pp. 1178-1199.

[2-11] Evenson, A. J. and J. L. Troy, "Introduction to the Architecture of a 288-Element PEPE", in Proc. 1973 Sagamore Conference on Parallel Processing, Springer Verlag, 1973, pp. 162-169

[2-12] Rudolph, J. A., "A Production Implementation of an Associative Array Processor - STARAN", in AFIPS 1972 Joint Computer Conference, 1972, pp. 229-241.

[2-13] Fernandez, E. B. and B. Bussell, "Bounds on the Number of Processors and Time for Multiprocessor Optimal Schedules", IEEE Transactions Computers, Vol. C-22, No. 8, August 1973, pp. 745-751.

[2-14] Ramamoorthy, C. V. and K. H. Kim, "Pipelining - The Generalized Concept and Sequencing Strategies", AFIPS Conference Proceedings, 1974 NCC, Vol. 43, pp. 289-297.

[2-15] Peebles, R. and E. Manning, "System Architecture for Distributed Data Management", Computer, Vol. 11, No. 1, Jan. 1978, pp. 40-47.

[2-16] Morgan, H. L. and K. D. Levin, "Optimal Program and Data Locations in Computer Networks", Comm. ACM, Vol. 20, No. 5, May 1977, pp. 315-322.

[2-17] Levin, K.D. and H. L. Morgan, Optimizing Distributive Data Base - A Framework for Research", AFIPS Conference Proceedings, 1975 NCC, Vol. 44, June 1975, pp. 473-478.

[2-18] Mahmoud, S. and R. S. Riordon, "Optimal Allocation of Resources in Distributed Information Networks", ACM Trans. Database Systems, Vol. 1, No. 1, March 1976, pp. 66-78.

[2-19] Chu, W. W., "Optimal File Allocation in a Multiple Computer System", IEEE Transactions on Computers, October 1969.

[2-20] Whitney, V.K.M., "A Study of Optimal File Assignments and Communications Network Configuration", Ph.D. Thesis, University of Michigan, 1970.

[2-21] Casey, R.G., "Allocation of Copies of a File in An Information Network", Proceeding 1972 Spring Computer Conference, AFIPS Press, Moutvale, N.J., pp. 617-625.

[2-22] Hsiao, D.K., Editor, "Data Base Computers", Collected Readings on a Database Computer (DBC), 2nd ed., Ohio University, 1980.

[2-23] McDonald, W.C., H.O. Welch, and J.D. Reynolds, "Distributed Simulation Host: A Distributed Testbed", Proceedings COMPSAC 80, October 1980, pp. 562-568.

[2-24] Hoffman, R.H., R.W. Smith, and J.T. Ellis, "Simulation Software Development for the BMDATC DDP Underlay Experiment", Proceedings COMPSAC 80, October 1980, pp. 569-577.

[2-25] Panel Session 1: Fundamental Concepts of Fault Tolerance, FTC 12th Annual International Symposium: Digest of Papers, June 22-24, 1982, IEEE Catalog No. 82CH 1760-8.

[2-26] Avizienis, A., "Fault Tolerance: The survival Attribute of Digital Systems." Proc. IEEE, 66-10: 1109-1125, Oct. 1978.

[2-27] Avizienis, et al., "The STAR Computer: An Investigation of the Theory and Practice of Fault-Tolerant Computer Design," IEEE Transactions on Computers, Nov. 1971.

[2-28] Parnus, D.L., "On the Criteria to Be Used in Decomposing Systems into Modules," Comm. ACM, Vol. 15, No. 12, Dec. 1972.

[2-29] Parnus, D.L., "Information Distribution Aspects of Design Methodology," Tech. Report, Dept. of Comp. Science, Carnegie Mellon University, Pittsburgh, Pa., 1971.

[2-30] Ma, P., et al, "On the Design of a Task Allocation Scheme for Time-Critical Applications," Proc. Real-Time Systems Symposium, December 1981, pp. 121 - 126.

[2-31] Kung, H.T., "Structure of Parallel Algorithms," Advances in Computers, Academic Press, New York, 1980, pp. 65-108.

3.0 CRITICAL IMPLEMENTATION ISSUES

INTRODUCTION

Distributed architecture design and implementation issues are considered critical if: (1) their solutions are necessary for the successful application of distributed data processing to a system and (2) no adequate solution approach has yet been established.

At the present time eight such issues can be identified, and solution approaches are currently under investigation by both industry and the academic community. These eight issues are the following:

- Real Time Control - research into both process and resource control at the multicomputer node and distributed computer levels
- Decomposition/Partitioning - the continued research into establishing the concepts, principles and rules which promote high-payoff design of the applications.
- Distributed Data Base Design and Management - research into the concepts, principles and rules which promote high-payoff data base design and real-time management
- Intranode Communication - research into protocols which promote high-payoff interprocess communication (IPC) and maintenance of a distributed data base with replicated files
- Highly Reliable and Fault-Tolerant Architectures - research into the design and control techniques, concepts, principles and rules which promote highly reliable and/or fault-tolerant architectures
- High-Performance Architectures - research into the design and development concepts, principles, rules and techniques which promote high-performance architectures
- Distributed Performance Modeling - research into the development of a methodology and performance models (both analytical and simulation) which provide high-confidence performance analyses during design and development
- High-Growth Architectures - research into the design concepts, principles and rules which promote high-growth architectures.

Of the eight critical issues, three: real-time control, distributed data base design and management, and communications are of major importance to the real-time operation of any fully distributed system. Such a distributed system could consist of distributed, asynchronously executing tasks which operate off of a data base which itself is distributed (i.e., partitioned and partially replicated) across a computer network. The issue of decomposition/partitioning, coupled with allocation (Reference Section 2.3) and distributed performance modeling (Reference Section 2.5) are system architecture design issues. Highly-reliable/fault-tolerant, high-performance and high-growth architectures are also architecture design issues, where architecture is intended to include the integrated design of the applications, data, control and hardware. In this section we will discuss those three critical issues of distributed real-time control (DRTC), distributed data base management (DDBM) and communications (COMM).

3.1 DISTRIBUTED CONTROL MODEL FOR CRITICAL ISSUE RESEARCH

In our research and experimentation [3-32] at the BMDATC Testbed [3.33] we have chosen to address the three critical issues all as issues of system control, each a key element of the distributed operating system (DOS) of a network (Figure 3.1-1). The distributed operating system will be cellular; a network of homogeneous DOS cells are distributed across the computer network, they cooperate to control the operation of the message based computer network to insure no central control/decision point and therefore no central point of failure.

Each DOS cell (**Figure 3.1-1**) contains five major functional components:

- Local Process Executive: controls the scheduling and dispatching of applications tasks within the local computer.

- Local Data Base Manager: controls the access/update of the global data base by all local applications tasks. The local DBM also edits each data base access/update request to determine whether it is either a remote file or a replicated file in which case the distributed data base manager is notified.

- Distributed Data Base Manager: controls the access or update of all remotely local files, and performs the synchronization of replicated data files once a local update is made.

- Real-Time Resource Manager: controls the network load balancing and load shedding functions to prevent local network overload. Also controls the dynamic reconfiguration of the network architecture in the event of a HW/SW "hard" (non-recoverable) failure.

- Communications: Controls the transmission and receipt of messages between computers within the network.

Of these five key functions the process executive and local data manager are quite similar to those functions which would exist within a real-time operating system for a centralized monolithic computer system; the main differences being the addition of requirements to support the distributed data manager and resource manager interfaces.

The DOS cell is considered to be the interface between the applications software tasks and the physical system. With this DOS model approach, several important design features are provided:

- Physical network architecture is transparent to the applications software, thus enhancing
  - SW testability
  - system reconfigurability for fault tolerance
  - system flexibility and growth characteristics

- Applications SW tasks are developed as though they execute on a centralized computer, thus improving the

SW development schedule, and simplifying unit level testing.

- The network DOS can be integrated and tested with only a subset (e.g., 3-computer network) of the entire network.

- Separated DOS and Applications provides a control research environment for critical algorithm performance evaluation.

With this distributed control model we can consider the issues, and candidate approaches for the three critical areas of distributed data base management, real-time resource management and communications.

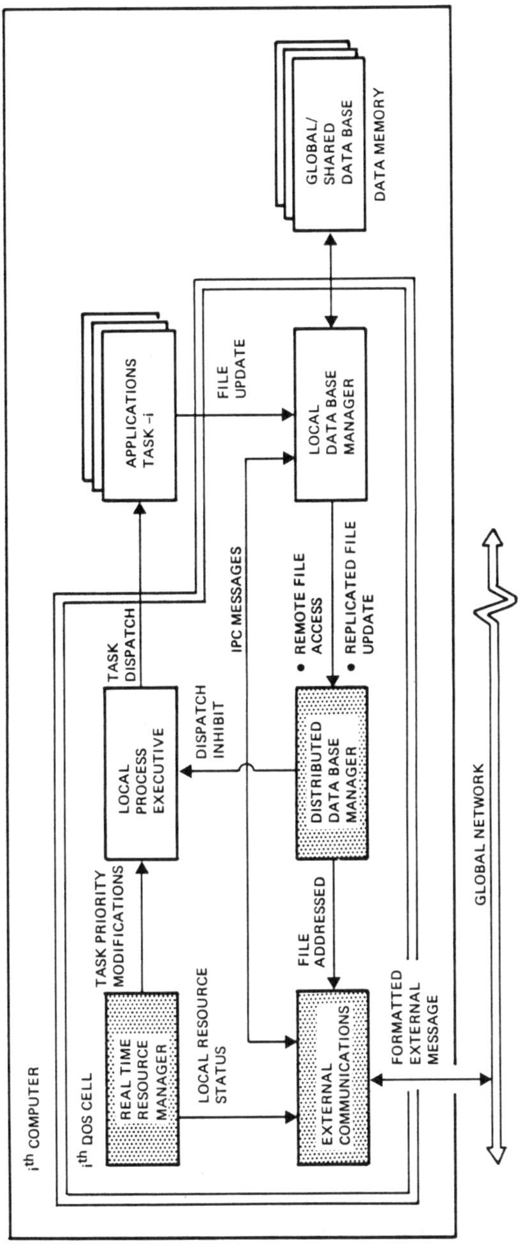

Figure 3.1-1. A Single Distributed Operating System (DOS) Cell

3.2 DISTRIBUTED DATA BASE DESIGN AND MANAGEMENT

The design and real time management of distributed data bases (DDB) are highly interdependent and are both major research areas, and perhaps the areas which commands the most significant change in the transition from centralized to distributed systems.

The data base design problem must be addressed during the early stages of distributed systems designs. No longer is the definition and structure of the global data base a secondary concern to be addressed after the software process design, as it has been for centralized system design*. With distributed systems design the definition, distribution and structure of the global data base becomes an immediate concern to be addressed concurrently with the software design. No longer can the access to the global data base be assumed instantaneous. No longer can data base updates guarantee coherency. Instead, data base accesses now can require networking delays, and concurrent accesses, resulting from parallel executing tasks, must be managed to insure global file coherency.

The distributed data base systems which will evolve to provide enhanced performance access response, reliability, availability, and survivability will involve both partitioned and replicated data bases (Figure 3.2-1).

For reasons of performance, reliability/availability/survivability, and security the data base design and real time management function will require advances to current technology. Most of the current research in distributed data bases has been oriented toward information management systems with relaxed real-time response requirements. As a result current research is typically concerned with the design and management of a centralized data base with distributed/remote users, as opposed to command and control systems with stringent real-time access requirements. Although some of the issues are similar (e.g., remote file access and deadlock prevention) for the real-time command and control problem, the fact that the data base will itself involve distributed and in many cases redundant data files creates unique issues such as replicated file maintenance, and further complicates the issues of file access, deadlock prevention and coherency. For such distributed data bases, there are seven critical issues associated with its design and management:

- <u>Data Structures</u>: file organization, including logical-to-physical organization
- <u>Data Partition and Allocations</u>: file definition and data base distribution across the network
- <u>Distributed Network Architecture</u>: network topology and communications protocol definition
- <u>Data Base Security</u>: file access/update management to insure against unauthorized data read or data corruption

---

* Software process design is that decision process which addresses the interaction of software units; which typically includes such decisions as enablement criteria, execution priorities, task-operating system interface, global file definitions, and global data base distribution.

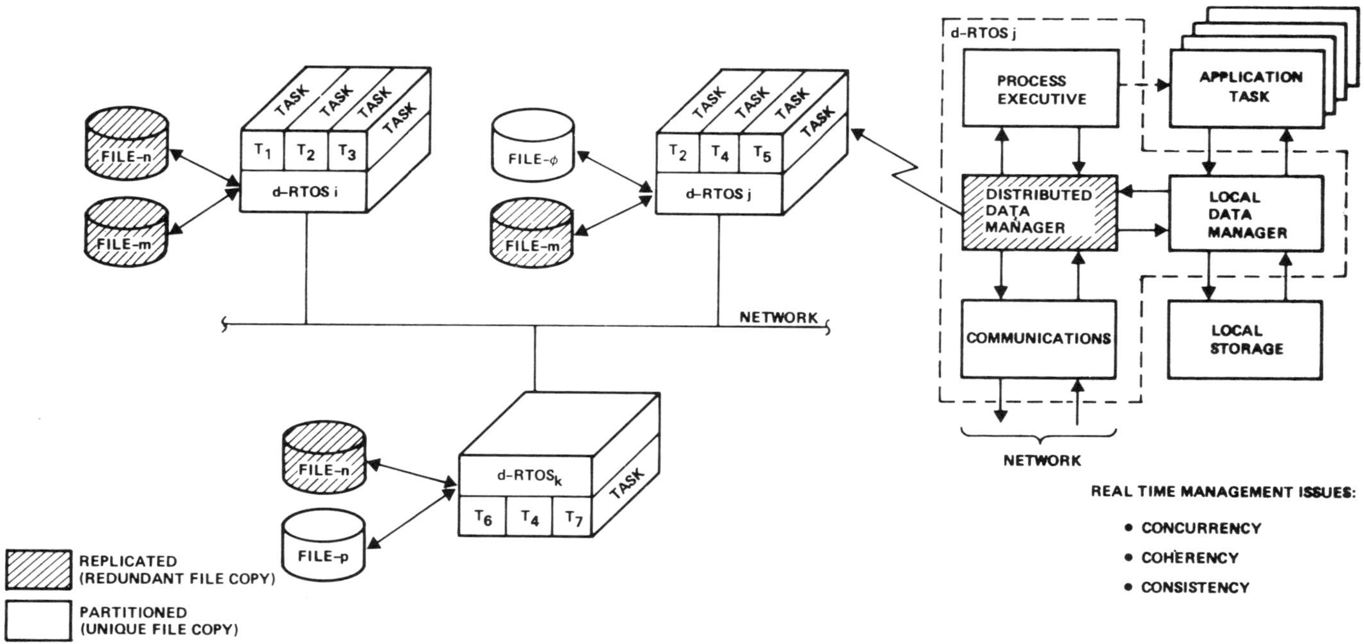

Figure 3.2.1. Distributed Data Base System Involves Both Partitioned & Replicated Files

- Real-Time Data Management: control of file access and update under conditions of,
    - remote data access by a non-local task
    - redundant file maintenance to insure coherency of replicated files/data
    - concurrent file access by parallel executing tasks

- Data Base Recovery: reconfiguration of the data base organization to insure continuity of data access

- Configuration Management: off-line maintenance of the data base contents, organization, distribution, and access/update pattern

The complexity of the distributed data base design and management problem can be illustrated by the interdependency of these issues (Figure 3.2-2). The dependency matrix represents the net results of a subjective analysis survey of distributed data base designers. The matrix illustrates that the network architecture design issue displays the highest coupling, with five "9's", followed by the allocation and structure design issues, and the remote access and security distributed data base management issues each with three "9" couplings. This strong dependency of the network design on the issues of file allocation, remote file access, redundant file maintenance, concurrency control and security suggests to the designer that a special emphasis be placed on the network analysis of any distributed system design. Many past experiences have substantiated the benefits of comprehensive network analyses, which include topology, hardware performance, and traffic analyses.

Some of the typical pitfalls which have occurred as a result of insufficient network architecture analysis have included:

- significant processor overhead due to I/O handling of message traffic associated with data base management

- unanticipated network traffic due to data base management messages

- remote file access delays due to unpredicted internal processor message handling SW delays

- poor network utilization due to (1) significant variations in message sizes under a fixed block transmission protocol, (2) unaccounted for header/trailer information, or (3) unaccounted for security header/trailer data.

A discussion of the distributed data base design and management problems, and the critical issues associated with each are discussed in the following paragraphs.

3.2.1 Distributed Data Base Design

Most systems requiring data base design are driven by the performance and cost concerns to minimize access delay, data management overhead and storage. In addition, considerations of reliability/availability and security often heavily influence the data base design. With these

CRITICAL DESIGN AND MANAGEMENT ISSUES	1	2	3	4	5	6	7	8	9
1. PARTITION		5	5	7	5	3	9	9	8
2. ALLOCATION	5		9	3	9	9	3	5	7
3. NETWORK ARCHITECTURE	5	9		2	9	9	9	9	7
4. STRUCTURE	7	3	2		9	8	8	9	9
5. REMOTE ACCESS	5	9	9	9		8	8	6	7
6. REDUNDANT FILE MAINT.	3	9	9	8	8		5	5	7
7. CONCURRENCY CONTROL	9	3	9	8	8	5		5	5
8. SECURITY	9	5	9	9	6	5	5		7
9. CONFIGURATION MGMT	8	7	7	9	7	7	5	7	

LEGEND:
0: COMPLETELY INDEPENDENT ISSUES
9: COMPLETELY DEPENDENT ISSUES

(1) DEPENDENCY IS A SUBJECTIVE ESTIMATE OF THE INFLUENCE OF ONE ISSUE ON A SECOND. THE INFLUENCE MAY INCLUDE THE ISSUES SOLUTION COMPLEXITY, OR THE OPERATIONAL OVERHEAD, OR PERFORMANCE ASSOCIATED WITH THE ISSUES SOLUTION.

Figure 3.2-2. Inter-Dependencies of Critical Distributed Data Base Design & Management Issues

considerations in mind the data base design problem typically includes three major decisions:

- Data Organization: definition of the file contents and their structure, both from the program's viewpoint (i.e., logical structure) and from the hardware's viewpoint (i.e., physical structure).

- Data Allocation: assignment of partitioned files to processors and global data memory across the node.

- Security and Recovery: definition of the techniques for assurance against unauthorized access of data, and reconfiguration in the event of hard or soft failures resulting in either impeded access or data corruption.

Each of these design decisions has implications on the physical storage size, the management/control approach to be used and the data management software to be selected/developed. Often the availability of data management software can influence, if not dictate, the data base design to be implemented. The desire to capture existing data management software can often lead to unacceptable performance overhead, or excess storage because of the lack of total compatibility of the current problem with off-the-shelf data management software. The software will always provide capabilities not required and fail to provide functions desired; the unused capabilities will result in extraneous overhead, and the addition of new functions will require additional software enhancements be developed.

For distributed data base systems, the use of off-the-shelf systems to date have led to problems in performance, such as poor file access, and unacceptable data management overhead. These inadequacies are a result of inherent inefficiencies in tailoring existing data base management systems (DBMS) for new applications. The approaches which are founded on enhancing existing DBMS' often result in embedded data management capabilities which are not used but which must be "paid for" in performance losses and extraneous resources.

3.2.2 Data Base Allocation

The allocation of files to processors is an important aspect of the distributed data base design process. An important aspect of the data base design process, and an area which has attracted a substantial amount of attention over the past ten years is the area of data base modeling and allocation. Most of the allocation models are based on file interconnect models. The interconnect model is formulated in a more general manner and file allocation can be considered if one can structure the problem to be represented by weighted factors and in terms of coupling coefficients. One such interconnnect model has been discussed (Section 2.3.3.2) for the allocation of tasks/processes across the computer network.

Other models have been developed by many different authors, the one summarized by D. Foster can be selected as an example [3-1]. Foster's approach is to divide the problem into two steps: (a) micro model, and (b) macro model. The micro model is used to solve the problem of obtaining the branching probability. The macro model takes the optimal branching probabilities as the initial starting point in the integer programming model. Other input to the macro model include the file accessing frequencies, length of each file, number of storage devices and their capacities. The output is the assignment of each file to the best device with the objective to minimize the difference between the optimal branching probability and the total accessing frequency to each device, subject to the input physical constraints which includes that file splitting is not allowed. If splitting is desirable, one can divide the file into several groups with similar access patterns to form new files and rerun the whole model again.

Another approach to the baseline DDB design issue is to analyze the types of DDB. Our research shows that there are three main types of DDB [3-2].

- Fully redundant (or replicated)
- Fully partitioned
- Partially redundant.

Remote access may be required in the last two types, therefore the amount of remote access required or allowed is also a very important consideration. In Figure 3.2-3, the relationship between 9 software related payoff measures and the 5 types of basic DDB design is shown. It is obvious that not every payoff measure can be considered equally in a given DDB design. For example, performance, the fully redundant DDB can easily provide the required performance requirements but the fully partitioned data base with moderate amount of remote access may have difficulty in achieving a high performance standard. On the other hand, the cost and deployability payoff measures are much easier to achieve for partitioned data base designs. Thus, depending on the overall system

Figure 3.2-3. Relating the Type of Distributed Data Base to the S/W Payoff Measures

Payoff Measures	Type of DDB				
	Fully Redundant	Fully Partitioned		Partially Redundant	
		With moderate Remote Access	With low Remote Access	With moderate Remote Access	With low Remote Access
Performance	5	1	2	4	4
Survivability	5	0	0	4	3
Development Cost	0	4	4	1	1
Availability	5	2	1	4	3
Reliability	3	1	1	3	3
Fault Tolerance	4	1	1	3	3
Deployability	1	3	3	2	3
Growth	2	1	2	2	3
O&M Cost	0	3	3	1	1

0-5 Degree of ease to implement the payoff measures
0 - Most difficult to implement
5 - Least difficult to implement

design goal, the designer may select one basic design approach over another. However, most often he will select a compromise approach, such as partially redundant data base which attempts to minimize remote access.

3.2.3 Baseline DDB Management

In the beginning of the chapter we introduced a cellular distributed operating system (DOS) model. We will now further explore the two major data management functions of the model:

- Local Data Manager
- Distributed Data Manager.

The local data manager as defined here is very similar to a data manager in a centralized or non-DDP environment. It provides facilities to define and create local files and to retrieve and update that portion of the distributed data base which is locally stored. There are several approaches to such a local data manager [3-3, 3-4]. The local data manager will serve as the interface between the local applications and the distributed data manager function. As a result it must recognize data base read/write requests which are either for remote data or redundant data and therefore necessitate action by the distributed data manager. It is the distributed data manager which performs those functions which are unique to the maintenance of distributed data. We will therefore turn our attention to the Distributed Data Base Manager (DDBM) to which we have devoted the major emphasis of this section.

In the following sections we provide more detail on the following areas related to the Distributed Data Base Manager:

- Operational model (requirements and assumptions)
- Functional elements or modules
- Preliminary top-level design of functional modules
- Detailed discussion on critical modules
- Current technology
- Future research directions.

Much of the discussion in the following paragraphs is based on work performed in the development of a distributed data base manager for a multi-VAX experiment for a stringent real time applications [3-35].

3.2.3.1 Operational Model

The DDBM will reside in either a single computer (centralized approach) or each computer (distributed approach) of the network. The DDBM will interface with several distributed operating system functions (Figure 3.1-1); the Local Process Executive, Local Data Base Manager and the External Communications. The DDBM - Local Process Executive function interface can exist to inhibit /lockout the dispatching of applications tasks which require data associated with files that are being updated. The DDBM -

Local Data Base Manager function interface will support the interface between the access/update of data which is locally resident and data which is remotely located. The DDBM - External Communications function interface will support all data access/update which occurs remotely over the network. The DDBM interfaces will exist regardless of whether the DDBM is centralized or distributed, and whether the distributed operating system functions are themselves distributed within a single network node. In the latter case a special function, such as the communication function, could reside in a communication frontend processor, while the local data manager or even the distributed data manager can reside on a specialized back-end processor [3-5].

Several factors effect the complexity of the distributed data base manager (DDBM) and its operating overhead. These factors include:

- number of remote files and access frequency
- number of replicated files and update frequency
- number of replicated data entities and update frequency (same data entity may exist in multiple files for performance or cost reasons)
- global consistency requirements of replicated files/data entities
- file access concurrency; number of simultaneous file accesses
- network heterogeneity, e.g., physical processor word size, memory structure, local file structures.

These factors are significant in that they all tend to complicate the DDBM functions and/or increase the resources required to perform its basic functions. These functions include keeping track of the distribution of the data, translation of user queries into physical data access/update actions, and maintaining the consistency and coherency of both a partitioned and replicated data base under concurrent user requests.

Because of the complexity of the operational environment, DDBM development usually occurs in increments of increasing complexity. For example, such an incremental approach has been employed in the development of a research DDBM for the Army*. In that system the DDBM was developed under two release environments, Model 1 and Model 2.

In Model 1 a fully partitioned DDBM with low or moderate frequency of remote file access (see Figure 3.2-3) was installed. However, some partially redundant files are needed for some file status tables and catalogs. In Model 2 a highly redundant system was installed with some of the data partially replicated for reliability, and others for performance. At the same time replicated status tables and catalogs are needed to maintain the partially replicated files. In each case the status tables and catalogs are maintained to determine physical file locations, and maintain the access availability of files.

---

* Contract DASG60-76-C-0088 "Distributed Processing Architecture Design", a multiyear research program commenced in CY1977.

Also in Model 1, in order to simplify the problem, the computers within the node are homogeneous. In addition, the data base structures across the network are also completely compatible so that no translations or conversions are necessary.

In model 2, the intranode computers are heterogeneous. Although the data base softwares may still be able to transfer from one computer to another without major redesign (the layer approach to software design), a translation and conversion module was added to convert and translate the data and even messages between one computer and the other within the same node. We will not discuss any implications for the internode communications, translation and conversion under these more stringent operational environment requirements, but instead emphasize the Model 1 environment, concentrating on the issues of concurrency control and synchronization replicated files.

3.2.3.2 Distributed Data Manager Overview

The design of the distributed data manager is driven by three basic functional requirements: concurrent access control, remote access and replicated file synchronization. The requirements of concurrent access control and replicated file synchronization are related and the most complex issues. Solutions to remote access are well known and are available with most all distributed data base managers. The issue of concurrency control is available with most commercial DBMS's. However, replicated file synchronization is still in the conceptual solution stage. Concurrency control requires that the DDBM manage simultaneous data update requests to insure that any two or more update requests do not interfere with each other in a way which would lead to either inconsistent results or an erroneous data base state. This problem can be further complicated in geographically distributed networks (e.g., ARPANET) with variable non-deterministic message delays. Because of these delays, the sequence of receipt of data update requests can no longer be assumed to occur in the same order in which the updates were issued. Replicated/redundant file synchronization requires that the DDBM insure that multiple file copies although physically distributed are consistent with each other at a reference time usually defined after a finite set of data base updates.

In both the management of concurrent file accesses, and replicated file synchronization, the protocol approach selected will be based on an analysis of the file, its reason for distribution (e.g., performance/ response, reliability), and the application's requirement on data freshness. Although several synchronization approaches exist in concept, none have been developed to a level of sophistication in which they appear as standard features in off-the-shelf DDBM's. There a two fundamental synchronization approaches, Lockout and Merging of Tagged Updates which can be based on physical or logical clocks. The lockout synchronization approach yields very good consistency across replicated files at the expense of poorer file access response. The tagged synchronization message approach yields very good file access response at the expense of poorer global file consistency. No single protocol provides both good consistency between replicated files and good file access response (Figure 3.2-4). As a result multiple protocol synchronization approaches are appearing (e.g., SDD-1 [3-5]).

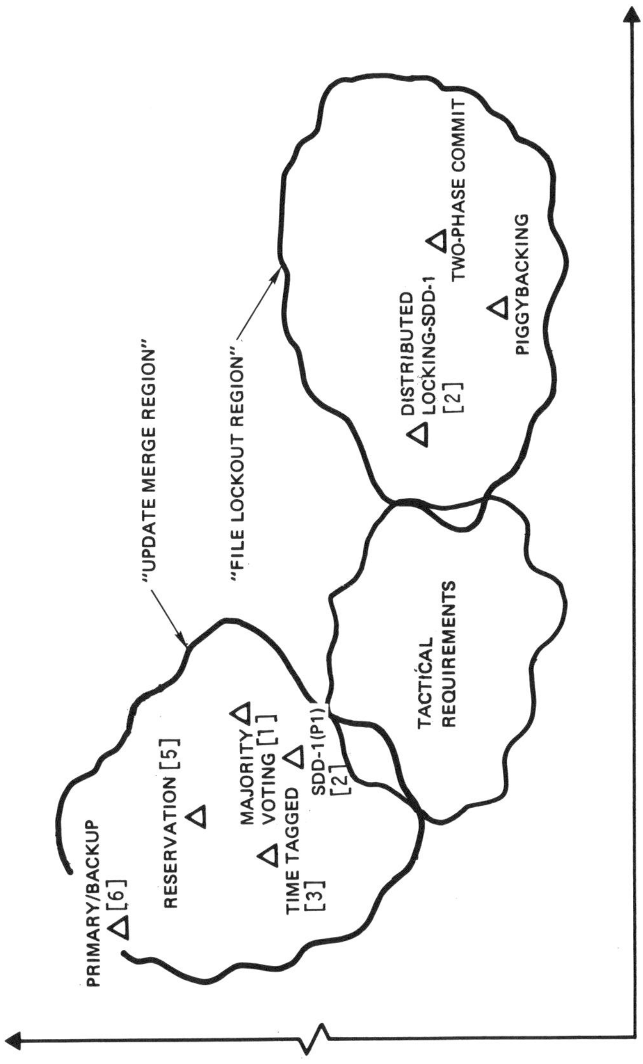

Figure 3.2-4. Fundamental DDBM Design Tradeoffs

The protocol selection is based on the type of file replicated, the application - file interaction characteristics and the applications requirement for data freshness. File types can include critical system status information on which resource management decisions are made. For such status information data timeliness and global consistency are most important for distributed resource management approaches. Application - file interaction characteristics, such as update frequency, file access rates, and whether these file accesses occur remotely, are key factors in selecting the replicated file synchronization approach to be used. High accessed files can result in high network communication requirements, and can strongly influence the file partitioning and allocation. Files may be further partitioned into smaller granularity to reduce the access frequency, and reallocated to reduce communications. Finally, the application's algorithms may be modified to permit the use of data which is less fresh. Current protocol approaches presented (Figures 3.2-4 and 3.2-5) resynchronize all copies of a replicated file after each file update. If file consistency is not of total necessity, updates may be queued at each file copy and then transmitted periodically to all file copies. This approach would reduce the communications message traffic and I/O overhead at the processors.

A second multi-protocol system is also being developed by TRW under Army contract (i.e., DASG60-79-C-0039). The system also uses multiple synchronization protocols with prioritized file update requests. The priority of the file merge request depends on the urgency of each update request, and is determined during the design phase on the basis of analyzing each application file combination in the system. A preliminary design currently exists and additional research and development was performed [3-35] to refine the design and implement a prototype (Figure 3.2-5) at the Army's Advanced Research Center (ARC) in Huntsville, Ala. [3-33].

The TRW DDBM consists of five basic functional modules, which interact to perform remote file access and replicated file synchronization. They are:

- Synchronization Transmit Module (STM)
- Synchronization Merge Module (SMM)
- Protocol Select Processing Module (PSPM)
- Data Base Status Maintenance Module (DBSMM)
- Remote Access Processing Module (RAPM)

For the heterogeneous network (Model 2) environment a sixth module, the Data Translation and Conversion Module (DTCM), must be added (Figure 3.2-5). The six modules will execute asynchronously on each computer of the network.

The Synchronization Merge Module (SMM) processes all local update requests from both the local data manager and from remote distributed data managers within the network. For heterogeneous networks, remote update requests will be translated by the DTCM prior to being serviced.

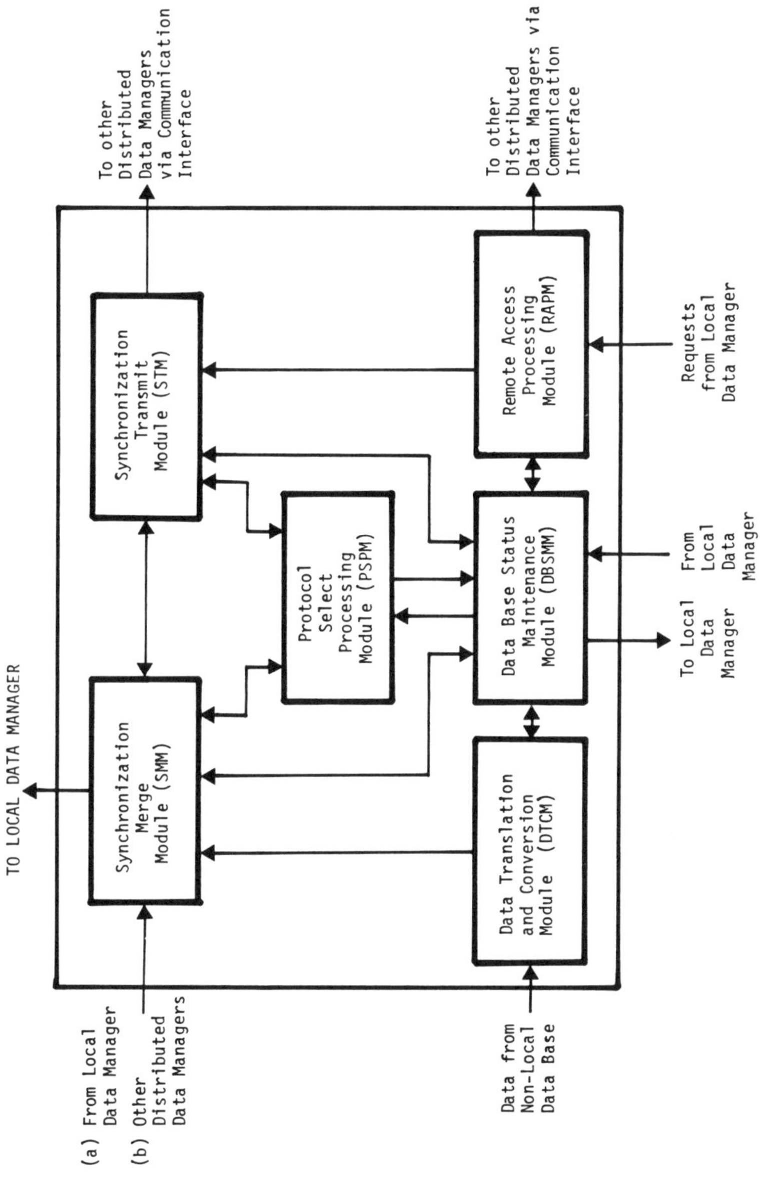

Figure 3.2-5. Distributed Data Manager Top-Level Modules

The Synchronization Transmit Module (STM) transmits all the valid update synchronization requests using a tailored protocol provided by the Protocol Select Processing Module (PSPM). The STM interfaces with other DDBMs via the network.

The Data Base Status Maintenance Module (DBSMM) is considered the heart of the DDBM, controlling the execution of all modules. The DBSMM maintains the status tables and data catalogs for all the local and remote data base activity. It is important to note that some of the status tables and catalogs are replicated files themselves. Because of the frequent access to these tables and catalogs, they must be maintained by the most efficient method possible. Hardware or firmware solutions with a hierarchical architecture [3-6] have been used to improve performance.

The other two modules in the DDM are less critical, we will not give any further details except to mention them here for completeness. The Remote Access Processing Module (RAPM), controls all the remote accesses to and from remote data bases to avoid deadlocks. There is much current research and development work in this area [3-7, 3-8]. The Data Translation and Conversion Module (DTCM) is required when there are heterogeneous computer and data bases within the node, and it can provide a central interface for converting and reformatting all the data so that the local data manager is exposed to a uniform data format and structure. Similarly there is active R&D work in this area also available [3-9, 3-10].

3.2.3.3 DDBM Preliminary Design

In this section we provide the top-level overview for the four modules associated with the replicated file synchronization function in the distributed data manager. They are:

- Synchronization Transmit Module (STM)
- Synchronization Merge Module (SMM)
- Protocol Select Processing Module (PSPM)
- Data Base Status Maintenance Module (DBSMM)

The top-level design provides only the flow of logic in function blocks which can be further broken down into subblocks and subroutines.

STM (Synchronization Transmit Module)

The top-level functional design of the Synchronization Transmit Module (STM) is presented in Figure 3.2-6. This module interfaces closely with the SMM and DBSMM modules. The STM module serves as the interface between the DDB remote access requests and the communications subsystem. Among the functions performed are:

- Process message transmit requests according to selected protocol(s)
- Invoke fast synchronization transmit protocol to update replicated status tables and catalogs

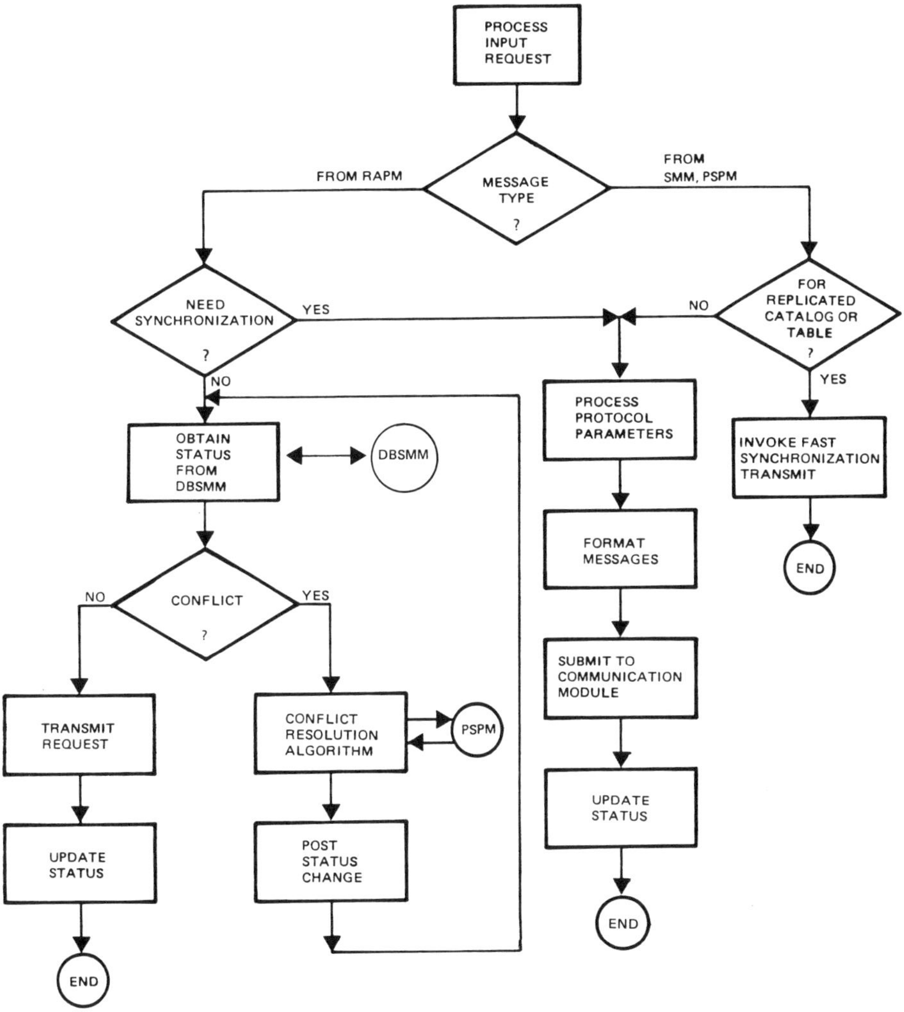

Figure 3.2-6. Top-Level Design of STM

- Process requests from RAPM for remote access
  - Transmits non-conflict request
  - Resolves conflicts by selecting alternate protocols
- Interface with PSPM to obtain the optimal protocol for synchronization transmit
- Interface with DBSMM to update catalogs and status tables
- Interface with SMM to coordinate synchronization merging.

<u>SMM</u> (Synchronization Merge Module)

The top-level functional flow diagram for SMM is shown on Figure 3.2-7. SMM manages all the update synchronization merge requests from both the local data manager and the remote DDM's within the node. It also processes the acknowledgements of all such merging requests. Among the functions performed are:

- Process data and update merging requests from
  - Local data manager or applications to update the following:
    - -- remote data bases
    - -- local data bases
  - Remote DDM to update local data bases
- Process messages from other DDM for
  - Acknowledgement of update requests(protocol dependent)
  - Requests or attempts to update local data bases
- Resolve contention and deadlock requests from both local data manager and remote DDM's
- Maintain merge lists or tables
- Interface with PSPM by providing the parameters of an update request for protocol selection
- Interface with DBSMM to obtain or update current DB status information
- Interface with STM for feedback and transmit messages (depending on protocol selected).

<u>PSPM</u> (Protocol Select Processing Module)

PSPM processes the replicated file update requests to select the optimal protocols for update synchronizations. Two types of algorithms are considered:

- locking (centralized)
- time tag merging

Some simulations have been performed by Garcia-Molina [3-11] comparing two algorithms similar to the above two types (see Section 3.2.3.5

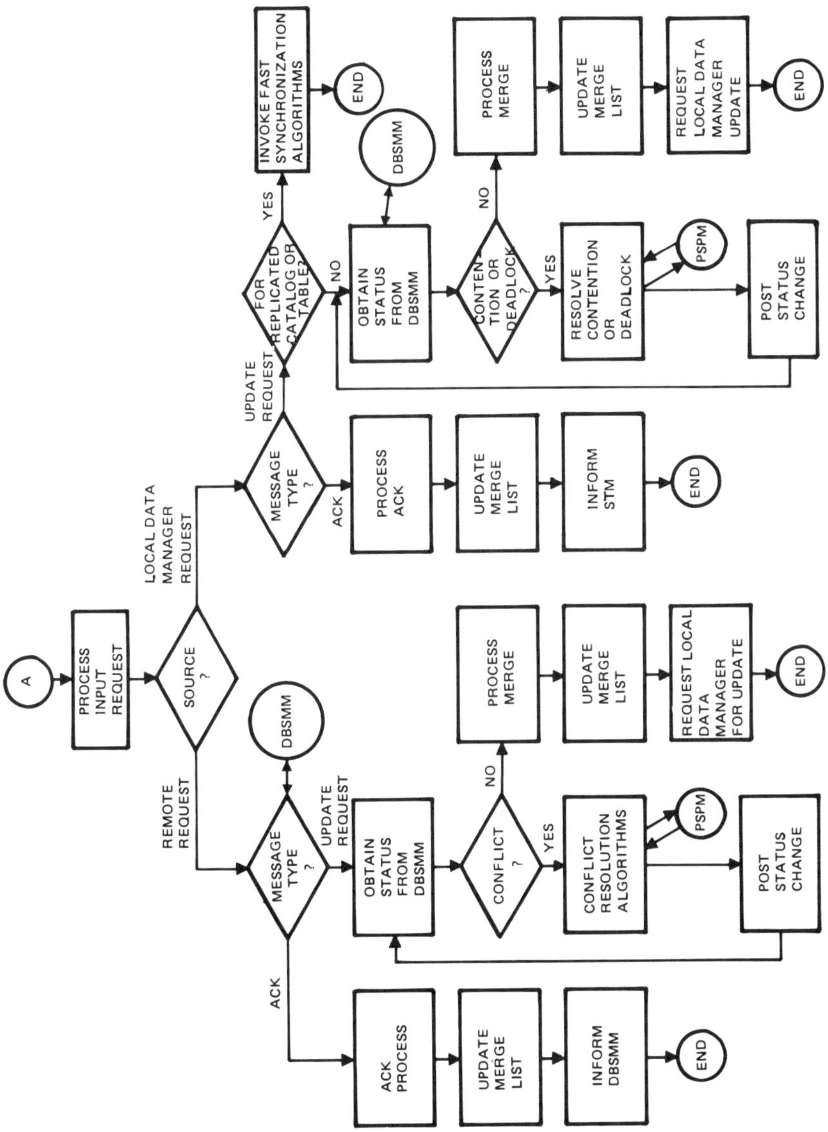

Figure 3.2-7. Top-Level Design of SMM

for more details). Many parameters can be involved in the selection of an optimal algorithm. The top-level structure of PSPM is depicted in Figure 3.2-8. The logic chosen requires the separation of the merging and transmit requests. However, it is possible to combine both together if the protocol selected does not require merging operations (e.g., in case of centralized locking algorithm). The major functional blocks are:

- Analyze the merging or transmit parameters
- Execution of protocol selection algorithm based on the input parameters
- Generate the protocol and the list of parameters which are required to govern the operation of the protocol
- Pass all information to the modules that will execute the protocol
- Update the information to DBSMM if needed
- A stand-alone function that can be a separate utility to maintain the protocol/algorithm tables or files which may be changed when new protocols are added or changes made.

DBSMM (Data Base Status Maintenance Module)

The data base status maintenance module (DBSMM) monitors the status of the files within the data base and coordinates the file access and update activities. The top-level design for the DBSMM is presented in Figure 3.2-9. Every global file which is either remotely accessed or replicated has its status maintained within this module. The DBSMM deals with two kinds of information:

- Status tables
- Data catalogs

Each of the above two types of information can be divided into two classes:

- Replicated information
- Non-replicated information

The replicated classes of status tables and catalogs require special handling compared to the non-replicated ones. In addition, two access patterns are normally required:

- Retrievals
- Updates or changes

The regular contentions and deadlocks have to be considered for both replicated and non-replicated classes. Moreover, for the update or change operations for the replicated status tables and catalogs,

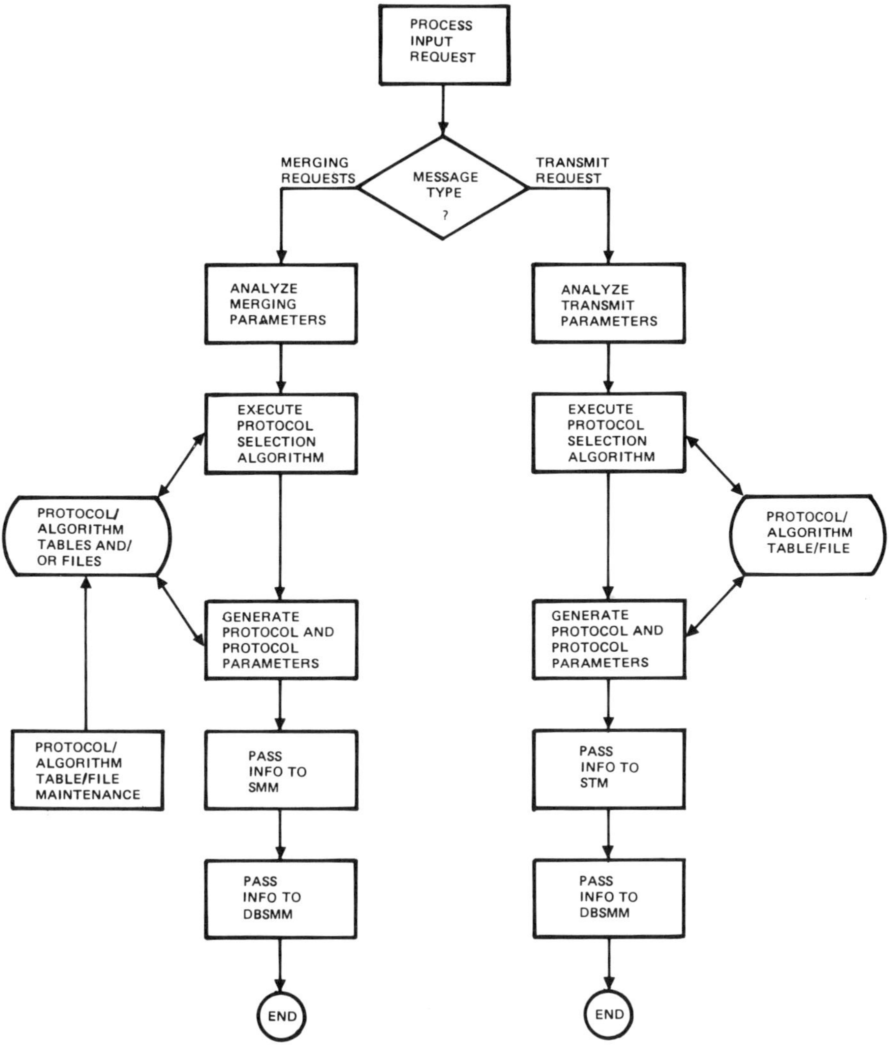

Figure 3.2-8. Top-Level Design of PSPM.

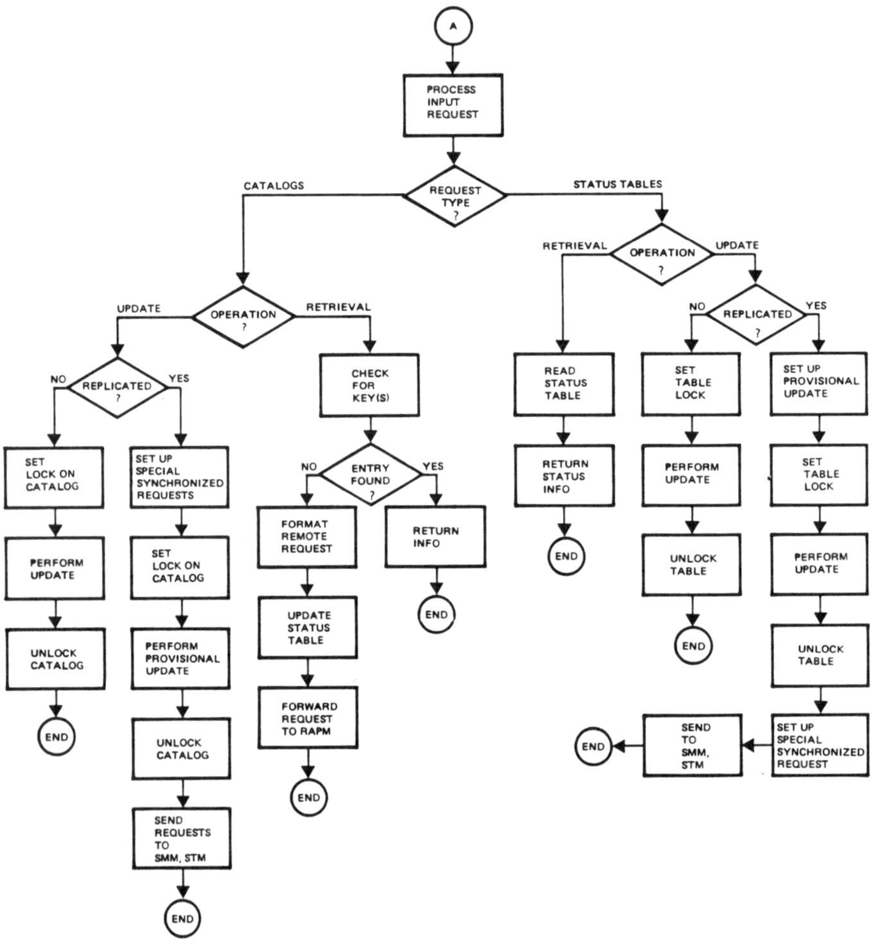

Figure 3.2-9. Top-Level Design of DBSMM.

synchronization procedures are needed. Because the fast response time and frequent accesses required on these data, special protocols must be used. For the status table fast lock and unlock procedures are used. For the catalogs, depending on the urgency and other coherency requirements, special requests are sent to SMM and STM for special processing.

The major functional blocks are:

- Classify type of request by catalogs or status tables
- Determine types of operations
  - Update
  - Retrieval
- For retrieval, access the data in the status tables or catalogs (local entry)
- For remote catalog entries, set up request via RAPM
- For updates - non-replicated tables or catalogs
  - Set lock
  - Perform updates
  - Release lock
- For updates - replicated tables or catalogs
  - Set up special synchronization requests
  - Set lock
  - Perform provisional updates
  - Release lock
  - Send request to STM and SMM.

3.2.3.4 Current Technology

Although there are many critical research issues in DDB, our current research emphasizes the methodologies of update synchronization. There are many proposed solutions to the synchronization problem; five were discussed in the IPC Workshop held at Atlanta on November 20-22, 1978 [3-12]:

- Logical clocks - L. Lamport [3-13]
  To implement a sequential (time ordered) processing in a distributed manner, i.e., "the waiting queue" may be used to achieve mutual exclusion.

- Physical clock - L. Lamport [3-14]
  Provide techniques on how to implement logical clock on a set of physical clocks (i.e., unique physical time frames)

- Logical clocks + Voting - R. Thomas [3-15, 3-16]
  Techniques to resolve conflicts between simultaneous/concurrent processes via a majority concensus voting scheme.

- Event count - Reed/Kanodia [3-17]
  An event counter and sequencers (tickets) are used to control processor events, some practical problem in

implementing resilient event count in case of failure or withdrawal of processor.

- Virtual ring with circulating tokens - G. LeLann [3-18]
  - without tickets
  - to achieve mutual exclusion
  - with tickets
  - to serialize and to express relationships between events

However, several important features which all of these solutions fail to address are:

1. The correctness or provability of correctness of the protocol

2. The actual implementation or simulation of the protocol

3. Means to verify and evaluate the protocol to provide quantitative measures or some form of figures of merit

Lacking the answers to the above questions, it becomes very difficult to implement the protocol even in an experimental environment. Fussell, et al, [3-31] use hypergraphs as a means of representing locking protocols, and the framework for proving serializability and deadlock free operation. However, Garcia-Molina of Stanford University shows in his paper [3-11] that some simulation as well as analytical analysis can be applied to these protocols and some form of quantitative data on performance. He introduces 10 parameters to test his models. Although there are many more parameters that can be used, the 10 he selected are meaningful for such evaluation. They are:

1) Mean interarrival time of updates at each node, Ar. The interarrival time is exponentially distributed with mean Ar. (That is, it is a Poisson process). This means that on the average 1/Ar updates per second arrive at each node.

2) Mean base set, Bs. The number of items referenced by an update transaction (the base set) is exponentially distributed with mean Bs. (Actually, it is a truncated exponential distribution; see (4) for details.) This means that updates that reference a small number of items will occur more frequently than updates that reference many updates. Out of the referenced items, some will be read-only items while the rest (at least one) will be read and write. We assume that the fraction of the read and write items (items in the write set) in an update is uniformly distributed with mean 0.5. That is, on the average, half of the items will be read only.

3) The number of items, M. This parameter is the total number of items in each data base.

4) The number of nodes, N. The number of nodes and data bases in the system is N.

5) Network transmission time, T. We assume that the time it takes any message to go from any node to any other node is a constant T. This is an acceptable assumption if the communications network is lightly loaded or if the distributed data base message traffic is only a small fraction of the total network traffic.

6) CPU time unit, Ct. The CPU computation time is the time it takes any CPU server to do a "small" computation. For example, in Ct seconds a processor can check and set a lock in memory, it can compare two timestamps in memory and maybe add something to a queue, or it can send a lock request to the central node.

7) CPU update time, Cu. If an update references x times, then the time to compute the actual update values is x times Cu. That is, once an update transaction has been accepted or all of its locks have been granted, it will need x times Cu CPU seconds before a message with the update values can be sent to all nodes.

8) IO time unit, It. This is the time it takes to read or write a lock or a timestamp from an IO device. For example, if a transaction at a node needs to read x timestamps, then it must get x times It seconds of service time from the IO server at the node.

9) IO item update time, Iu. The time needed to read or write one item value from or to the IO device is Iu.

10) Retry delay time, Rt. This last parameter is special since it only applies to the distributed voting algorithm. The retry time is the time a node must wait before retrying a rejected update transaction.

The two algorithms he picked for the evaluation are:

- A centralized locking algorithm (CLA) [3-19]
- A distributed control system as represented by Thomas' distributed voting algorithm (DVA) [3-15, 3-16]

The following series of 6 plots taken from [3-11] (see Figures 3.2-10 to 3.2-15) depicts the important parameter of response time R plotted against various parameters. The abbreviation CLA stands for the centralized locking algorithm and DVA stands for the distributed voting algorithm in all figures. The values of the parameters are as shown and are as explained before. Such analysis illustrates the quantitative trades which supports relative performance of the synchronization options. These metrics offer a far superior mechanism than that of counting the number of message exchanges required for synchronization.

3.2.3.5 Future Research

Both hardware and software solutions to distributed data base management are currently under study. Hsiao [3-36] provides a good discussion of

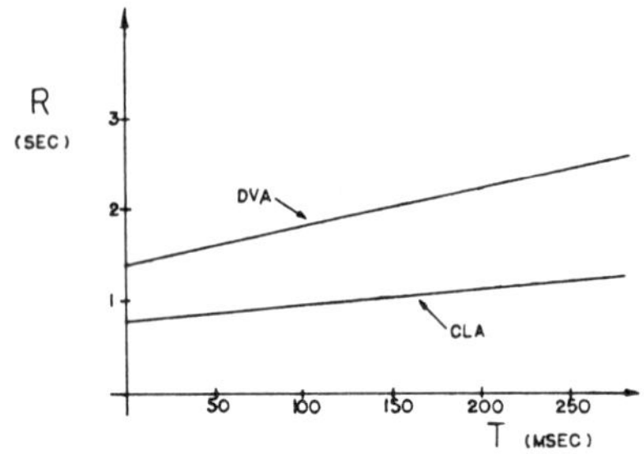

Figure 3.2-10.

The average response time of updates, R, versus the network transmission time, T. (N=6, Ar=7, M=1000, Bs=5, It=Iu=0.025 sec., Rt=1 sec., Ct=0.1 msec., Cu=1 msec.)

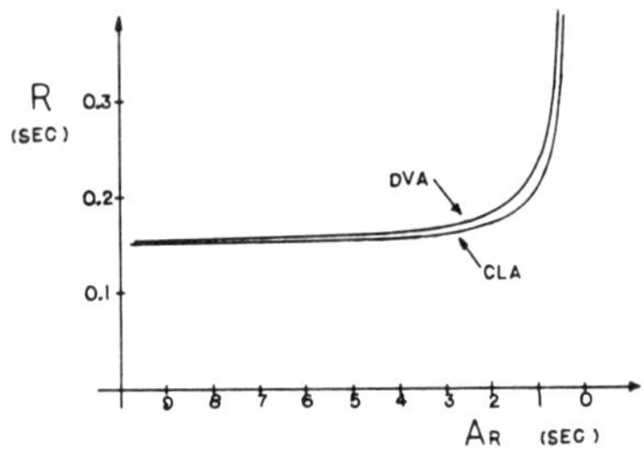

Figure 3.2-11.

The average response time of updates, R, versus the interarrival time, Ar, for a special case. (N=3, M=1000, Bs=3, It=0 sec., Iu=0.025 sec., T=1.25 msec., R=1 sec., Ct=0.1 msec., Cu=1 msec.)

Where:

N = number of nodes and data base systems in network.

Ar = mean arrival time of update transactions.

M = total number of items (e.g., records) in each data base.

Bs = mean base set (e.g., number of items referenced) per each update transaction.

It = Iu = time for read/write.

Rt = retry delay time

Ct = CPU computation time.

Cu = CPU update time.

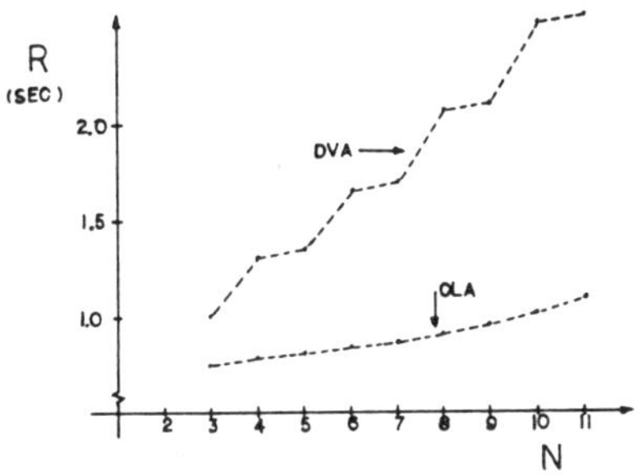

Figure 3.2-12.

The average response time of updates, R, versus the number of nodes, N. (Ar=10, M=1000, Bs=5, It=Iu=0.025 sec., T=.1 sec, Rt=1 sec., Ct=0.1 msec., Cu=1 msec.)

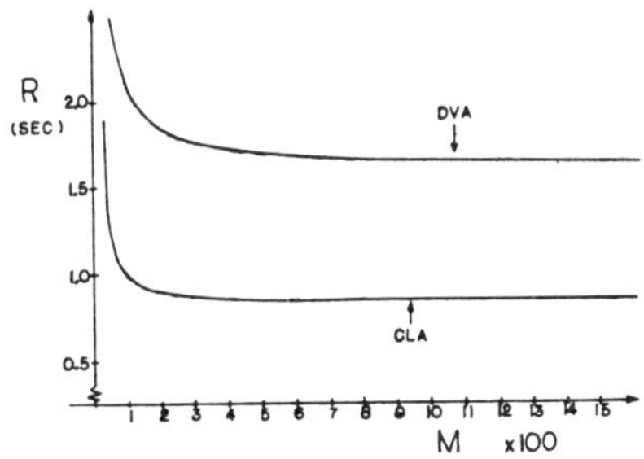

Figure 3.2-13.

The average response time of updates, R, versus the total number of items, M. (N=6, Ar=10, Bs=5, It=Iu=0.025 sec., T=.1 sec, Rt=1 sec., Ct=0.1 msec., Cu=1 msec.)

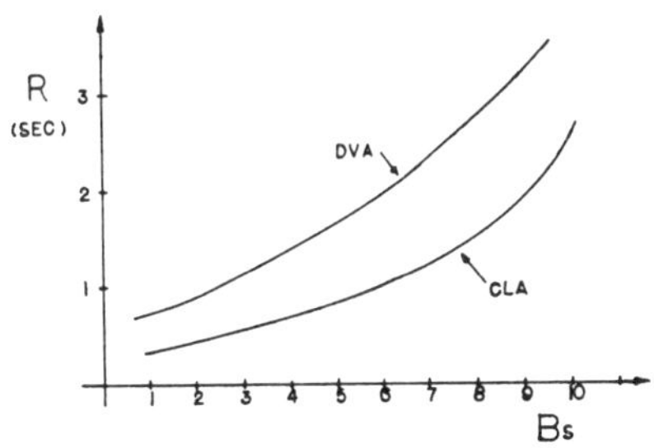

Figure 3.2-14.

The average response time of updates, R, versus the average number of items in the base set, Bs. (N=6, Ar=10, M=1000, It=Iu=0.025 sec., T=.1 sec., Rt=1 sec., Ct=0.1 msec., Cu=1 msec.)

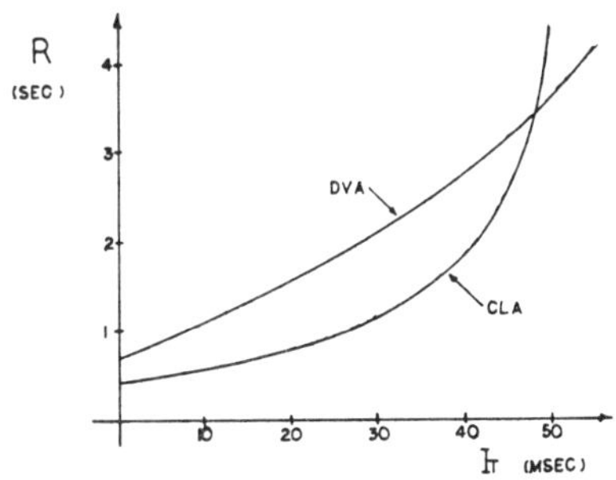

Figure 3.2-15.

The average response time of updates, R, versus the IO time unit, It. (N=6, Ar=7, M=1000, Bs=5, Iu=0.025 sec., T=.1 sec., Rt=1 sec., Ct=0.1 msec., Cu=1 msec.)

the current status of hardware solution concepts to the data base management problem. In a recent survey of software research and development in this field by Rothnie and Goodman [3-2], they cited 61 references with the majority of the papers published since 1975. However, despite the intensive work progress in actual implementation and experimentation is still limited. One of the areas that need additional work is the evaluation of the synchronization protocol in order to provide quantitative performance data as well as means to verify the correctness and applicability of the protocol. As discussed in Section 3.1 the synchronization protocols tie in very closely with the other two critical implementation issues;

- Real-time control/resource management which must operate from redundant data and programs.

- Communication which must support the real time data base maintenance operations of remote file access and replicated file synchronization.

It is therefore necessary to define the scope of research in this area, while taking into account work and progress in the related issues of real-time control and communication. As an example, if the communication delay is on the order of seconds instead of msecs, decision to replicate data and which file to replicate, and the approach for the synchronization protocol may well change in order to optimize the total system performance.

The preliminary design of the distributed data manager as reported in this report is the first step in the iterative process of DDM design. A separate but parallel effort is the protocol evaluation which can be divided into three major activities:

- Perform analytical analysis of the protocol model to derive quantitative performance measures.

- Develop high fidelity simulation models to obtain similar and/or different performance data.

- Develop techniques to verify the correctness and applicability of the protocols.

The results from these activities will bring improvements to current protocols or even lead to design of new ones. This information is then fed into the preliminary DDM design step -- especially to the Protocol Select Processing Module (PSPM).

The first iterative process of DDM design will produce a first cut detail design which will be analysed by a functional simulation model. The results of the simulation modelling can then be fed back into a second pass of an iterative design process. At the same time critical modules can be coded and evaluated under a well controlled experimental environment. With the results of the implementation and experiment, additional input can be fed back to the design process. Each iterative cycle can provide a better and improved design. Very few DDM systems exist which have been developed ground-up from a distributed data base model. Most have evolved from an environment which is based upon a central data base and multiple, distributed users. We will see most of the early DDM systems evolve from industry's applications rather than research. It will be the industrial applications upon which distributed data models will be developed. The early Bank of America models will be replaced with more complex, more fully distributed data base system for which new DDM systems must be developed.

3.3 REAL-TIME CONTROL

Real-time control is an implementation issue in the development of distributed data processing systems. Three major control levels can be identified, (Figure 3.3-1),

- Systems Level
- Data Processing Subsystem Level
- Local Computer Level

Control at the systems level will be dependent on the specific system (i.e., C^3, Sensor control, Satellite Ground Station, Tactical Weapons System) developed. The system level functions will include the optimal control/allocation of subsystem resources; such as the deployment of interceptor resources, or the allocation of search volumes among multiple sensor/radar subsystems. At the subsystem level each subsystem will itself be controlled under the direction of the system control functions. The data processing subsystem control can be decomposed into three basic functions: (1) process control -- aka the computer real time operating system, (2) network control and (3) distributed data base management. These functions are basic to any distributed data processing subsystem regardless of the system which they support. The key to successful implementation of all control functions, regardless of the level, is the distribution of the decision making capacity across the network processors to preclude single point failures and loss of control.

The process control function is the basic real time operating system which exists at each computer in the network. The network control function manages the utilization of the network processing resources under overload and hardware failure conditions. The distributed data base management function (reference Section 3.2.3.2) maintains the global/shared data which supports the execution of the distributed application. The implementation of both the network control and distributed data base management functions have received a significant amount of research attention. This chapter deals with the techniques and concepts of the network control functions.

3.3.1 Real-Time Network Control

In attempting to design advanced high-throughput computer systems, the designer will commonly elect to use multiple processors or computers. While taking advantage of inherent software concurrencies to maximize processing speed such architectures create problems unknown in the single processor computers. As the application is distributed over multiple resources the designer must consider the pros and cons of integrating the distributed resources. Global resource control would permit load leveling and shedding across resources as an alternative to building in the additional hardware resource head room to handle the worst case load at each resource in the distributed system.

The dynamics inherent in most applications environment often make the use of load leveling and load shedding a desirable alternative.

The resource management algorithm supports global resource

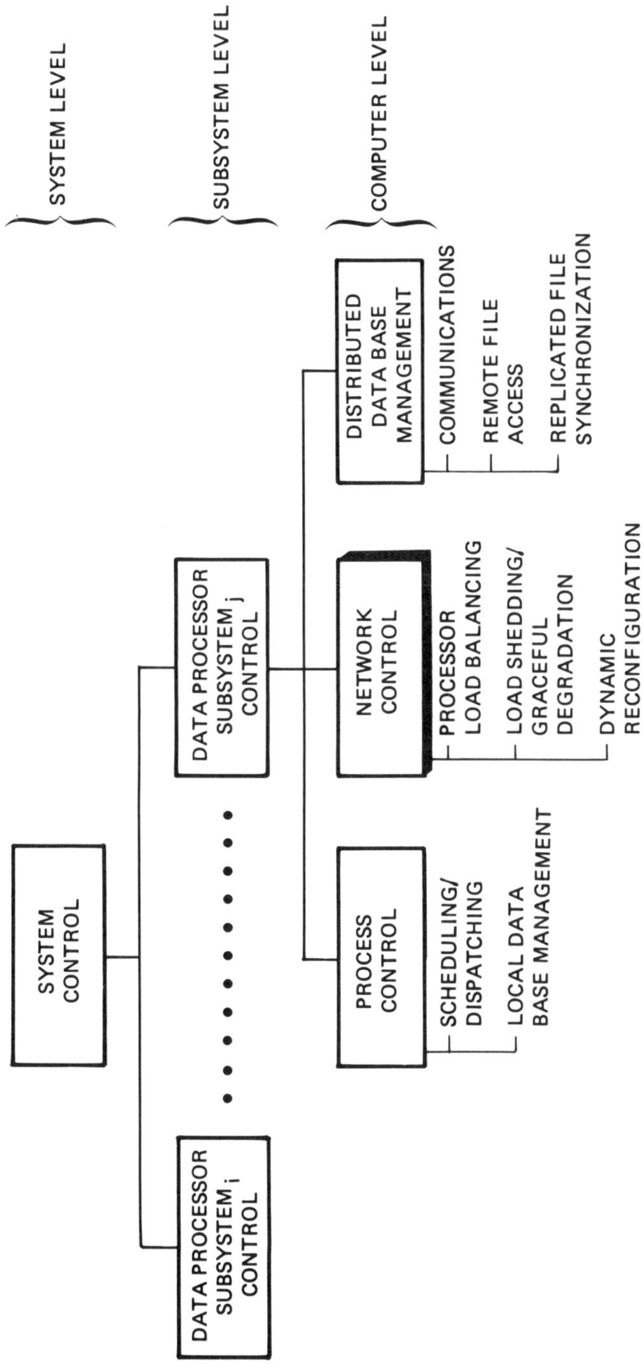

Figure 3.3-1. Real Time Control Hierarchy

redistribution under adverse or off-nominal loading conditions at localized points through the architecture. The same function is performed for centralized systems under nominal conditions through the task scheduling algorithm of conventional operating systems.

Unlike centralized systems control, the control of multi-resource distributed systems are substantially more complex due to the difficulty of maintaining the status of system wide resources. Centralized system status is instantaneously available, however due to networking delays inherent in distributed systems the system status must be based on the integration of multiple system component states, states which represent different time snap-shots. Similarly, control directives which can be applied instantaneously in centralized systems must be networked in distributed systems. Such distributed system networking delays makes the system state a prediction issue; the system state must be predicted into the future at the time the potential control directive would be implemented. The complexity of this problem may be better appreciated by considering three examples typical of off-nominal situations:

- An unacceptably large work load occurring at only one or a few of the computers,
- An unacceptably large work load at all of the computers, or
- One of the computers fails entirely.

Dealing with problems such as these requires a more sophisticated approach than found in the typical real-time operating systems of single computer systems. The specific nature of the resource management system will be explored in the following sections.

3.3.2 Resource Management Objective and Approach Overview

Before discussing specific areas of resource management requiring particular attention it would be helpful to first ask what one requires such a system to do. Referring to the three off-nominal cases cited earlier we can briefly examine the appropriate response of a resource manager to each situation.

In the first case the resource manager, after being made aware of the local overload condition, determines which other computers in the network have sufficient reserve processing capacity to accept some or all of the excess work load. Then the resource manager takes whatever actions are required to implement this transfer, such as informing the accepting computer to activate the required processing software, transferring the work load itself (usually data instances), and perhaps disabling some of the software in the previously overloaded computer.

In the second case, with all of the computers overloaded, the resource manager, after learning of the overload, will first determine the extent of each computer's overload and perform as much load-balancing as the situation will allow. However, in some situations load balancing will not suffice and certain decisions will have to be made regarding a qualitative degradation in the applications processing. Again the resource manager will act to implement the load balancing and degradation decisions.

In the third, and most stressing situation the resource manager would act as in the earlier cases; that is distribute the overall work load uniformly among the remaining computers and, if necessary, implement some form of degraded processing to reduce the overall work load. The resource manager may be forced to accept quantitative performance losses, perhaps by skipping processing entirely on certain selected inputs.

From these three situations one can establish a common objective; that is the ability of the resource manager to distinguish the particular system anomaly which exists (i.e., local overload, global overload or processor failure) and the resource reconfiguration approach to pursue.

Another aspect of resource management illuminated by these examples is the breakdown of the management function's responsibilities. Three distinct functional areas are identifiable. The first is that of monitoring and detection, that is, periodically collecting system state data and the detection of critical system failures. The second area is identified as assessment; using the gathered data to make a decision regarding the need for some degree of reconfiguration and the type of reconfiguration required. The third functional area is that of reconfiguration determination and implementation, that is, deciding what form the system reconfiguration should take and then carrying out the necessary actions to reconfigure the system.

One of the major areas of concern, and a principal subject of research interest, is the manner in which the above identified functional areas are allocated to the computers in the network. At the highest level this is primarily a question of relative distribution of functional responsibility. One way of illustrating the questions which arise in this area is to consider three degrees of management distribution: centralized, partially distributed, and fully distributed.

Figure 3.3-2 schematically depicts a system with a centralized resource manager. In such a system one computer has a role distinctly different from that of the other computers. As the diagram shows all inputs and outputs flow through this computer, thus allowing it to perform job allocation and data routing very easily. If a system fault occurs or one of the computers reports an overload status the resource manager, located in the central processor and cognizant of the conditions in each of the subprocessors, can easily make a reconfiguration determination as well as carrying out the necessary commands to the subprocessors to implement such a decision.

In contrast to this situation is the case of the partially distributed resource manager, one example of which is shown in Figure 3.3-3. Unlike the centralized case, all inputs are available to all the computers, each of which selects only those inputs relevant to its assigned processing. The fact that the resource manager resides at only one processor at any single time interval disturbs the system symmetry slightly, since even that processor is assumed to have applications processing assignment. As in the centralized case all the other processors file their status reports with the resource manager, including the processor at which the manager resides. In the

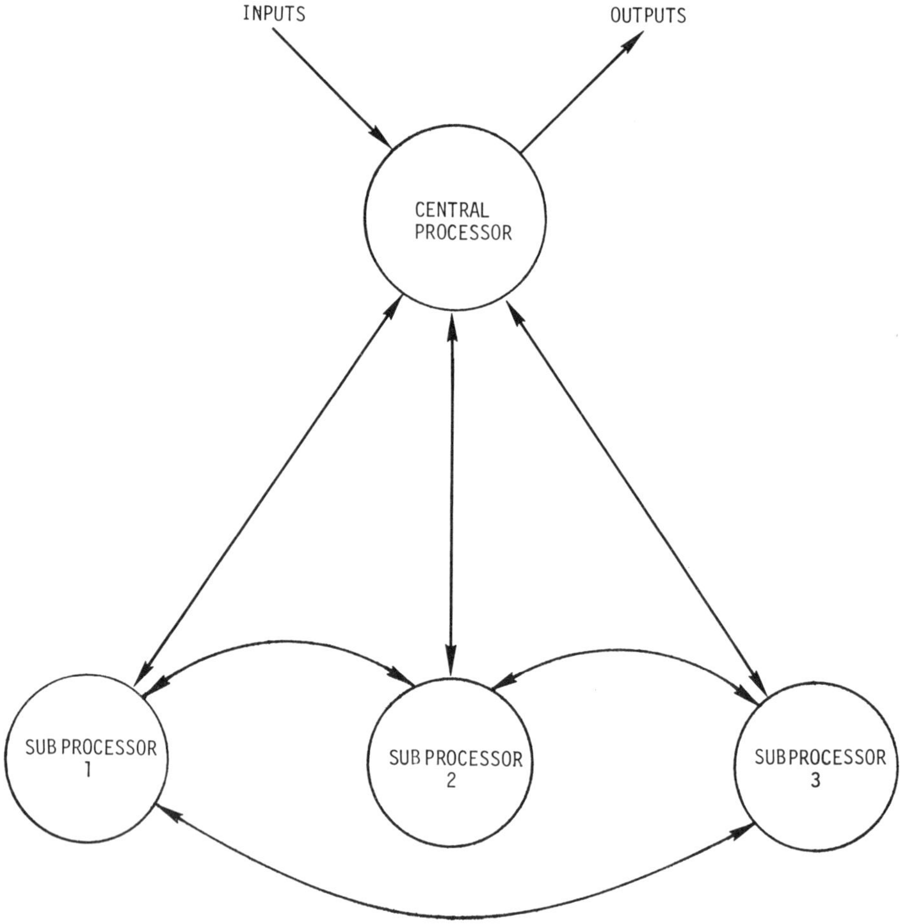

Figure 3.3-2. Centralized Resource Management

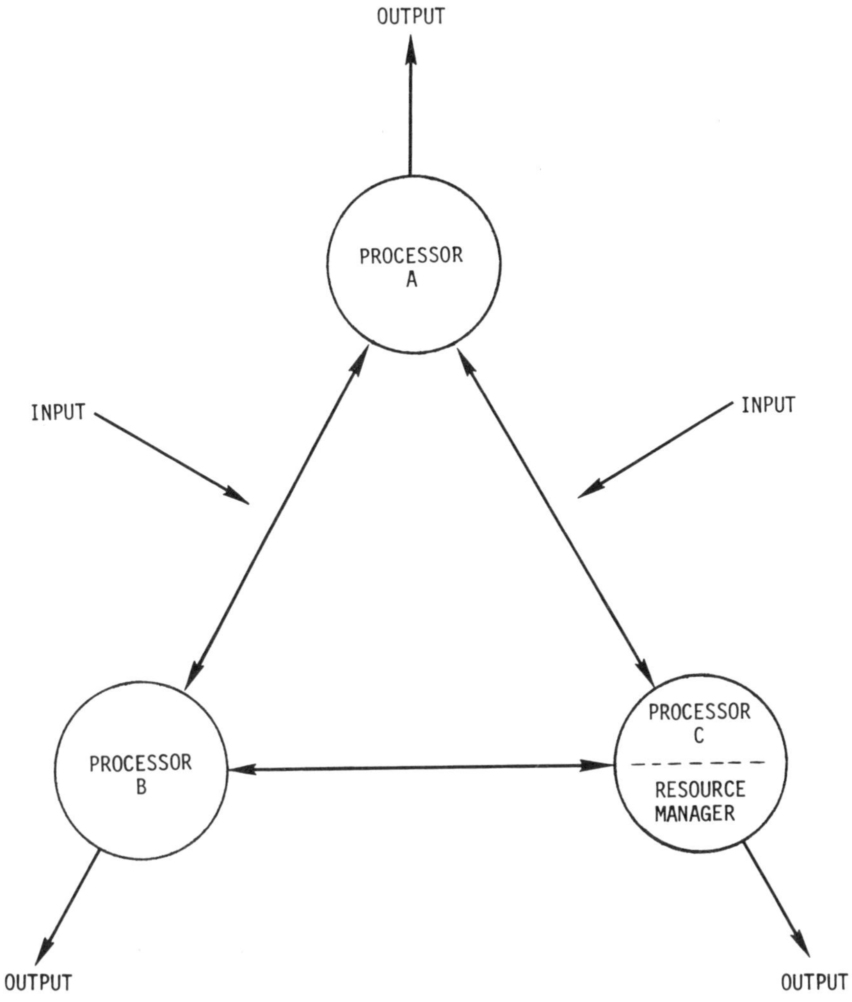

Figure 3.3-3. Partially Distributed Resource Management

event of stressing load situations the manager would take the command role of determining and implementing specific reconfiguration schemes. Unlike the centralized network this construct, because of its symmetry, allows the resource manager to migrate around the network under the direction of an appropriate protocol (see [3-20]). Such preset migration eliminates the essential weakness of the centralized scheme: the danger of losing the entire system if the central processor fails.

The fully distributed resource management scheme outwardly appears identical to the partially distributed one in that no processor resides in a physically distinguished position in relation to the others. Unlike the other two cases, however, no processor has the monopoly on resource management responsibilities either. Rather the resource manager is distributed among the participating processors; that is the resource management decision is based on an integration of all distributed resource managers. This last type of resource manager, where management responsibility is shared among the processors, has great appeal from the standpoint of eliminating single point failures. Unfortunately, such systems require novel protocols and implementation to make them work effectively. Research results in this area will be described in the next section.

Another important area of research concern, albeit on a lower system level than the previous considerations, is the subject of real-time reconfiguration algorithms. These are the specific schemes for determining the details of processing reassignments for the individual computers. Three broad classes of reconfiguration algorithms have been investigated and the results will be described later.

3.3.3 Resource Management Distribution Schemes: Fully Distributed Case

The fully-distributed resource management construct is one in which no single processor is distinguished from the other processors as possessing unique authority over the others. Furthermore, no single processor is internally configured to act individually as the system resource manager. We are left with a "democratic" scheme in which all processors participate to some extent in the decision making process. Three versions of democratic schemes have been identified and briefly explored during early research at TRW. Each will be briefly described.

In the first management scheme, called "bidding", each processor performs its own internal monitoring and assessment of reconfiguration requirements. When a processor determines it is overloaded it determines the extent of the overload and sends this information as part of its periodic health reports to the other processors. Upon receiving such a report each processor will examine its internal status and determine how much, if any, of the excess load it can absorb and report this bid to the threatened processor. After receiving all the bids the first processor will assess which are the best and notify those processors as to what actions they should take. Thus crisses are resolved without reference to a central authority. Even the case of a processor's failure may be handled within this scheme if certain adaptions are made. The primary weaknesses of such a scheme are that it suffers from long negotiation periods before a crisis is resolved, and the bidding message traffic causes increases in processor overhead during the critical period.

A second possible scheme, called "demand" management, requires each processor to monitor its internal status and periodically transmit the details to each of the other processors. In this way when a processor discovers itself to be in trouble it already has the entire system's status at its disposal for decision making purposes. Thus it needs only activate its own internal reconfiguration algorithm, determine the best alternative configuration, and then transmit the appropriate commands to the other processors, who must obey. Again the possibility of a processor's failure can be worked into this scheme as well. The problem with the "demand" scheme is that it is quite conceivable that two or more processors will find themselves issuing conflicting commands to the remaining processors, and depending on the period of the status messages, the system status may not reflect the actual current system state.

The potential for conflict is reduced in the third scheme, called "management by concensus". Each processor monitors its own status and transmits all the details to the other processors. If any processor is seen to be threatened then all the processors take the same actions. Each will activate its own reconfiguration algorithm and determine the best new system configuration and how that will affect the individual processor. Under this scheme each processor operates under the identical control algorithm usually with an a priori specified conflict resolution procedure. Given identical system status, the processors will come to the same resource management decision.

3.3.4 Reconfiguration Algorithms

Reference has been repeatedly made to the activation of reconfiguration algorithms. Regardless of the type of management scheme selected one is generally placed in a position of using all of the system state data to make a decision as to reassigning processing among the different computers. The ways in which this decision can be made are quite numerous and vary considerably in speed and quality of solution. Three broad classes of reconfiguration algorithms have been investigated and will be described briefly.

Before discussing the individual algorithms it is necessary to introduce the fundamental concept of the cost function. No matter which reconfiguration scheme is chosen it can only make decisions to reassign processing to other computers if that reassignment will improve matters by some objective standard. The system cost function represents such a standard. To give some feeling for what such a function would look like the following function was proposed: If t_{ij} is the expected execution time of task i in processor j, based on that processor's speed and the number of instances waiting to be processed by that task, then one definition for the system cost function is

$$Z = \sum_j \left| t_{ij} - t_{avg.} \right|$$

Thus the objective function is defined as the sum of the variance between each processor's execution time and that of the average processor. If one designs a reconfiguration algorithm to shift processing loads among the processors with the aim of minimizing the above function then the ultimate effect will be to achieve a set of uniformly loaded processors, a generally desirable, though not a strictly necessary nor cost effective situation.

Regardless of how the cost function is defined one must still lay down ground rules for the operation of the chosen algorithm. For the initial investigation described below, the algorithms were restricted in the following ways:

1) The task code is not regarded as a factor in any reconfiguration decision. It is assumed that each processor possesses a copy of every task. When speaking of transferring a task from one processor to another it is the input instances which are being referred to.

2) A task's work load (instances) may be moved from one processor to another but may not be split among two or more processors.

Given these restrictions three different classes of algorithms were explored for suitability to the real-time environment: Optimal solutions, heuristic programs, and table-driven schemes.

3.3.4.1 Optimal Solutions

The optimality being referred to is in fact that certain assignments of task loads to processors represent a minimum value of the cost function. In general, strict minimization is not a necessary condition, usually reducing the value of the function below some threshold value Z_M suffices.

Optimal solutions are rarely sought in real-time situations because efficient solution techniques rarely exist; because one must often enumerate all possible assignments and test the cost function for each. Since the total number of unrestricted assignments of m tasks to n processors is given by the exponential relationship,

$$n^m$$

it is easy to see why such solutions are not attempted in real-time. Still, such solutions are important as benchmarks for other algorithms. A qualitative assessment of optimal solutions follows.

OPTIMAL SOLUTIONS - GENERAL REMARKS

- Program complexity: Moderate to considerable
- Storage requirements: Small to large
- Speed: Poor
- Solution: Optimal

3.3.4.2 Heuristic Programs

Since it is quite obvious that exhaustive state space searches would be too time consuming to make the optimal solution a practical approach, other avenues must be explored. One such possibility is the class of programs which conduct limited state space searches under guidance of some solution seeking rule, or heuristic. These programs may vary considerably in their complexity, depending on the sophistication of the heuristic. The advantage of such a program lies in the fact that when one considers a state-space representation of the problem the current state will typically be "close to" some feasible solution state if the reconfiguration algorithm was called soon after the cost function exceeded the threshold value Z_M. Thus an iteration of only a few steps may well suffice to find an acceptable reassignment.

One simple such heuristic [3-21] takes all processors and breaks them into two classes, those with excess loads and those with slack capacity, and sorts them within each class by either decreasing excess or slack, as appropriate. Each program step then consists of attempting to shift the largest (in time) task from the most burdened processor to the processor with the most spare capacity after which the processors are again sorted within class or, if an excess-load processor is reduced below the load threshold, moving the processor to the other class. The procedure continues until no processors are overburdened.

A qualitative evaluation of such programs follows.

HEURISTIC PROGRAMS - GENERAL REMARKS

- Program complexity: Moderate to considerable
- Storage requirement: Moderate
- Speed: Usually reasonable
- Solution: Rarely optimal - often unpredictable

3.3.4.3 Table-driven Schemes

While the heuristic program approach will yield solutions much faster than the optimal scheme it has the drawback that there is little guarantee of finding a good solution unless the heuristic is made fairly sophisticated. One remedy to this problem is to allow more sophisticated types of transition steps but to replace the real-time computation and decision making process with tables of previously computed transition decisions. In [3-21] a detailed plan for developing such algorithms was outlined. Only the barest details will be given here.

The basic requirement in table look-up algorithms is to be able to generate an integer representation of the state space without sacrificing too much descriptive detail. A first step is to select those parameters which one regards as being important in the representation of each processor's, and hence the system's state. In the example described in the above reference, two parameters were chosen: (1) the total processing time for each processor and (2) the maximum task processing time for each processor. These then become the components of a two-dimensional state vector for each processor.

The next step is to partition the range of each parameter for each processor and assign an integer value to each subinterval. Figure 3.3-4 shows how such a partitioning might look for a three-processor system. Note that the subintervals may vary from processor-to-processor to reflect differences in speed or other factors. One now has an integer-valued

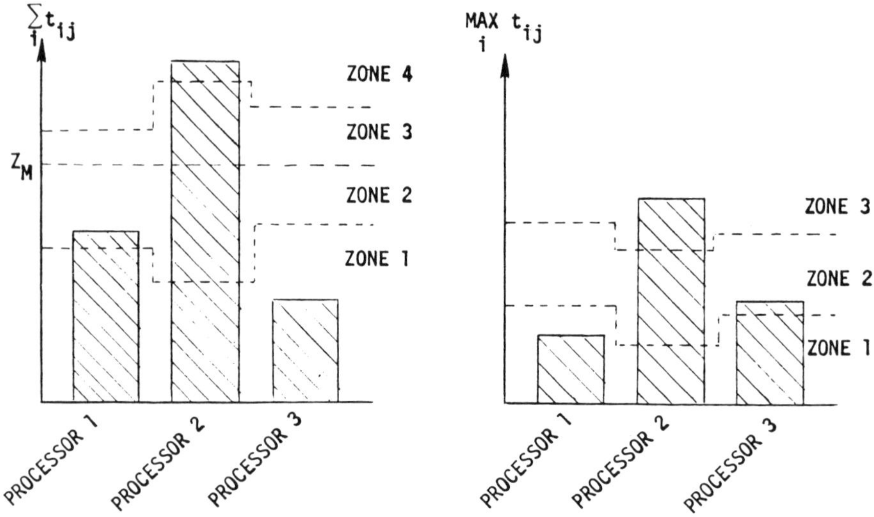

$$\vec{U}_1 \rightarrow [\vec{U}_1] = (2,1) \qquad \vec{U}_2 \rightarrow [\vec{U}_2] = (4,3) \qquad \vec{U}_3 \rightarrow [\vec{U}_3] = (1,2)$$

$$\vec{U} \rightarrow [\vec{U}] = ([\vec{U}_1],[\vec{U}_2],[\vec{U}_3])$$

Figure 3.3-4. Integerization of State Vectors

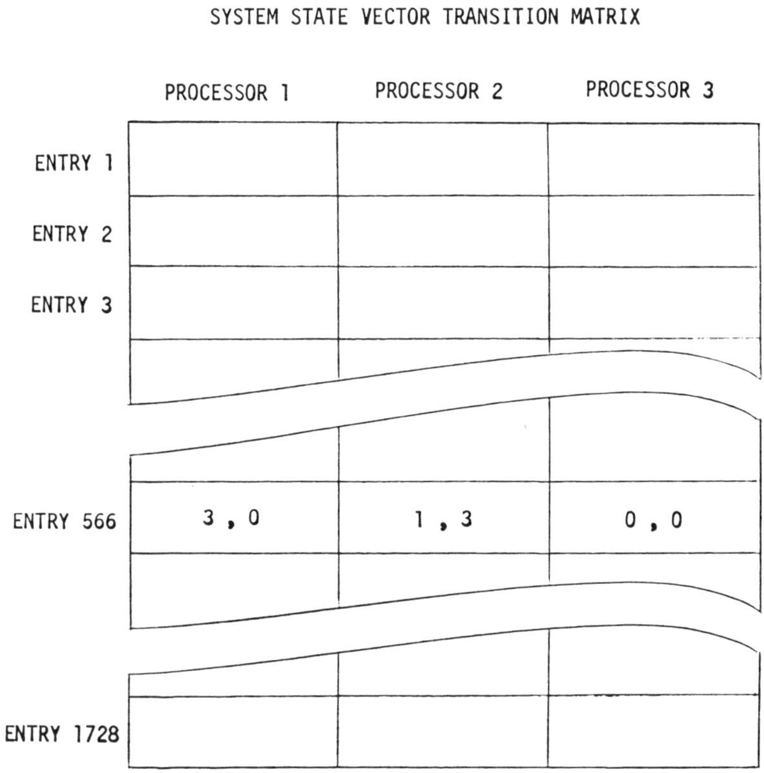

Figure 3.3-5. Sample Content of Transition Matrix

vector with a manageable number of states. In the diagram each processor has a total of twelve (4 x 3) integer states, thus a total of 1728 states for the entire system.

The next step is to combine the integer valued state vectors into a single integer. This is most easily accomplished by the standard matrix indexing rule. When applied to the numbers of our current example a value of 566 is obtained. This then becomes the table index to be used in locating the required transition directions. Figure 3.3-5 illustrates what such a table might look like. In the indicated entry we are directed to move the largest task of processor 1 to processor 3, move the largest and second largest tasks in processor 2 to processors 1 and 3 respectively, and leave the tasks in processor 3 untouched.

The only remaining detail in such a scheme is how to generate the table. This is really the basis of making the scheme useful. In general, one would operate in a reverse manner from the table index to the table entry. In detail this would consist of finding the integer state vector which is mapped to the index, then generating a representative system state which maps into this integer state vector. Finally, one would apply the techniques of the optimal solution to this state and determine the best transition possible. Now the fact is that while the entry in the table represents the optimal solution for this representative state it may not be optimal for other states which are mapped to the same table index. On the other hand if one has chosen a cost function which is suitably continuous over the problem state space, then states which map to the same table index will also have optimal solutions which are in close proximity. Thus one will not be too far off.

An assessment of table driven schemes follows.

TABLE-DRIVEN RECONFIGURATION SCHEMES - GENERAL REMARKS

- Program complexity: Very simple
- Storage requirements: Potentially vast
- Speed: Very fast
- Solution: Good

3.3.5 Candidate Experimental Algorithm

As previously discussed there are three fundamental algorithmic approaches; i.e., optimal, heuristic and table-driven. The latter two, heuristic and table-driven, are suboptimal but, in general, are less complex and therefore, faster executing than optimal approaches. If we acknowledge that one of the potential benefits of distributed data processing is the potential of far lower hardware cost, the software development cost and execution resource cost of optimal control algorithms may outweigh the potential hardware cost savings which optimal algorithms may provide. Instead, a very viable alternative under current hardware trends is sub-optimal control and designing in additional hardware resources.

Regardless of the algorithmic approach, one must recognize that implementation feasibility will depend on the performance and dynamic stability of the algorithm. The algorithm's effectiveness can be measured in terms of the net resources saved,

$$\gamma_{eff} = \left(\sum MIPS_{saved} - \sum MIPS_{cost}\right)$$

where: $MIPS_{saved}$ can be thought of as the additional hardware resources needed (i.e., headroom and redundancy) if the algorithm were not used, and $MIPS_{cost}$ are the resources required by the reconfiguration algorithm.

The dynamic stability on the other hand will be the ability of the algorithm to satisfactorily control the resources without causing instability in the system resource loading. A fundamental hypothesis is proposed concerning the relationship of resource instability and the operational environment in which the algorithm performs:

> THE STABILITY OF THE CONTROL ALGORITHM IS A FUNCTION OF THE RELATIONSHIP BETWEEN THREE KEY FACTORS: (1) ALGORITHM EXECUTION SPEED, (2) DEGREE OF THE THRESHOLD VALUE Z_m AND (3) THE RATE OF CHANGE OF LOCAL LOADING REQUIREMENTS

The speed of the algorithm execution is dependent on three factors: (1) its inherent computational complexity, (2) the resource's architecture structure/configuration and (3) the inherent computational power of the architecture on which it will execute.

The optimality (η) of the algorithm can be viewed as the degree to which the unused resources of the network can be used to shed local processor overloads. One view of optimality (η) considers the loading variance of the network:

$$\eta = \sum_{i=1}^{N} \left(MIPS_i - MIPS_{MEAN} \right)$$

For optimal algorithmic approaches that ratio should be very close to 1.0. For suboptimal algorithms the ratio should be substantially less, perhaps as low as 0.5. Suboptimal algorithms will require the architecture designer to design in higher margins of resource headroom than required for optimal algorithms. The threshold value, Z_m, used can affect the networking loading variance. For low values of Z_m the network will tend to exhibit very small load variations. For high values of Z_m, the network will exhibit very large loading variances.

The dynamics of the resource requirement at local points of the architecture will bound the execution time permissable for the control algorithm. The more dynamic the loading, the less time permissable for control algorithm execution. We have started by hypothesizing a maximum time permissable, $MAX(\lambda_t)$, for execution of resource control; i.e., from initial overload detection to completion of resource reconfiguration:

$$MAX(\lambda_t) = \frac{(\Delta MIPS_i)_{Reserve}}{2 * \Delta MIPS_i/Sec}$$

where,

$(\Delta MIPS_i)_{Reserve}$: is the designed-in headroom of the ith local resource.

$\Delta MIPS_i/Sec$: is the rate of change of throughput requirement at the ith local resource.

The relationship first says that each resource under the control of the global control algorithm must not permit utilization of all 100% of its available resources. Instead, some finite amount can be considered as useful for control; i.e., the threshold value,

$$Z_m = (MIPS_i)_{Useful} = (MIPS_i)_{Avail} - (\Delta MIPS_i)_{Reserved}$$

Where the useful throughput is determined to be that which is (theoretically) available minus that which must be retained in reserve to accommodate the local perturbations in the resource load. We note that the faster the control algorithm can execute (λ_t) the lower the reserve requirement. In addition, the same reduction in the reserve requirement can be achieved by reducing the rate of change in the local resource requirement. Through a judicious design of the architecture, for example using parallel processing for resources handling potentially high data rates, the local architectures resource loading can be desensitized to the threat perturbations; that is the rate of change in throughput loading (i.e., $\Delta MIPS_i$/sec) can be reduced.

Summarizing the above discussions we conclude with the following:

- The need for optimal versus suboptimal control approaches has not been established - the decision is one of a system level trade between HW cost and SW cost for a fixed performance requirement.

- The algorithm design and its architecture implementation will be based on considerations of:

  - SW/HW implementation COST
  - Control execution speed
  - HW headroom required
  - HW resources required for control algorithm execution

With these considerations in mind, an initial algorithm has been formulated [3-34] with which to investigate the resource control phenomenon The algorithm is not intended to represent a preferred solution to the fully distributed resource control problem. Instead we suggest the algorithm as an initial basis for perhaps experimental examination of the control problem.

3.3.5.1 Resource Control Algorithm Overview: Load Balancing/Load Shedding

The control algorithm is viewed as consisting of three principal functions (Figure 3.3-6), overload detection, overload prediction and resource redistribution. All three functions will exist at each computer of the network. Both the resource overload detection and prediction functions will monitor local resource status and operate independent of the other resources of the node. The resource redistribution function must have status knowledge of all resources in the node, and will operate in conjunction with all resources in the node.

The overload detection function will search for, detect and isolate resource overload situations in the system. The function will typically execute at high rates on either a time or interrupt enablement basis. One such approach would be to coordinate the execution with the operating system scheduler/dispatcher function.

The overload prediction function will predict the resources required to offset the detected overload condition. The function will also determine the ability of the local resource to handle the resource requirement,

PROVIDE CAPACITY TO PERFORM INTRA-NODE REAL TIME DISTRIBUTION OF RESOURCES

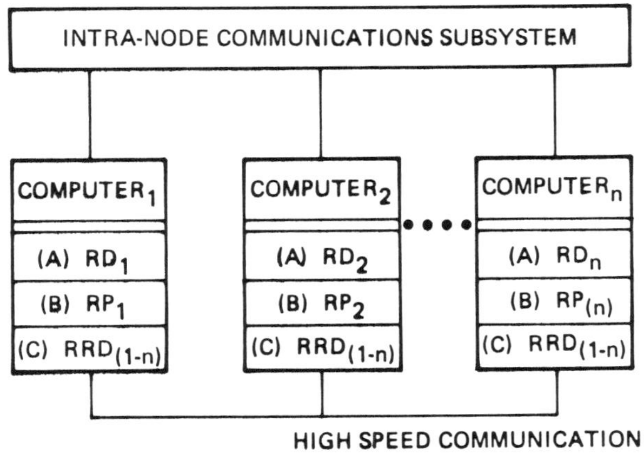

A.	RESOURCE OVERLOAD DETECTION (RD):	BASED ON INDIVIDUAL MONITORING OF TASK QUEUE BUILDUP (Q_i) AND TASK EXECUTION DELAY (T_{w_i})
B.	RESOURCE OVERLOAD PREDICTION (RP):	BASED ON EXTRAPOLATING RESOURCE REQUIREMENT FROM CURRENT UTILIZATION
C.	RESOURCE REDISTRIBUTION (RRD):	DETERMINATION OF NEW VALUES FOR CONTROL VARIABLES (e.g., BASED ON INTEGRATING BIDS FROM ALL COMPUTERS)

Figure 3.3-6. Resource Control Algorithm Overview

and if necessary, enable the resource redistribution function to support load balancing or shedding across multiple resources.

The resource redistribution function will determine and implement the required redistribution of processing load across the multiple available resources. This algorithm may be based on optimal or suboptimal techniques, and will execute at a much lower execution frequency than either the overload detection or prediction functions.

The three functions together represent the potential of a high resource requirement in themselves. An experimental model for resource control is discussed in the following paragraphs.

3.3.5.1.1 Resource Overload Detection Function (RODF)

The RODF will continuously monitor the local resource requirement of each computer in a multicomputer node. The function will continuously project the computation timeline necessary to meet the data load. The RODF operates at a high frequency relative to the other functions of the resource manager. The function will interface with the local operating system (OS) of each computer. The RODF will execute following each execution of the local scheduler/dispatcher function of the OS. The RODF will monitor the process level parameters of

- computer utilization (%)
- task queue length (# instances)
- task execution frequency (exec/sec)
- task execution cost (MIPS/exec/instance)
- task execution wait delay (msec/exec.)

Each of these parameters will be maintained by the scheduler/dispatcher function of the computer OS. The task execution cost function will be determined a priori as a function of execution overhead and the number of instances processed. This function may also be tuned during execution using actual resource cost data.

The current approach to overload detection is based on projecting the local computer throughput in millions of machine instructions (MMI_i) required to insure that all data awaiting processing meets the port-to-port (PTP) response requirements. The approach acknowledges that the PTP requirement may vary depending on the particular data to be processed. It also recognizes that one data type may indicate a potential overload situation but that the overload may be internally accommodated if other data loads are small.

The current detection algorithm (Figure 3.3-7) will monitor the data buildup of each task executing on the respective computer. The machine instruction count (10^6 INST) required to deplete all data instances (w_i) awaiting processing by each task i is then determined using a linear function,

$$MMI_i = A_i \delta + B_i (w_i)$$

This function may be determined a priori, or the values of A and B tuned during real-time operation using actual data. We are determining the function prior to execution.

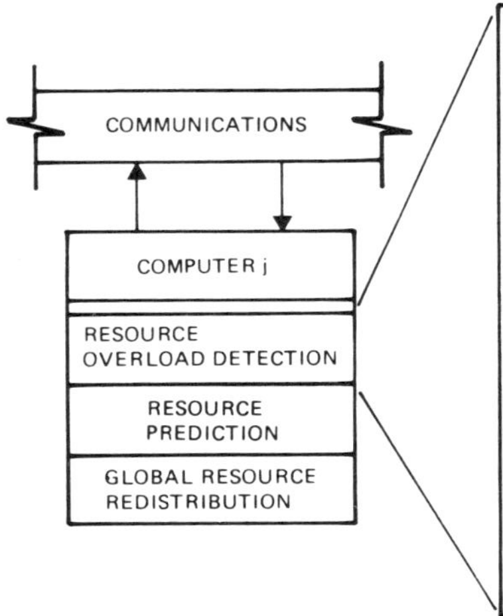

OVERLOAD DETECTION FUNCTION:

$MMI_i = \sum \{A_i \delta \left(\frac{w_i}{m_i}\right) + B_i (w_i)\}$

$MMI_j = \left[\sum MMI_i\right]_j$

$t_{ij} = \frac{MMI_i}{MIPS_j} + \Delta t_{w_{ij}} \, \delta \left(\frac{w_i}{m_i}\right)$

$\Delta t_{ij} = t_{ij} - \{(t_{P\text{-}T\text{-}P})_i \, w_i\}$

$\Delta t_j = \sum \Delta t_{ij}$

IF $\Delta t_j \geq MAX_j$, THEN GO TO RESOURCE PREDICTOR

WHERE:

MMI_i = MACHINE INSTRUCTION REQUIREMENT OF THE ith TASK (10^6 **INST) TO DEPLETE ENTIRE INPUT QUEUE.**

$\Delta t_{w_{ij}}$ = i^{th} TASK AVERAGE EXECUTION WAIT DELAY **ON jth COMPUTER.**

$MIPS_j$ = j^{th} **COMPUTER THROUGHPUT (10^6 INST./SEC)**

w_i = NUMBER OF DATA INSTANCES AWAITING PROCESSING BY i^{th} TASK

m_i = MAXIMUM THROUGHPUT OF ith TASK PER EXECUTION

$\delta(x)$ = TRUNCATED INTEGER VALUE OF FLOATING POINT VARIABLE (x)

(tp-T-P)i = PROCESSING RESPONSE BUDGET FOR THE ith TASK

Δt_j = TOTAL TASK TIMING ERROR BUILDUP IN THE jth COMPUTER

ISSUES

(1) Δt_{w_i} IS HIGHLY DYNAMIC OVER TIME

(2) MMI_i IS HIGHLY DYNAMIC OVER TIME; w_i IS HIGHLY DEPENDENT ON TASK'S DEPLETION RATE **AND DATA LOAD.**

(3) $MAX_j \overset{?}{=} MAX_{j+1}$; EACH VALUE OF MAX_j MAY BE DEPENDENT ON LOCAL PROCESSING **AND PROCESS DESIGN AND MAY VARY ACROSS COMPUTERS.**

Figure 3.3-7. Resource Overload Detection Algorithm

Following the computation of the total instructions required to deplete data awaiting execution by the ith task, the clock time (t_{ij}) is determined. This time represents the projected wall clock time required to totally deplete all data currently awaiting processing on the local computer. The time is based on the local computer's throughput rating ($MIPS_j$) and includes task execution wait considerations based on a past history of the task. The final time (t_{ij}) is then used to represent that time at which the last instance in the queue will be processed, and is compared with a stored value of a PTP response budget. The difference (Δt_{ij}) represents a response time error buildup for that task. The same procedure is performed for each task executing on the local computer, and may be performed in parallel. The sum of all task error buildups (Δt_j) is then compared with a stored threshold value (MAX_j) for the computer.

Both the computer throughput rating ($MIPS_j$) and the timing error threshold (MAX_j) are design variables. The value selected for $MIPS_j$ may not be identical to the actual throughput rating of the computer and instead, may have a value less than the actual rating. Such a decision would permit accounting for operating overhead, resource contention, or needed resource headroom.

3.3.5.1.2 Resource Prediction Function (RPF)

The resource prediction function (RPF) will be enabled by the RODF if a local computer overload condition is detected. As a result, this function will execute at a significantly reduced rate from that of the detection function. The RPF will project those total resources required to insure that all data awaiting execution meet their respective port-to-port budgets. In addition, the function will survey available resources within the node to determine the potential of redistribution. If redistribution is determined impossible due to the unavailability of sufficient resources, a graceful degradation mode will be entered. If sufficient resources do exist then the reconfiguration function will be enabled.

The current approach to RPF is to determine the overload resource requirement in terms of a throughput * time product (i.e., $MIPS_j * \Delta t_j$) (Figure 3.3-8). The time value of the overloaded computer (i.e., $+\Delta t_j$) is broadcast to every computer in the hetwork (Every computer maintains a throughput capability table of the MIPS available at each computer in the network). Upon receipt of the broadcast time (Δt_j), each computer responds by transmitting its own projected time error buildup (Δt_j) back to the overloaded computer. The overloaded computer then takes the projected time error buildup to check for available network resources LIMIT. If the sum throughput * time product of the network is less than that required by the overload then a "Graceful Degradation" state is entered. If the network product is less then redistribution is initiated by ordering the individual tasks by decreasing magnitude of execution time (i.e., t_{ij}).

Once the ordering is complete, the redistribution algorithm is enabled.

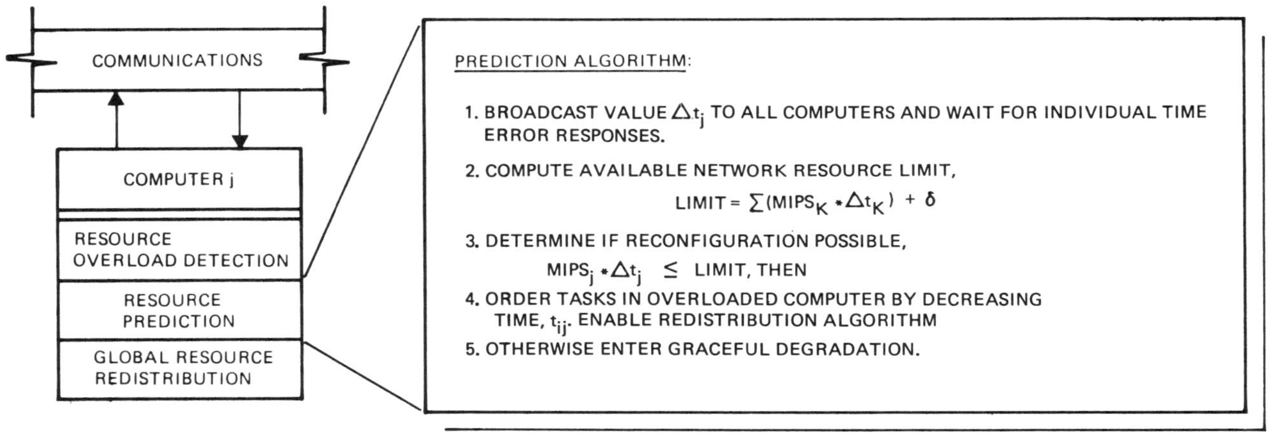

ISSUES:

(1) "LIMIT" VALUE IS DEPENDENT ON ARCHITECTURE AND CONTROL OVERHEAD, MAY ALSO BE A FUNCTION OF ΔMMI_j, Δt_i, OTHER.

(2) "LIMIT" VALUE ALSO DEPENDENT ON **UNCERTAINTY AND EXECUTION TIME OF RECONFIGURATION ALGORITHM (δ).**

Figure 3.3-8. Resource Prediction Algorithm

3.3.5.1.3 Resource Redistribution Function (RRF)

The resource redistribution function (RRF) will execute only in the event that a local overload is detected, and the resources are determined available to support redistribution. The redistribution algorithm may take two forms, either optimal redistribution or suboptimal redistribution. The difference between the two forms is the efficiency with which the hardware resources are used, and the execution cost of the algorithm. The suboptimal reconfiguration algorithm will usually cost less to execute but produce less efficient use of hardware resources than the optimal reconfiguration algorithm. We have chosen to initially pursue the suboptimal algorithms, the main rationale being that they provide better response and the associated hardware inefficiency is not significant in distributed data processing environments where the individual computer throughput requirements are low enough to correspond to low per MIPS cost. Centralized or slightly distributed architectures may require high throughput computers which operate in the high cost regions of the throughput-cost curve.

The current approach which we are pursuing (Figure 3.3-9) is based on a suboptimal heuristic algorithm. The approach performs resource redistribution in a sequential manner, simultaneously at each of the multiple computers of the node. The redistribution is performed in the order of decreasing resource overload; i.e., computer with the highest overload time (Δt_j) first. For each overloaded computer the reassignment is performed in order of decreasing task time error buildup (t_{ij}) to computer with maximum excess reserve capacity (i.e., throughput-time product: $MIPS_k \cdot \Delta t_k$). The same algorithm is executed at each computer of the network, and each computer receives all ordered lists of task execution time requirements for each computer in the network with detected overload condition. This approach improves the response time of the redistribution algorithm by allowing simultaneous computation of the reconfiguration with sequential implementation of the redistribution commands. The algorithm has a high bandwidth requirement due to the broadcast of the ordered execution times of those computers detected as overloaded. This bandwidth may not be significant unless many simultaneous overload conditions are detected for complex networks containing several computers.

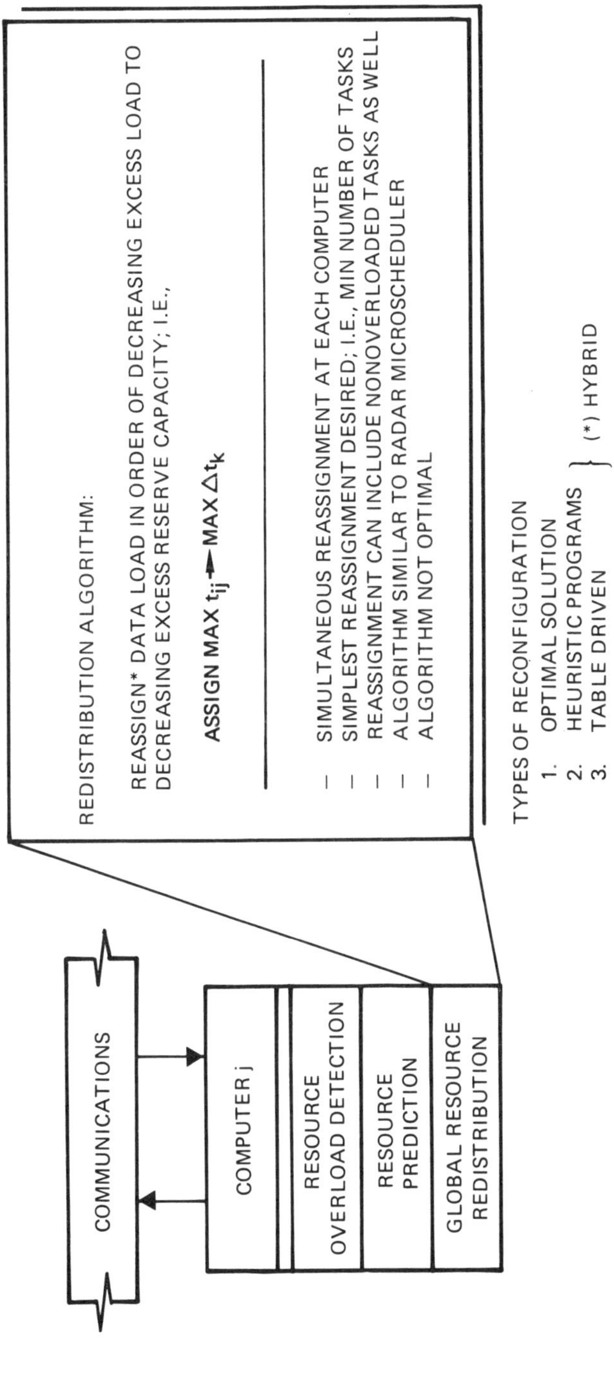

Figure 3.3-9. Resource Redistribution Algorithm

3.4 INTERPROCESS COMMUNICATIONS (IPC)

High response approaches to interprocess communication via messages are of major importance to the success of distributed systems for real time systems. Four classes of IPC traffic typically exist in most distributed systems. These four classes of messages are the following,

- CLASS 1: IPC of Process Control messages for maintaining the flow of control from one task in a logic thread to the next.
- CLASS 2: Distributed Data Base Access/Update messages which execute the read and write of remote global data by applications tasks.
- CLASS 3: Network Resource Management messages which provide continuous status updates of the network resources, and control directives which reconfigure the system resources in the event of resource overload or hardware failure.
- CLASS 4: Hardware Synchronization messages which provide the necessary synchronization of processor time sources to a universal or central time reference.

Unfortunately these four message classes have quite diverse message characteristics (Figure 3.4-1). Acknowledgement of the diverse characteristics of these four message classes is of major importance during the design selection of the communications subsystem, if the system is to meet real time response requirements. As the Figure indicates for example, the messages associated with IPC for process control will almost always be characterized by high message response requirements (i.e., < 1msec), with a moderate to high relative message rate. However, the message size will usually be relatively small. Messages associated with distributed data base management activities are noticeably different from process control messages. The DDBM messages will typically require less stringent message response, and operate at a lower frequency. They will also be based on much larger message size. The first two classes are of major interest since they will often constitute the major percentage of the communications message traffic under normal system operations.

The principal payoff criteria in the design of IPC for the tightly coupled computer system are performance (response times and ability to handle required data volumes), reliability, cost, deployability and capability to grow and accommodate changes in nodal structure. These payoffs are all affected by the communications architecture, complexity of interaction protocols, and transmission line characteristics. Emphasis is given to the formulation of protocol levels for communications (Figure 3.4-2).

3.4.1 A Preliminary Model: Multilevel Protocols for Transparency

A preliminary model of nodal communications is described and used as the basis for this IPC discussion. The model assumes that commu-

MESSAGE TYPE	MESSAGE RESPONSE TIME	MESSAGE RATE	SIZE (WDS)
I INTERPROCESS COMMUNICATION (IPC)			
1. TASK ENABLEMENT	<1 MSEC	10^2-10^3HZ	1-10 WDS
2. CONTROL INTERRUPT	<1 MSEC	1-10 HZ	1-10 WDS
II DISTRIBUTED DATA BASE MANAGEMENT (DDBM)			
1. REDUNDANT FILE SYNCH.	1-10 MSEC	10^2-10^3HZ	10-10^2WDS
2. REMOTE FILE ACCESS	<1 MSEC	10 -10^2HZ	10^2-10^3WDS
3. FILE STATUS INFORMATION	<1 MSEC	10 -10^2HZ	1-10 WDS
III RESOURCE MANAGEMENT (RTRM)			
1. RTRM ENABLEMENT REQUEST	1-10 MSEC	1-10 HZ	1-10 WDS
2. RESOURCE STATUS	10-100MSEC	10-10^2HZ	1-10 WDS
IV HARDWARE SYNCHRONIZATION	<1 MSEC	1-10 HZ	1-10 WDS

Figure 3.4-1. General Requirements on Control Messages and Data Transfer Messages

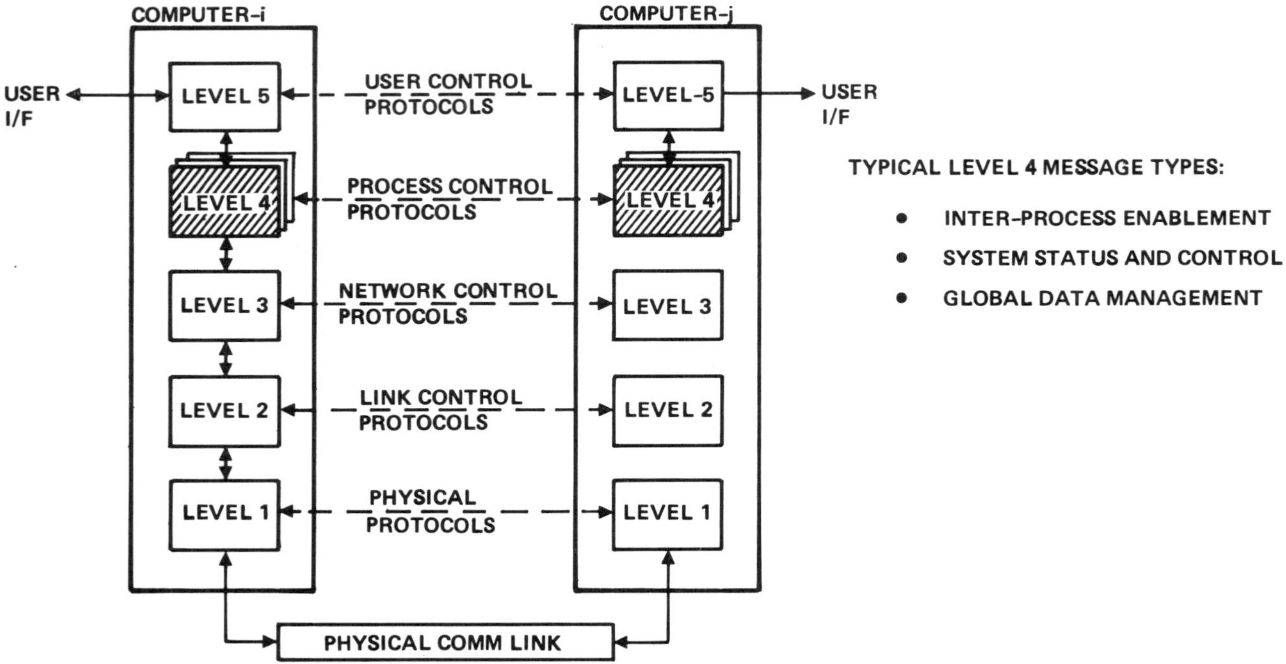

Figure 3.4-2. A Candidate Communications Protocol Hierarchy

nications take place between application processes* (LEVEL 4) only (from application process through three levels of communications protocols at the sending computer then through three levels of protocols at the receiving computer to the destination application process).

There are numerous definitions for process that convey its dynamic nature or its structure. In the present model, a process is a program module that can be assigned for concurrent processing to one or more processors of the network. In addition to such application processes, there are control processes associated with each network computer's operating system, and processes that manage various devices in the computer and their interactions (e.g., communications processes, data management processes).

Processes are created and terminated in the course of computations. They can be in several states (e.g., active, waiting, blocked, ready). They communicate by sending and receiving messages. Concurrently active processes can be cooperating with each other, but they can also interfere with each other in the use of shared resources (e.g., buffer space) or operating on data base (e.g., attempt to access the same data record simultaneously). Thus, rigid controls must be designed into the system to permit concurrent processing in an orderly manner.

Figure 3.4-3 illustrates a possible structure of the network. In this structure, the following assumptions hold:

A. Communications take place between processes only: from application process to a communication process (under the control of or via the control process) and from there to the communications process of the addressed computer and then to the application process that was specified. The use of communication processes may be avoided when the communicating processes are in the same processor.

B. Within the network, certain a priori assignments of computing tasks to processors are made, such that the associated programs are pre-stored in those processors and dynamic assignments of tasks to processors need not be made. Similar assignments are made for data sets.

C. For load sharing and fault-tolerance reasons, provisions are made in the design of the network for assigning the same tasks to several processors. One of the processors would be the primary choice for executing a task, others would serve as backups that can be enabled to perform the task in the course of processing.

D. Each of the processors will contain parts of the control process: the Real Time Operating System (RTOS), and the Resource Management (RM) system. Subsystems of RM are Load Balancing (LB) and

---

* We define process as the basic (dynamic) units of computation that are scheduled and dispatched by the operating system of each computer in the network.

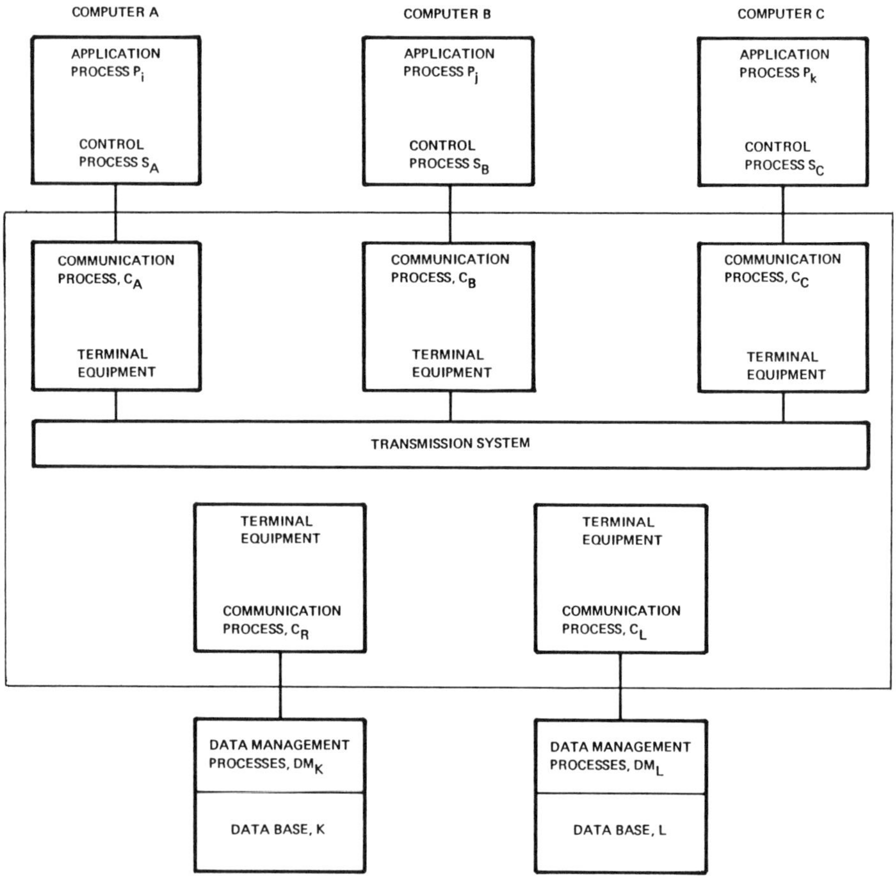

Figure 3.4-3. Structure of a Network

Dynamic Reconfiguration (DR) modules (reference Section 3.3.1). Application processes communicate through the control processes. The overall control mode may be described as a "partial autonomy" in that individual processors can proceed asynchronously until some synchronization is needed. Each computer also has its own "health monitoring" process as a part of the RM module. The control processes also maintain processor state variables for query by other control processes.

3.4.2 Interprocess Communication

Given the model described in the previous section and the distribution of functions among the several processors of the network, a number of application, control, device management, and data management processes will be active concurrently. Interprocess communication involves communicating messages containing control information or data between these processes.

The set of rules which completely define the way two processes can communicate is called a <u>protocol</u>. Typically, establishing a communication path between two processes and preparing one of the processes to send a message and the other one to receive involves several interchanges of messages. The protocol specifies precisely the sequence of these interchanges and the format and content of messages communicated. There are several processes and hardware subsystems involved in IPC, starting with the application processes and ending with the data transmission link hardware. In order to permit structuring of computer networks from heterogeneous computer systems and permit concurrent processing of many different processes, it is useful to develop standard protocols at different levels of the IPC function. The purpose is to isolate the higher levels from the lower ones, such that at each level only those communication functions that are pertinent to the level are addressed. For example, error control in the transmission systems is not a concern to application processes in that they should not be required to know anything about how error control is achieved. Neither do they need to know what data links are used to effect the connection.

There are a number of ways for defining protocol levels. In general, there are the following classes (where each class may have additional protocol hierarchies):

A. <u>Data network protocols</u> that take care of picking up the message at computer A and delivering it correctly to computer B. These are end-to-end data transmission protocols.

B. <u>Process level protocols</u> that pick up the message from process p_i in computer A and deliver it to process p_j in computer B (making use of the lower level network protocols as applied to communication processes).

C. <u>Standard formats</u> for message types communicated between processes (e.g., control, data transfer) and private formats for applications processes.

D. <u>Functional-level protocols</u> that have been agreed upon for processes -- interpretations of the message content for performing computations required for the functions. Involved is the syntax and semantics of messages.

In terms of the model in Figure 3.4-3 network protocols govern data transmissions in the communication system (which includes the communication service processes, terminal equipment and transmission system); process level protocols are implemented in the control processes and application processes, and functional-level protocols deal with interface data that are computed by the application processes.

3.4.3 Data Network Structure

Interconnection of computers within a tightly couple local computer network is a special case of computer-to-computer communications networking in that distances are very short and transmission systems such as radio, satellites, microwave, etc. are not to be used. Instead, all computers in the network system will be connected by electrical or optical cables. Even then, there are a number of network structures to choose from. Based on a classification system developed in Reference [3-22], these structures and some of their attributes are listed in Figure 3.4-4. The classification system used is based on the following classification dimensions:

A. Transfer strategy from sender to receiver

(1) Direct (D) transmission of messages with no routing decisions made in transit.

(2) Indirect (I) transmission in which an intervening operation (switching, rerouting) is required.

B. Transfer control method (applies for indirect transfer strategy only)

(1) Centralized (C) routing where a single control center switches all messages.

(2) Decentralized (D) routing in which a number of switching points have control over transfer routing.

C. Transfer path structure

(1) Dedicated (D) transfer path (point to point)

(2) Shared (S) transfer path; accessible to more than two points (sources of destinations of messages, or switching nodes).

In both cases, the path could be either uni- or bidirectional and bit-serial or bit-parallel. Not included in this classification dimension is the message protocol choice that deals with how connections are maintained: circuit switching, message switching, packet switching, and various multiplexing schemes.

Important characteristics of the communication system structure examined in [3-22] and summarized in Figure 3.4-4 are the following:

A. Performance of the communication system, described in terms of the following:

(1) Transit time - time for a message to reach its destination

(2) Bottlenecks - problems that may arise and adversely affect transit time or maintenance of overall high level performance.

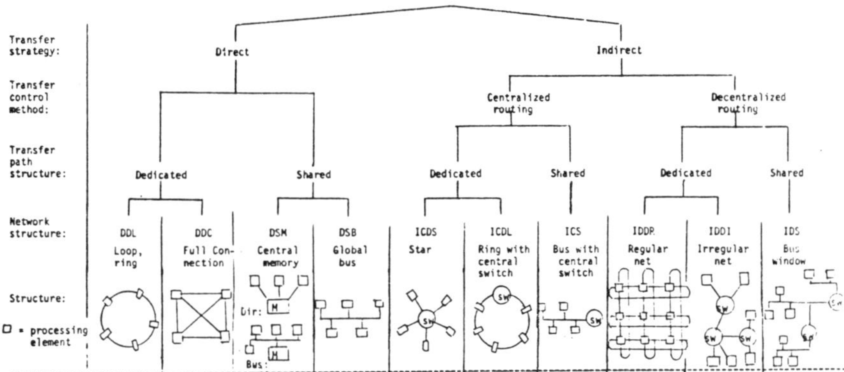

	DDL	DDC	DSM	DSB	ICDS	ICDL	ICS	IDDR	IDDI	IDS
Performance										
Transit time:	Variable (store and forward)	Good	Good (if memory used for comm. only)	Good	Variable (slowed by switch)	Variable (due to sw. and ring)	Good (some sw. effects)	Variable (routing)	Variable (sw.)	Variable (sw.)
Bottlenecks:	Bandwidth Saturation	None	Memory bandwidth, use	Bus bandwidth Contention	Switching capability Contention	Switching Loop bandwidth	Switching Bus bandwidth Contetion	None	Switching (if on critical path)	Critical switches Deadlock
Logical complexity:	Low (interaction with neighbors only)	Moderate (location addressing needed)	Low	Variable (depends on protocols)	Moderate (routing tables in switch)	Moderate (less than ICDS)	Moderate (less than ICDL)	Moderate (routing, regularity)	High (routing requires knowledge of topology)	High (grows rapidly with levels of switching)
Fault tolerance:										
Fault-effect:	Poor	Good	Proc: Good Mem: Poor Bus: Poor	Proc: Very good Comm: Poor	Proc: Good Sw: Poor	Proc: Good Comm: Poor Sw: Poor	Proc: Good Bus: Poor Sw: Poor	Variable (depends on routing discipline)	Good (if redundant paths)	Moderate
Reconfigurability:	Poor (bypass needed)	Good (relay messages)						Very poor (regularity required)		
Growth capability:										
Cost-modular: (Proc = adding a PE; Comm = increasing capability)	Very good	Poor	Dir: Variable (depends on available memory ports) Bus: Good	Proc: Good Comm: Poor	Proc: Good Comm: Poor Sw: Poor	Good	Good	Very poor (regularity requirement)	Good	Good
Place-modular:	Very good	Good	Very good (can add PEs arbitrarily)						Very good	Very good
Connection flexibility:	None	None	None	Good	Poor (path to switch)	Improved over ICDS	Good	None	Good	Moderate (less than IDS)
Application consideration:	In systems where performance & reliability requirements not high	Geographically dispersed systems, but not large systems	Multiprocessors; large messages quickly delivered	Aerospace systems; real-time control	Widely used; handles sophisticated IPC needs	Experimental; handles sophisticated IPC	Experimental	Experimental	Geographically dispersed networks	Complex distributed systems, networks

Figure 3.4-4. Network Structures and Their Attributes

In addition, there are a number of other ways that performance can be measured: connection establishing time, transmission times (end-to-end, message plus acknowledgement of receipt, turnaround time), and data transfer rates (bits/sec or characters/sec).

B. Logical complexity of the communication system - the nature and number of routing decisions that must be maintained in the system for supporting this.

C. Failure tolerance of the network in terms of effects of errors and ease of recovery. Two dimensions are used in Figure 3.4-4.

(1) Failure-effect on network - what effect will a single failure have on the network operation

(2) Reconfigurability - how easily can the system be restructured or message traffic rerouted to resume operation.

D. Growth capability - the ability to add new processors to the network, or new communication links, or to increase the capabilities (e.g., the bandwidth, throughput) of the communication system.

(1) Cost-modularity characterizes the cost of incremental addition of one processor, or incremental improvement of communications system capability.

(2) Place-modularity characterizes the ability to choose the location in the network where incremental addition or increase is to be made.

(3) Connection flexibility refers to the availability of choice in deciding how to connect the additional capability (processor, communication link capability) into the network.

Also included in Figure 3.4-4 are assessments of the suitability of various network structures for various types of applications.

3.4.4 Network Functions

The purpose of the communications system (network) is to pick up messages from a source (e.g., computer A) and deliver them correctly and efficiently to the destination (e.g., computer B). There are a number of functions to be performed that are essentially independent of the contents of the messages being transmitted and that are dependent on the structure of the communications network. These functions are implemented in a hierarchy of protocols in the network. Following the model defined in Figure 3.4-3, all the following functions will be performed by the communications service process, C_i, of computer i. The input to this process is assumed to consist of the ID of the receiver process, a priority indication, ID of the sending process, a security indication, indication of the message type, indication of the message length, indication of whether or not a response is expected and what kind (all of which appears as message header and trailor), and the message text.

The following functions are performed in the communication system:

A. Locating the destination process - the communications service process of the sending computer, C_A, maintains an addressing table from which it can determine the location of destination process, p_j. It is highly likely that computations in the nodal computer system must be totally preplanned for normal operation, overload conditions, and for reconfiguration to circumvent failures. Thus, the IDs and locations of all possible processes are known in advance and can be stored in fast-access tables. If a process really needs to be moved then these tables would have to be updated.

B. Exercising flow control. Determining whether or not the destination computer can receive the message and maintaining message transmission at a rate that will not exceed the ability of the receiver to accept the message. In some protocols this involves sending a message to the destination communications service process to establish the connection and have a buffer space reserved for the message, especially if data is to be transferred. Here, the sending process p_i may be in contention with other processes in other computers for establishing a connection with computer B where the destination process p_j is located (prevention of deadlocks).

C. Routing of messages (from p_i or from communications process C_A) from computer A to computer B (or to data bases, as the case may be). The specifics depend on the nature of the communication system, e.g., circuit switched, message switched, virtual circuit switched or packet switched, and also on the structure of the network as shown in Figure 3.4-4. In networks with direct transfer strategies (ring, bus, full connection, and shared memory) no routing is involved (except when redundant paths exists for reliability or performance enhancement purposes). In these networks priority assignments can be used to capture the shared transmission channel for rapid access to the destination computer.

D. End-to-end security control to assure that messages transmitted are not compromised or placed in situations of potential compromise in networks where multi-level security is implemented. This includes control over possible misroutings.

E. Error control. Use of techniques in the network for assuring that messages are correctly transmitted and received.

F. Configuration management to handle problems with failures and assuring that connectivity of processors is not broken for any reason.

Most of these functions will have their counterparts in lower levels in the network (switching node level, link-to-link) and other functions may be added, such as handling packets in packet-switched networks, handling conflicts in requesting network resources, performing multiplexing operations, and so forth. A variety of techniques are involved for handling messages, managing queues, and tracking messages through the network. Performance of these functions introduce delays in data transmission, and requires adding headers and other house-keeping data fields to messages, as well as requiring acknowledgements of correct reception (or retransmission in case of errors, contention, collisions, or flow control). This reduces the useful data rate of the communication system. These overhead aspects of message transmission can be taken into account in a measure of efficiency of a protocol in a given communication system structure, such as the average ratio of time required to transmit the text of a message to the time to transmit (including establishing connections and performing other network functions).

3.4.5 Network Protocols

Network protocols are procedures and message formats that are specified to standardize interfaces within networks and between networks and processors. They depend on the network structure and data transmission techniques used. For the purposes of the design of a communication network for the local computer networks, it appears useful to discuss protocol requirements from the point of view of the system's application which ranges from special-purpose through general-purpose capabilities, with some intermediate steps.

Protocols are used to implement the functions described in the previous section, and to deliver messages from applications and system processes to their destinations reliably and with minimum delay. In general-purpose systems, protocols also implement network functions such as connect or disconnect a terminal (or a computer) to/from the network, or log-in or log-off a user. In the local communications network these may not be necessary if response requirements are too stringent. Instead network connections may be defined and fixed at system generation and there may be no man in the loop.

Protocols are standardized interchanges of messages, in standardized formats, between the sending and receiving processes (in their various levels of the protocol hierarchy). As discussed previously, two major types of messages are involved:

A. Control messages (TYPES I, III and IV) that initiate actions, request status information, or send status information for network operation. They are used in the communications processes (C_X) and control processes (S_X) of the component computers X, and in data base management processes, DM_Y, of data bases Y.

B. Data messages (TYPE II) which convey data between applications processes (where the "data" may be anything needed by applications processes, including control of application processes themselves).

Some messages may be constant in that they have a single meaning (e.g., ACK for positive acknowledgement, NACK for negative acknowledgement, or EOB end of block). Most of the messages, however, have one or more variable fields, such as message ID, destination and origin addresses, parity and checksum values, and status codes. In data messages the data fields are, of course, variable.

Typically a message consists of three parts: a header, the body, and a trailer. The header contains information necessary to deliver the message from sender to receiver and to indicate its attributes:

A. Identification number of the message - a unique quantity that shouldn't be assigned again. It may have several components for example, also the number of the data block that it is a part of, and the sequence number in the block.

B. Addresses of the destination and the origin. Addresses can be in several levels: IDs of the sending and destination processes, IDs of the sending and the destination units (computers, data bases), IDs of the sending and destination nodes of the network, and even more detailed hardware IDs, routing information, and so forth.

C. Priority level of the message in networks where there is contention for transmission channels, queues, etc.

D. Security level of the data.

E. Control codes indicating beginning of message, whether it is a retransmission, what type of acknowledgement is requested, the length of the message, the type of access requested, type of error control used, and so forth.

The data part of the message is variable-length (and may be totally absent in the control messages for the communication network). Messages are usually nested in that a total message can be the data part of another message -- usually the process-to-process message is the data part of a computer-to-computer message as more header information is added when the message is passed down to communications and network protocol levels and processes. Figure 3.4-5 illustrates such nesting.

The trailer of a message usually contains information for error detection/correction purposes and network control codes such as "end of message". Error control may be implemented in a variety of ways: parity over all characters of the message, checksum, or use of polynomial coding (division). The error correction filed in the trailer will contain the error checking results obtained prior to transmission to be compared with results computed independently after reception.

The dynamic part of the protocol is the sequence of message interchanges between the various levels in the transmitting computer, communication network, and receiving computer. Such sequences can be described as graphs (or sequential machine state diagrams). Such graphs show states of the communication processes (e.g., sending, receiving, dormant, waiting to receive, waiting to send, busy, etc.) and transitions between states and messages communicated in the process. Graphical representation is used as a design aid and a means for verifying protocol correctness. Examples are given in [3-23].

Important from the point of view of communication system performance is the complexity of the protocol (i.e., the number of sender-receiver interactions required until the message is completely and correctly delivered). Additional complexity may be required to increase the

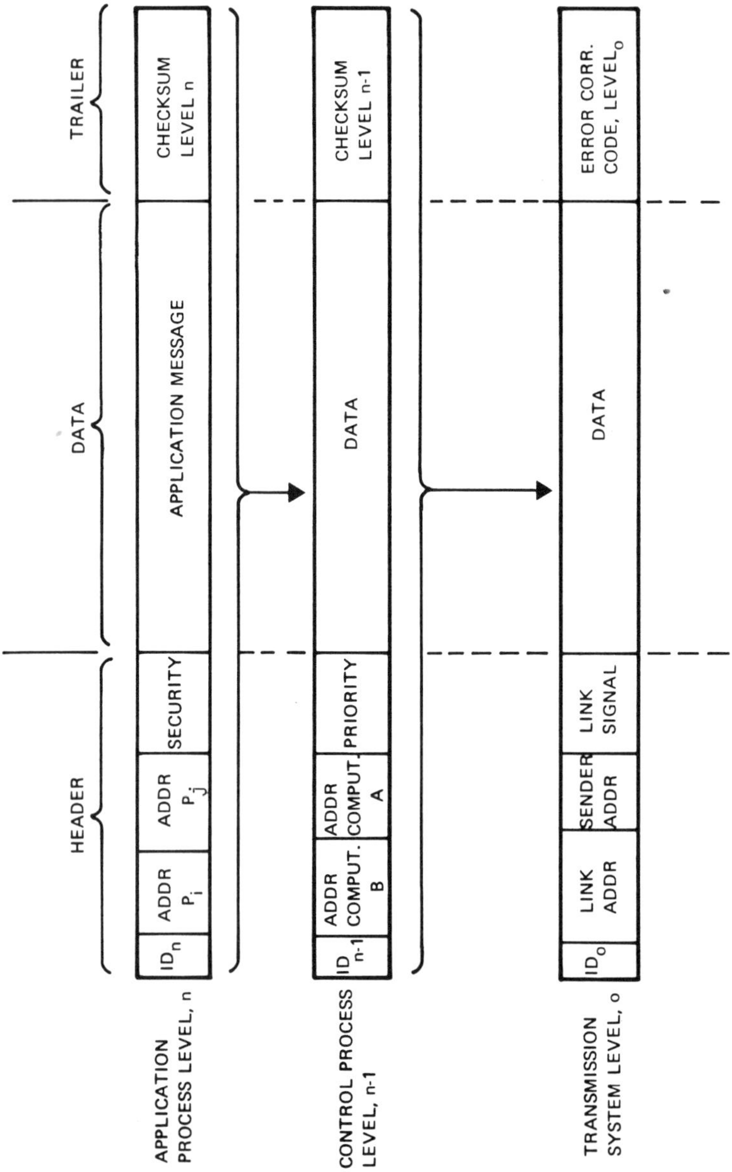

Figure 3.4-5. Protocol Levels and Corresponding Nested Messages

probability that the message will be correctly delivered when a transmission attempt is made, but at the expense of longer response time. For the nodal computer network communication system a performance analysis must consider both factors.

3.4.6 Local Network Selection

As discussed earlier, the principal payoff criteria in the design of the communications network and interprocessor communication protocols for the local network are:

A. Performance (response time, ability to handle specified data volumes)

B. Reliability and fault-tolerance

C. Deployability and growth capability

D. Cost

Within the local network complex there will be a relatively small number of computers and data base modules, and the physical distances between them will be small (i.e., they may all be in the same room). Thus we are dealing with local networking where the following network structures (see Figure 3.4-4) are usually employed:

A. Directly connected (DDC)

B. Loop (DDL)

C. Central memory (DSM)

D. Global bus (DSB)

E. Star (ICDS)

Figure 3.4-6 combines the logical model of interprocess communication depicted in Figure 3.4-3 and the above choices for network structures. Also indicated are components of the overall message transmission time. These are defined in the next subsection. A distinction is made between data-carrying messages (data messages) and control messages. The latter include application system control messages that originate from processes, system control messages that originate from RTOS, and communication network control messages that originate from communication processes, C_X, of computer X. The length of text in a data message will be designated as M units (bits or bytes), and the "burdened" length of the message (includes headers and trailers) is designated by M^*. A control message length (text) will be designated by C_a, C_s or C_c to correspond with applications, system and communications control messages, respectively. The corresponding burdened lengths are $C_a{}^*$, $C_s{}^*$, and $C_c{}^*$.

3.4.6.1 Performance Considerations

There are several ways that performance can be measured in terms of communication times:

PROBLEM: INTRA NODE COMMUNICATIONS APPROACH MUST BE ADAPTABLE TO MANY NODE DESIGN VARIABLES WHICH ARE PROBLEM DEPENDENT

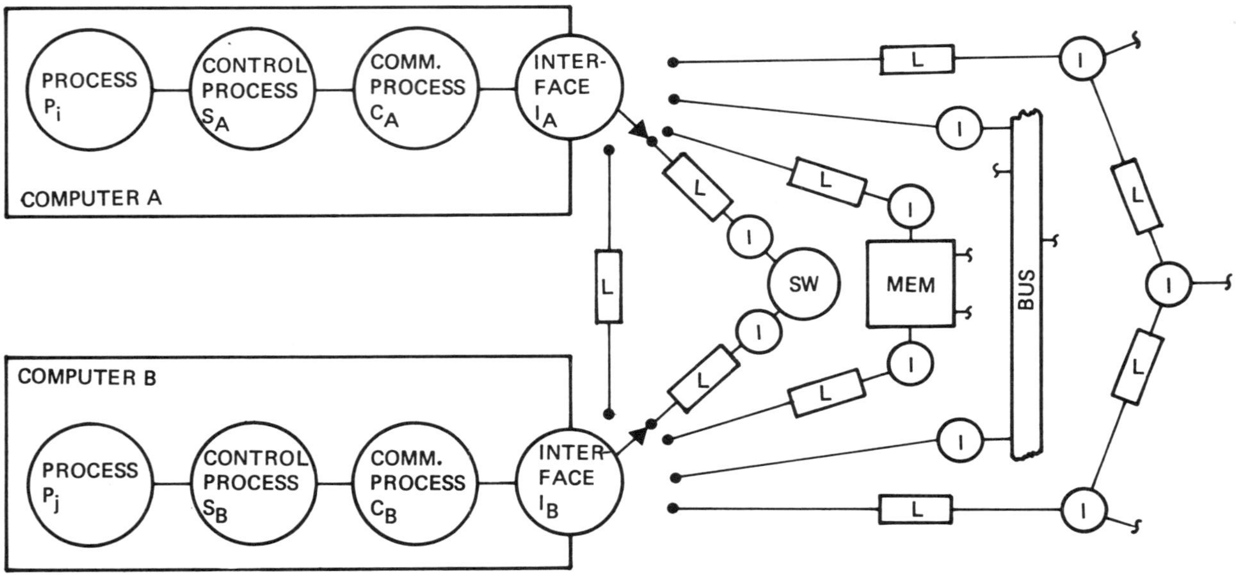

OBJECTIVE: DEVELOP AN APPROACH TO INTRA-NODE COMMUNICATION PROTOCOLS WHICH SUPPORTS HIGH RESPONSE COMMUNICATION WHILE OFFERING RESILIENCE TO DESIGN

Figure 3.4-6. Communications Model

1. T_{ppa} -- Overall process-to-process communication time with acknowledgement to the sending process of receipt by destination process. Time count begins when process p_i initiates communication action to send a message (data or control) to process p_j and receives back an acknowledgement from p_j that the message was correctly received.

2. T_{pp} -- Overall process-to-process communication time from process p_i to process p_j without acknowledgement back to p_i.

3. T_{cca} -- Computer-to-computer communication time from computer A to computer B, with acknowledgement (when computer B is known to be ready for reception -- no flow control protocol included).

4. T_{cc} -- Computer-to-computer communication time without acknowledgement.

The time T_{ppa} includes the full front-end and back-end protocol execution times up to the highest (application level) protocol level, and for data messages is dependent on the overall burdened message length and on the transmission time, $T_{xmit}(M^*)$, in the network. The latter is dependent on the structure of the network. The other times defined above are components of T_{ppa}. These can be further decomposed into the following times as shown in Figure 3.4-7:

1. T_{sp} -- Time required for the sending process p_i and the control process S_A in computer A to prepare the message and hand it over to the communications process, C_A. This includes assembling the message text in a buffer and generating the process-level header (addresses of p_i and p_j, security information, priority level, length of message text, etc.).

2. T_{scp} -- Time required for the communications process C_A to prepare the message for transmission. This includes the time for constructing the final header and trailer, and the time, T_{scf}, of performing the flow-control function protocol (communicating with the destination computer to prepare it for reception of a data message). Assume that flow control need not be performed for control messages.

3. T_{acc} -- Time to gain access to the network for sending messages. This is a function of priority assigned to the message, the security classification, nature of the network, and activity in the network.

4. T_{xmit}-- Time to transmit a message through the network to the destination computer. This depends on the nature and length of the message and on the structure of the communication network. It includes times for any network-level protocols (such as link-level error control, packet operations if packet switching is used, etc.).

5. T_{rcp} -- Time required by the receiving communication processor to accept the message, perform end-to-end error control operations, and pass it on to the control processor in the destination computer. A component is the time required to generate an acknowledgement of correct receipt for sending back to the originating computer and/or process, T_{ack}.

6. T_{rp} -- Time for the control process, S_B, in computer B to deliver the message to the destination process, p_j.

Depending on the protocol and network structure some of the above time components may be more or less significant. Furthermore, some of the functions may be more suitable for implementation in hardware at the lowest protocol levels (e.g., interface units) rather than in the control processors (modules of the RTOS) or communications processes. Determination of these questions requires a much more detailed level of design than considered in the present report. Figure 3.4-7 illustrates the timing relationships in a typical interprocess communication activity for control and data message transmission that involves two round-trip transmissions to accommodate a single data transmission.

The process-to-process message communication time, $T_{ppa}(M)$, is then expressed as:

$$T_{ppa}(M) = T_{pp}(M) - T_{rp}(M) + T_{pack}(M)$$

$$= T_{sp}(M) + T_{scp}(M^*) + T_{cc}(M^*) + T_{pack}(M)$$

While in varying degrees all of the above times are dependent on both the structure of the protocols at the various levels process-to-process, computer-to-computer, or between communication system nodes or across communication system nodes or across communication system links), the computer-to-computer transmission times of data messages, $T_{cc}(M^*)$, and control messages, $T_{cc}(C^*)$, are particularly dependent on the communication network structures, especially on the amount of sharing of the communication channels with other computers. The access times to the communication network, $T_{acc}(M^*)$ and transmission times, $T_{xmit}(M^*)$, for the five network structures of interest (see beginning of Section 3.4.6) are compared in Figure 3.4-8. In this figure, $T_{link}(M^*)$, is the time to transmit M* units over a single link, R_{mgs} is the rate of generating message data units by sending processes in computer A, R_{mgr} is the rate of being able to process arriving messages in the destination computer B, and R_{link} is the data transmission rate of a link. It is also assumed that links have the same bandwidth in all network structures considered (i.e., T_{link} is the same in all). Figure 3.4-9 illustrates the relative computer-to-computer transmission times of the various network structures as a function of qualitatively expressed traffic volume in the network. These curves show qualitative properties only; they are not based in any quantitative modeling or simulation.

Based on previous discussion and figures, it appears clear that the best performance in terms of smallest time delay in message transmission is to be expected from the fully connected network of computers: both the protocol complexity and computer-to-computer transmission time are minimal.

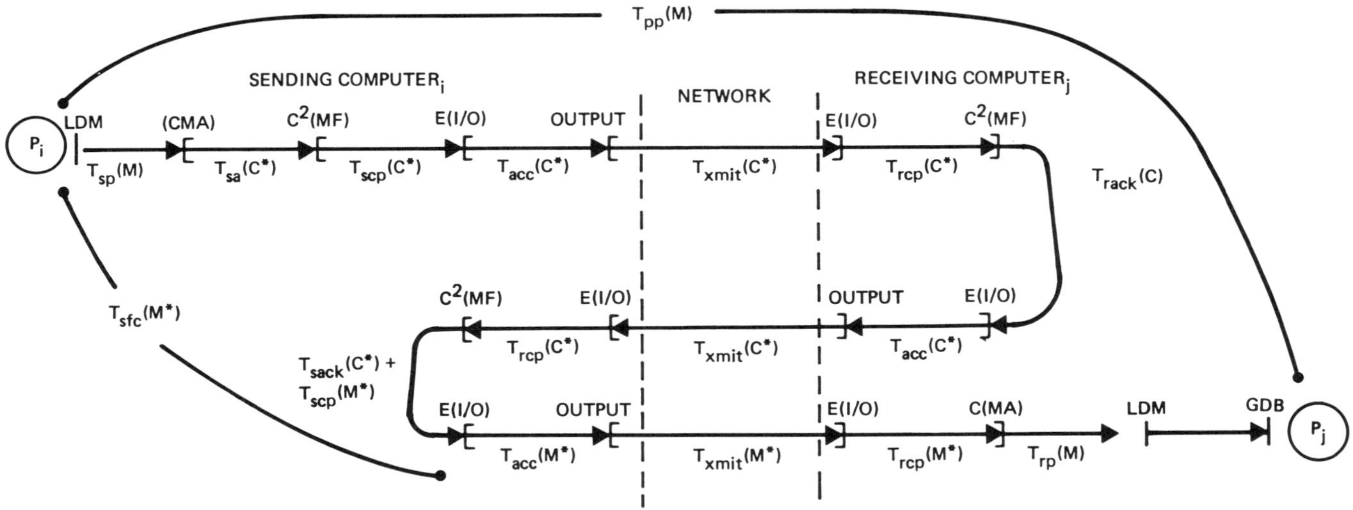

*DATA MESSAGE COMMUNICATIONS WITH OVERHEAD

Figure 3.4-7. Illustrative Timing Diagram for Data Message Communication

Network type	Time to gain access, $T_{acc}(M^*)$	Transmission time, $T_{xmit}(M^*)$
1. Fully connected, DDC	Minimal; dedicated links are available between any tow computers	$T_{xmit} = T_{link} = M^* R_{link}$
2. Star (centralized switch), ICDS	A shared switch is used. Access time depends on the length of the queue for use of the switch (which depends on the activity in the network and priority of the message to be transmitted, as well as on transmission protocol used).	$T_{xmit} = 2\ T_{link} + T_{sw} = 2\ M^* R_{link} + T_{sw}$ T_{sw} depends on the nature of switching: relatively small when circuit switching is used, larger when message switching is implemented.
3. Central memory, DSM	Communication is via mail boxes in shared memory. Access time depends on number of access ports and the way that memory sharing is implemented, and on the traffic volume. If each computer has independent access, access time is minimal. Otherwise, contention for shared access ports ensues.	$T_{xmit} = 2\ T_{link} + T_{mem} = 2\ M^* R_{link} + M^* R_{mw} + M^* R_{mr} + T_{mdly}$ R_{mw} and R_{mr} are memory read and write rates, respectively. T_{mdly} is the time required for computer B to check its mailbox for message .
4. Global bus, DSB	Bus may be operated in various ways, such as FDM or TDM. If the computer A has a fixed time slot for its use and the time slot becomes available evety T_{bA} time units, the expected delay is 1/2 T_{bA}. If N computers share the bus channel, waiting time is 1/2 N times as long as for dedicated channel.	$T_{xmit} = T_{link}$ since transmission time in the bus is essentially the same as in the link (since badnwidths are assumed to be the same).
5. Loop structure, DDL	The transmission level protocol involves passinge messages around the ring from computer ring interface to another. Computer A may be able to put its message on the ring if there is an empty slot or by holding up another message. If traffic volume is low, T_{acc} is minimal.	$T_{xmit} = N(T_{link} + T_{rint})/2$ on the average where T_{rint} is the time required for the message to pass through a ring interface unit.

Figure 3.4-8. Relative Computer-to-Computer Transmission Times

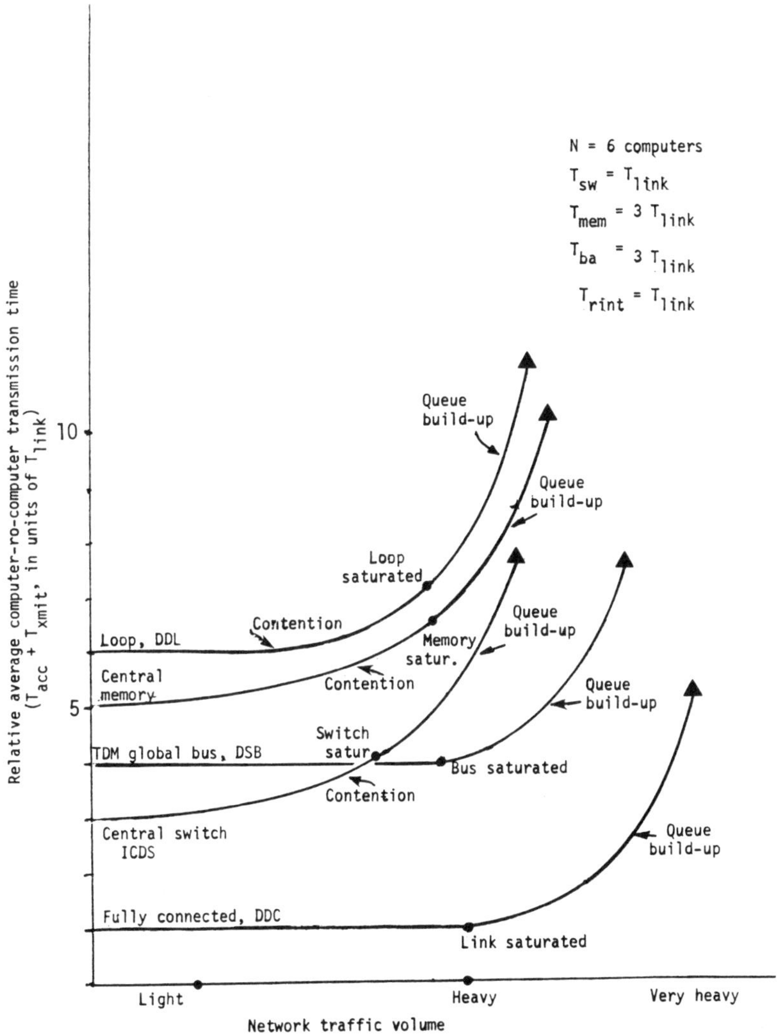

Figure 3.4-9. Qualitative Comparison of Network Structures

3.4.6.2 Data Transmission Rates/Distances

In the previous paragraphs, we have discussed the importance of communications protocols, and the network structure on the IPC message responsiveness. In fact, we have implied that a major part of the overall message delay is due to the IPC protocol and number of protocol levels through which any message must past before it reaches the physical network medium. However, an important contribution to any communication network performance is the medium over which the messages will pass, and the available data rates of the physical network.

The rates that can be achieved are widely variable and depend upon what technology and communications network structures used. Fiber-optics communications has advanced significantly such that it can be considered a viable technology option to standard wire-implemented systems. Fiber-optics research and development has stressed serial transmission technology primarily for high rate point-to-point communications over kilometer distances. Recent attempts to implement local networks with fiber optics technology have been reported [3-30]. Wire technology (usually coax/triax or twisted pair cables) has also emphasized high rate serial communications for distances usually beyond the reach of parallel channel implementations. Implementation cost is a very significant factor in the decision to utilize serial vs. parallel implementations of either fiber-optics or wire. It is technically possible, for example, to utilize fiber-optics in parallel fashion to implement digital communications but the economics, when compared to either serial fiber-optics or any wire type implementation are not clear. An indication of data communications rates that have been attained for various wire and fiber optics communications systems is provided in Figure 3.4-10. Included are point-to-point communication rates for some standard parallel I/O channel types.

3.4.6.3 Reliability, Deployability, and Cost Considerations

Reliability of the communication network affects the ability to transmit messages from computer A to computer B during the duration of the use of the nodal computer complex. In general, increased complexity in protocols when providing for sharing of parts of the intercommunication network, and increasing sharing of some central resource (e.g., memory, switch, communication channel) reduces the reliability of the overall network unless special provisions are made to provide backup for the shared resource.

From the overall network reliability and fault-tolerance point of view, the fully connected network is again advantageous, especially when provisions are included for relaying of messages between computers when direct links are not available. That is, at the expense of performance more reliability is provided. The other network configurations require more extensive use of redundancy links or other shared resources to obtain a comparable level of reliability and fault-tolerance.

Deployability and growth considerations favor network structures which are simplest to expand (either in the number of computers serviced or in bandwidth of the communication channels). This can be measured in terms of the number of new links that have to be installed, and amount of changes to the interfaces. Here the fully connected network is the least attractive: to add the N+1st computer requires N links to the

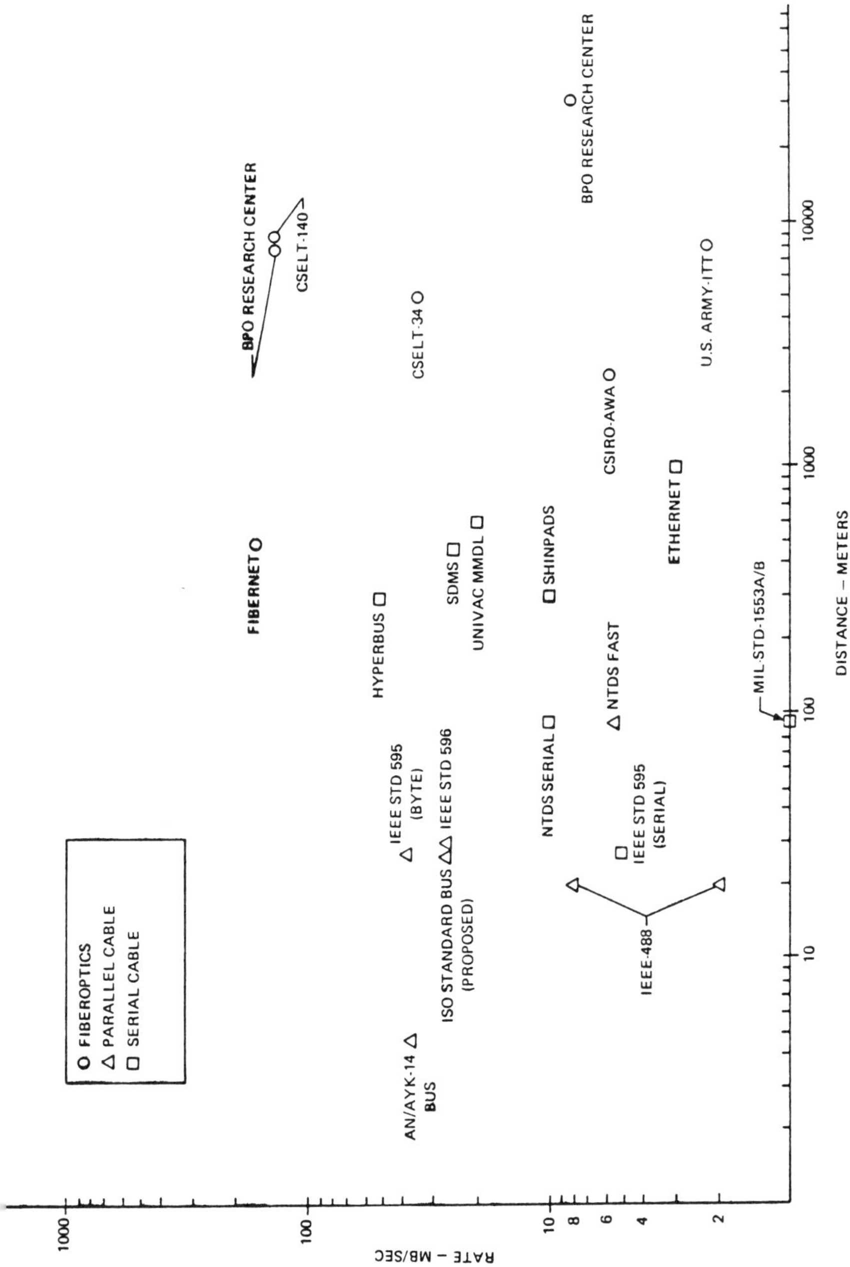

Figure 3.4-10. Rate Versus Distance of Various Communications Systems

existing computers and another switching position in each of the network interfaces. Adding another computer in a loop, however, requires only one link.

Cost of a communications network structure can be expected to be proportional to the number of transmission links required to effect communications between N units (computers or data base modules), the number of interface units, and any central units. The complexity of the interface units also affects the cost. A comparison of the costs of various structures requires information on relative costs of links, interfaces, and central switches or memories. At the present time we have not collected quantitative data for permitting such comparisons. For example, data is needed to determine whether a centralized memory of sufficient capacity and access speed to handle the specified communications load between N computers is more or less costly than N(N-1)/2 communications links (possibly of lower bandwidth) in a fully connected network that can handle the same communications load.

Figure 3.4-11 lists some of the quasi-quantitative considerations in comparing cost, reliability and growth capabilities of several network structures.

3.4.6.4 Cost Tradeoffs

The principal tradeoffs appear to be between performance and reliability on one hand (as represented by strongly connected network structure) and ease in growth capability on the other hand (as in global bus or in loop and shared memory structures). Of course, a higher bandwidth global bus may be able to meet the performance advantages of a fully connected structure, and its reliability may be improvable through redundancy techniques in associated electronics.

Another approach to a structure that has most of the desireable features involves hybrid structure. For example, in networks where the number of units, N, is too large to make full connection attractive, units could be formed into clusters and clusters interconnected by a backbone network that need not be concerned with growth requirements since all growth could be done in clusters (the number of clusters would be increased only rarely). In such a system, partitioning of the application tasks would emphasize keeping tightly coupled parts in the same cluster. Further study is needed in the design and design tradeoffs using the clustering concept. Figure 3.4-12 illustrates several cluster-based network structures.

3.4.7 Protocol Considerations

Implementation of interprocess communication and network control protocols involves tradeoffs between levels in the communication process where the various protocol functions are to be implemented, and tradeoffs involving implementation in hardware, firmware or software. The functions to be performed depend on the network structure and on the types of messages to be communicated.

Network structure	Cost	Reliability	Growth (Adding the (N+1)st unit)
1. Fully connected	Links: N(N-1)/2 links are required. Interfaces: N interfaces (each with an N-place switch and routing data).	Failure of link from A to B affects direct transmission between A and B only. Failure of interface at A affects communications with computer A only.	N new links must be added, and a new switching position must be available at each computer interface with the network.
2. Central switch	L: N links are required. I:2N simple interfaces (no switching or routing). Centralized switch with routing data.	Failure of link from A affects all communications with A. Same when A's interface fails. Failure of the switch affects all communications in the network.	One new link must be added. One new switching position is needed in central switch. One new interface.
3. Central memory	L: N links are required. I:2N simple interfaces. Memory with N mailbox storage areas and mailbox addressing.	Failure of link or interface at A affects only communications with A. Failure of the memory affects all communications in the network.	One new link must be added. One new interface. One new mailbox area in the memory.
4. Global bus	L: One link (bus) is required. I: N interfaces (must have capability to recognize message addresses and transmission time slots).	Failure of the link (bus) affects all communications in the network. Failure in the interface affects communications with A only.	One new interface unit must be added to the bus.
5. Loop	L: N links are required I: N interfaces (with buffering and addressing capability)	Failure of any link or interface affects the entire network	One new link and one interface unit.

Figure 3.4-11. Cost, Reliability and Growth Considerations (N Units -- Computers or Data Base Modules)

Typical functions implemented in protocols include the following:

A. Request to send a data or control message (at the application process level).

B. Construction of the message at the control process (operating system) level: header (addresses, security level, priority) and trailer (high-level error control, if desired).

C. Flow control action at the communication process level -- is the destination computer ready to receive the message?

   (1) Construct control message

   (2) Gain access to network and transmit

   (3) Wait for reply

D. In destination computer: receive control message, make provisions for receiving the applications data message. Transmit reply to originating computer.

E. Message transmission action

   (1) Gain access to communication network and transmit

   (2) Wait for positive acknowledgement of receipt

F. Message reception action in the destination computer

   (1) Receive and apply error control techniques

   (2) If error detected, request retransmission from the originating computer

   (3) If no error, send positive acknowledgement

   (4) Extract message to be passed on to higher level (control process and then application process).

The design of interprocess communication protocols for various communication system structures and techniques for their validation are currently topics of intensive study. Graph models [3-23], protocol machine approach [3-24], and finite state representation [3-25] are being used to develop protocol sequences. For larger (non-local) networks standards are being developed for various computer families [3-26] as well as for national or international use in general [3-27, 3-28]. These protocol development approaches as well as applicability of new concepts such as the "monitor" based systems exemplified by the KOCOS system protocols [3-29] must be studied to develop an approach for designing effective interprocess protocols for the tightly coupled computer network.

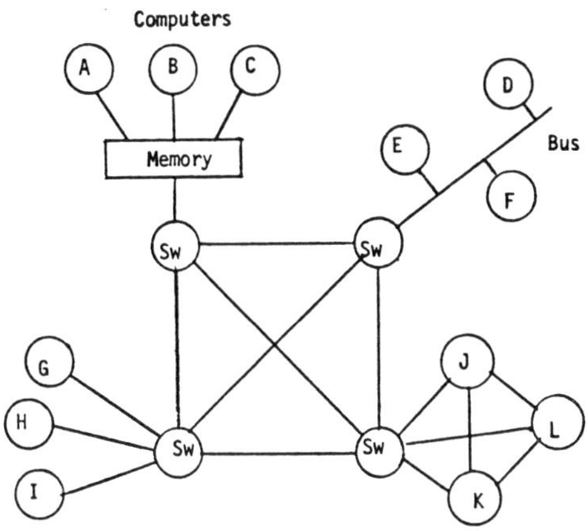

a) Fully connected back-bone net, various cluster-level networks

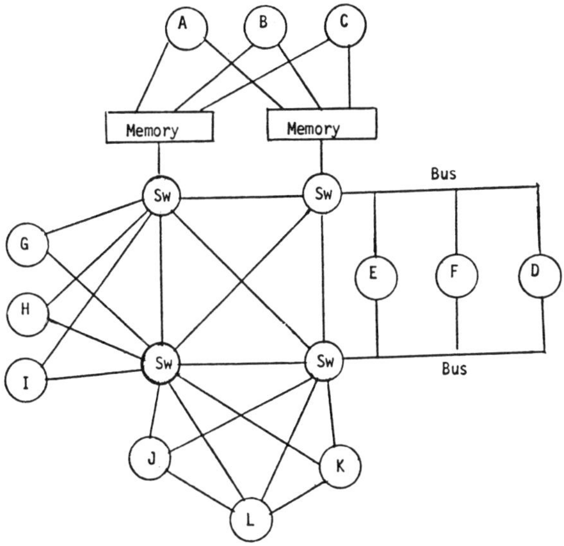

b) As in (a) above, but with redundant connections of the cluster to the backbone network

Figure 3.4-12. Hybrid Network Structures

3.5 REFERENCES

[3-1] Foster, Derrell V.; Dowdy, Lawrence W.; and Ames, James E., IV., "File Assignment in a Star Network" Department of System and Information Science, School of Engineering, Vanderbilt University, Nashville, TN. 37235.

[3-2] Rothnie, James B.; and Goodman, Nathan (Computer Corp. of America, Cambridge, MA). "A survey of research and development in distributed data base management.", Proc. 3rd Int. Conf. on Very Large Data Bases, Tokyo, Japan, October 6-8, 1977, IEEE, New York, and ACM, New York, 48-62.]

[3-3] Fry, J.P.; and Sibley, E.H., "Evolution of Data Base Management Systems", Graduate School of Business Administration, University of Michigan, Ann Arbor, MI. Comput. Surv. (USA) Vol. 8, No. 1, 7-42, May 1976.

[3-4] Mohan, C. "An Overview of Recent Data Base Research", Data Base, Vol. 10, No. 2, Fall 1978, pp. 3-24.

[3-5] Lowenthal, E.I., "A Survey - The Application of Data Base Management Computers in Distributed Systems", Proc. Third International Conf. on VLDB, October 1977.

[3-6] Madnick, S., "INFOPLEX: Hierarchical Decomposition of a large Information Management System Using a Microprocessor Complex", Proceedings of NCC, 1975.

[3-7] Lehon, A., et al., "Distribution of Access and Data in Large Data Bases", Tech. Rep. DAT 517, IRIA, France, March, 1976.

[3-8] Lomet, D.B., "A Practical Deadlock Avoidance Algorithm for Data Base Systems", Proceedings SIGMOD International Conference on Management of Data, August, 1977.

[3-9] Lum, V.Y., et al., "A General Methodology for Data Conversion and Restructuring", IBM Journal of R&D, September, 1976.

[3-10] Housel, B.C., "A Unified Approach to Program and Data Conversion", Proceeding of the Third International Conference on VLDB, October, 1977.

[3-11] Garcia-Molina, Hector, "Performance Comparison of Two Update Algorithms for Distributed Data Bases", Proceedings of the Third Berkeley Workshop on Distributed Data Management and Computer Networks, August 29-31, 1978.

[3-12] Lee, Edward Y.S., "Trip Report on IPC Workshop", TRW IOC #30451-78-054, 28 November 1978.

[3-13] Lamport, Leslie, "Time, Clocks and the Ordering of Events in a Distributed System", Massachusetts Computer Associates, Inc., CA-7603-2911, March 29, 1976, to be appearing in Comm. ACM.

[3-14] Lamport, Leslie, "The Implementation of Reliable Distributed Multiprocess Systems", Computer Networks 2 (1978), pp. 95-114.

[3-15] Thomas, Robert H., "A Solution to the Update Problem for Multiple Copy Data Bases Which Uses Distributed Control", Bolt Bernarek and Newman, Inc., BNN Report No. 3340, July, 1976.

[3-16] Thomas, Robert H., "A Majority Consensus Approach to Concurrency Control for Multiple Copy Data Bases", Bolt Bernarek and Newman, Inc., BNN Report No. 3733, December, 1977.

[3-17] Reed, D.P.; and Kanodia, R.K., "Synchronization with Event Counts and Sequences", MIT Report (1976).

[3-18] Le Lann; Gerard, "Algorithms for Distributed Data-Sharing Systems which Use Tickets", Proceedings of the Third Berkeley Workshop on Distributed Data Management and Computer Networks, pp. 259-271.

[3-19] Ellis, C.A., "Consistency and Correctness of Duplicated Data Base Systems", Proc. 6th ACM Symposium on Operating Systems, November 1977.

[3-20] "Resource Management Overview", TRW IOC 30451-78-052, from S. Katz to M.P. Mariani, 15 November 1978.

[3-21] "Reconfiguration Algorithms", TRW IOC 30451-78-060, from S. Katz to M.P. Mariani, 27 November 1978.

[3-22] Anderson, G.A. and E.D. Jensen, "Computer Interconnection Structures: Taxonomy, Characteristics, and Examples", Computer Surveys, December 1975, pp. 197-213.

[3-23] Postel, J.B. and D. Farber, "Graph Modeling of Computer Communications Protocols", Proceedings, Fifth Texas Conference on Computing Systems, October 1976, pp. 66-77.

[3-24] Gouda, M.G. and E.G. Manning, "Protocol Machines: A Concise Formal Model and Its Automatic Implementation", Proceedings, Third International Conference on Computer Communications, 1976, pp. 346-350.

[3-25] Bochmann, G.V., "Finite State Description of Communication Protocols", Computer Network Protocols (A. Dahine, ed.), University of Liege, Belgium, 1978, pp. F3-1 - F3-11.

[3-26] Conant, G.E. and S. Wecker, "DNA: An Architecture for Heterogenous Computer Networks", Proceedings, Third International Conference on Computer Communications, 1976, pp. 618-625.

[3-27] Emmons, W.F., "Data Network Protocol Standards", 1977 Computer Network Symposium, National Bureau of Standards/IEEE, 1977, pp. 9-17.

[3-28] Hertweck, F. et al, "X25 Based Process/Process Communications", Computer Network Protocols (A. Dahine, ed.), University of Liege, Belgium, 1978, pp. C3-1 - C3-21.

[3-29] Aiso, H. et al., "The System Software for KCOS", Minicomputer Software, (J.R. Bell and C.G. Bell, eds.), North Holland Publishing Co., Amsterdam, 1976, pp. 41-51.

[3-30] Rawson, E.A., et al., "Fibernet: Multimode Optical Fibers for Local Computer Networks", IEEE Transaction on Communications, July 1978.

[3-31] Fussell, D.S., et al., "A Theory of Correct Locking Protocols for Database Systems", Proceedings Very Large Data Bases, Sept. 1981, IEEE Catalog No. 81CH 1701-Z.

[3-32] Green, M.L., et al., "Session 6: Distributed Operating Systems: Case Study", Proceedings of Distributed Data Acquisition, Computing and Control Symposium, Dec. 1980, IEEE Catalog No. 80CH1571-9.

[3-33] McDonald, W.C. and Smith, R.W., "A Flexible Distributed Testbed for Real-Time Applications", IEEE Computer, Oct. 1982.

[3-34] Majumdar, S. and Green, M.L., "A Distributed Real Time Resource Manager", Proc. Distributed Data Acquisition, Computing, and Control Symposium, Dec. 1980, pp 185 - 203.

[3-35] Lee, E.Y.S., "A Distributed Data Base Manager", Proc. Distributed Data Acquisition, Computing, and Control Symposium, Dec. 1980, pp. 194 - 201.

[3-36] Hsiao, D.K., "Data Base Computers," Advances in Computers, Academic Press, New York, 1980, pp. 1 - 59.

4.0 DISTRIBUTED ARCHITECTURE CONCEPTS

The early computer systems of the 70's emphasized internal concurrency as a means of achieving greater throughput. This concurrency typically occurred through multiplicity of hardware. The same concept of multiplicity can also be seen in today's contemporary distributed architectures and networks which cooperate to solve a single homogeneous* problem. Early schemes [4-1A, 4-1B] for classifying computers based on their approach to concurrency has proved successful for single processors, and other approaches based on topology have been defined [4-2, 4-3] to handle more complex architectures. This scheme used instruction and data streams as the basis of classification:

SISD: Single instruction stream - Single data stream

SIMD: Single instruction stream - Multiple data stream

MISD: Multiple instruction stream - Single data stream

MIMD: Multiple instruction stream - Multiple data stream

In distributed architectures there exists multiple computers and/or processing units. They may be either homogeneous or hetergeneous, and each may be classified individually according to one of the four basic classes. However, when the distributed architecture is viewed globally from the system level as a processor network such a classification becomes much more complex. There now exists many levels of classification besides the streams associated with instruction and data fetches from memory. We can have separate program and data memories, multiple memory units, multiple functional units within a single processor, multiple processors, multiple levels of process control, and others. All of these levels represent a level of the architecture in which concurrency can improve performance. Almost contempory all computers employ some degree of internal concurrency to increase performance. The evolution of super computer (e.g., CDC 7600/7700, PEPE, STARAN, ILLIAC, STAR 100, CRAY) of the 1970's was based on increased internal concurrency through hardware multiplicity. These computers employed multiple functional units which could execute concurrently. In some cases (CDC 7600, CRAY) these functional units themselves were segmented to allowing pipelining of operands.

---

* This cooperation of resources is a key distinction from those networks which support multiple problems and users such as ARPANET, UCI's DCS or other SW development networks.

4.1 DISTRIBUTED ARCHITECTURE CONCEPTS - SELECTED OVERVIEWS

To date distributed architectures have been based on networks of conventional processors, with the early emphasis on topology and control. Perhaps the earliest networks were the research networks of Carnegie Mellon University (C.mmp) and of University of California (DCS). The CMU C.mmp is a homogeneous network of modified PDP-11 processors which operated as a multiprocessor under the control of a distributed operating system. The UCI DCS was a ring network of heterogeneous processing clusters which operated in a more autonomous fushion than the LSI-11 processors of the C.mmp. Each cluster of the DCS was based on off-the-shelf computers. Following the C.mmp, CMU developed another prototype multiprocessor system the Cm*, which is also based on homogeneous LSI-11 processors. With the Cm*, a hierarchical bus interconnect structure replaces the cross-bar switch of the C.mmp. One example of a theoretical machine which has yet to be developed as a prototype multiprocessor network, is the CHOPP. The CHOPP employs a direct connect structure between selected processors of the network. The CHOPP topology is based on very large scale processor configurations (10^5-10^6 processing elements). Another prototype computer which is of interest is the PEPE designed and developed by SDC/Burroughs under contract to the Army. The PEPE was a parallel processor which employed up to 288 processing elements each of which was a multiprocessor.

Two commercial based architectures which are considered interesting is the STARAN developed by Goodyear Aerospace, and the AN/UYK-7 developed by Univac. The STARAN is an associative processor while the AN/UYK-7 is a multiprocessor.

An overview discussion is provided for each of these distributed architectures in the following paragraphs.

- C.mmp (multi-miniprocessor computer)
- Cm* (computer modules)
- CHOPP (Columbia homogeneous parallel processor)
- DCS (Distributed Computer System)
- STARAN
- AN/UYK-7

Each architecture is distinctly different from the others. C.mmp is a multi-minicomputer system with a crossbar switch for common memory access. In Cm*, multi-microprocessor clusters are interconnected through buses. STARAN is a well known SIMD machine with great potential still to be developed. The novel idea of combining processing elements in the range of 10^5-10^6 has been analyzed in the CHOPP proposal. An example of ring topology is DCS which supports process to process communication. With the building blocks of the AN/UYK-7, a variety of systems meeting different requirements can be configured.

The STARAN and the AN/UYK-7 are commercially available while the others are research based systems. The research systems are in various stages of development: C.mmp, Cm*, and DCS have been in experimental use for some time; CHOPP has not yet been built.

In the following six subsections, the distinctive features, of each of the selected architectures are summarized. Most of the diagrams are reproduced from the papers describing the systems.

4.1.1 C.mmp

C.mmp is a multi-miniprocessor system designed by William A. Wulf and C. G. Bell at Carnegie-Mellon University (CMU) [4-4]. The objectives of the system were to satisfy the computational requirements for artificial intelligence and systems programming, as well as to explore computer structures. As the block diagram shows (Figure 4.1-1), up to 16 processors share 16 modules or primary memory through a crossbar switch, Smp. The total size of the primary memory is 2^{21} bytes (2 Megabytes). Each processor is a complete minicomputer (modified DEC PDP-11) with its own local memory, peripheral devices, and Dmap, which maps the (16 bit) addresses generated by the processor to the (21 bit) primary memory addresses or addresses used by Unibus.

Each processor can evoke a certain function on any collection of processors through a mechanism provided by the interprocessor bus, a controller, and the interface between them.

Applications of the system include speech understanding, parallel tree search, data base management, and integer programming.

4.1.2 Cm*

Cm* is a modular, multi-microprocessor developed by R. J. Swan, S.H. Fuller, and D.P. Siewoirek at CMU [4-5, 4-14]. All processors share access to a single virtual memory address space (Figure 4.1-2).

A computer module consists of a DEC LSI-11 processor, a local switch, LSI-11 bus, memory, and devices. The primary functions of the local switch, Slocal, are to direct references from the processor selectively either to local memory or to the Map Bus, and to accept references from the Map Bus to the local memory. Up to 14 computer modules and one mapping processor, Kmap, form a cluster. The Kmap consists of three major components: Kbus, Pmap, and Linc. The Kbus arbitrates and controls the Map Bus. The Pmap is a microprocessor: The basic configuration has1K x 80 bits of writable control store and 5K x 16 bits of RAM for holding tables, etc. The Linc provides the interface to two inter-cluster buses which allow communication between clusters.

The Cm* can support up to 256 clusters on the inter-cluster bus, although an initial Cm* configuration is being developed as a 10 processor 4Kmap (cluster) system.

4.1.3 STARAN

STARAN is an associative processor developed by Goodyear Aerospace Corporation [4-6, 4-7, 4-8]. Since its successful demonstration in an air traffic control environment in 1971, the system has been applied in text searching, command and control, image processing, signal processing, etc. A simplified functional block diagram is shown in Figure 4.1-3.

The unique capabilities of the machine are derived from its

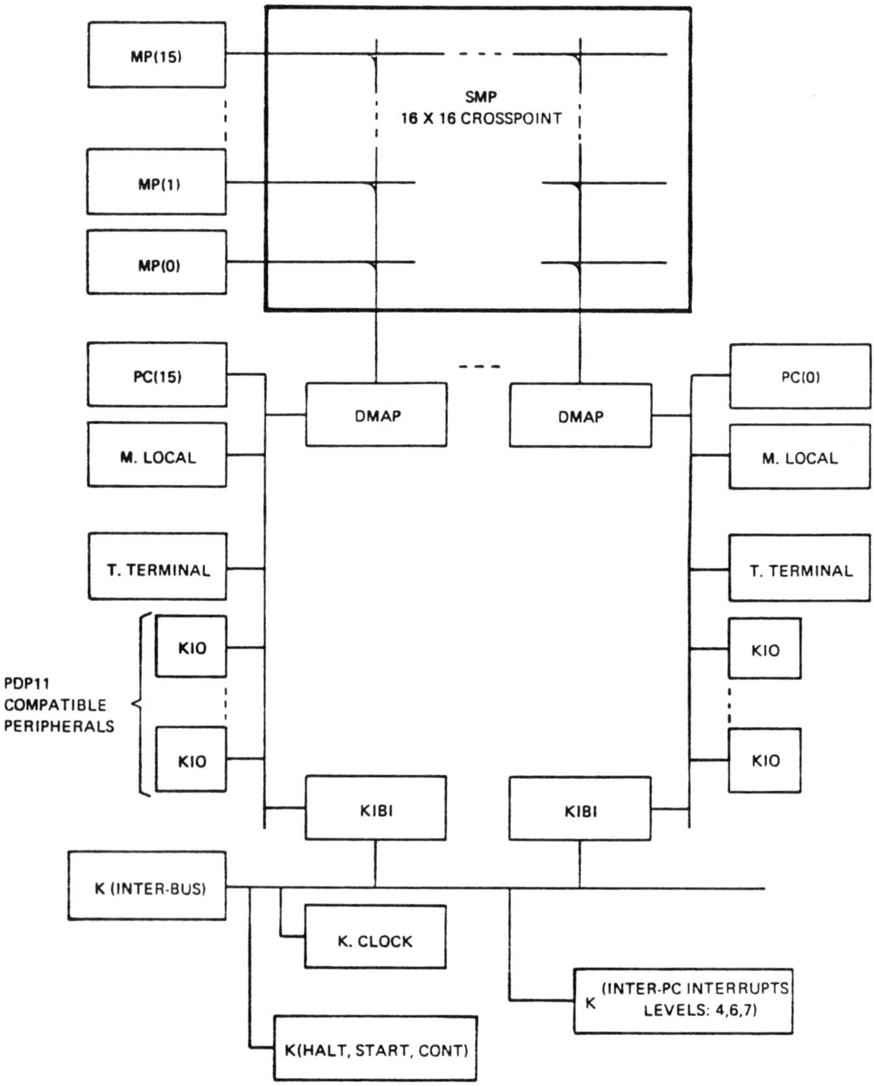

Figure 4.1-1. C.mmp Block Diagram

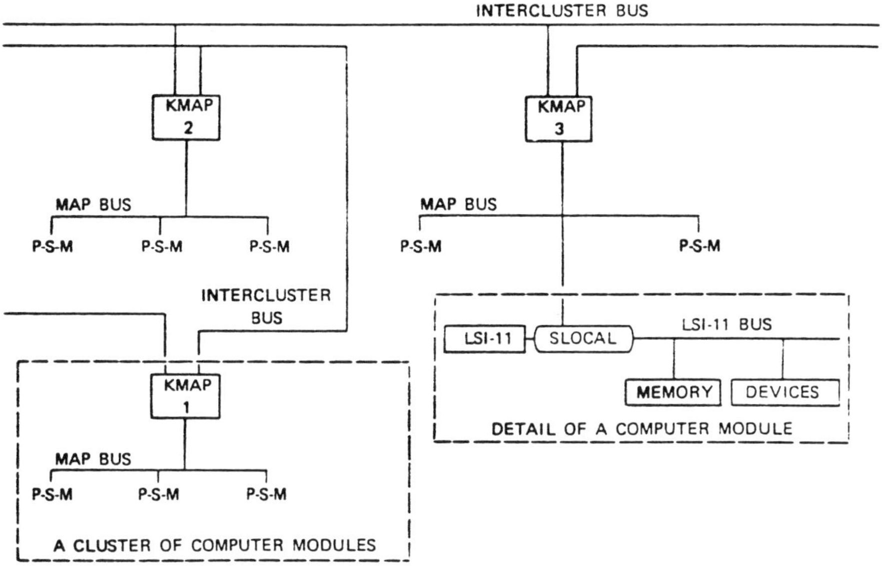

Figure 4.1-2. Cm* Block Diagram

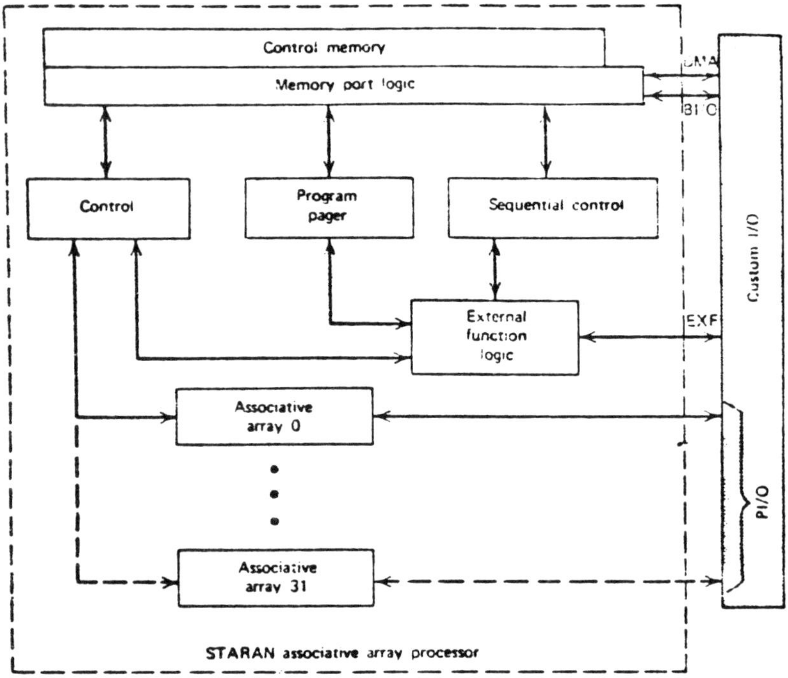

Figure 4.1-3. STARAN Block Diagram

associative array architecture, which consists of three components:

- Array Memory of 256 Words (MDA = Multi-Dimensional Access)
- 256 Processing Elements (PE)
- Flip Network

In early configurations the memory word size was 256 bits, subsequent configurations employed word sizes in improved models, it ranges from 1K to 64K bits. The flip network permutes data on transfers between PE's and MDA as well as among PE's. (Thus, the array is called Multi-Dimensional Access Memory). A basic machine configuration has one associative array; up to 32 arrays can be included in a single system.

The control memory is partitioned into three (0, 1, 2) pages of fast memory, a high speed data buffer, and bulk core memory. The word size is 32 bits. In actual processing, instructions stored in page 1 or 2 are executed while the other page is filled with new instructions.

STARAN is an example of a SIMD machine, a single control operation is performed in lock-step fashion in all or selected associative arrays, with each array operating on different data. Such an architecture is most effective which applications with large data arrays and in line logic are employed. One of the biggest problems associated with any array architecture is communications both inter-array and external. In all known applications, STARANs are interfaced to host systems through custom designed I/O. Honeywell 6180, CDC 6400, IBM 360/75, XDS Sigma 9, and Univac 1230 are among the host systems.

4.1.4 CHOPP

CHOPP is a homogeneous parallel processor proposed by H. Sullivan and T. R. Bashkow [4-9]. After analyzing various network structures, including ring, bus, crossbar switch, spatial arrays, hierarchy of buses, and full access networks, they concluded that the Boolean n-cube network is best for large systems consisting of 10^5-10^6 processing elements.

The Boolean n-cube has 2^n nodes and edges interconnecting them. Each node is identified by an n-bit address; each edge connects two nodes with only one bit different between their addresses. In the CHOPP architecture (Figure 4.1-4), N ($=2^n$) processors at the nodes are interconnected by full duplex links along the edges. All processors are identical; each of them consists of an application processor and a communication processor, and has local memory and an interface to the network.

Two notable characteristics of CHOPP are:

- The maximum link distance between any two processors is n.
- Any processor can send a message to all other processors in just n steps.

For the CHOPP architecture, key concepts on operating systems and high level language programming are available in published articles [4-4].

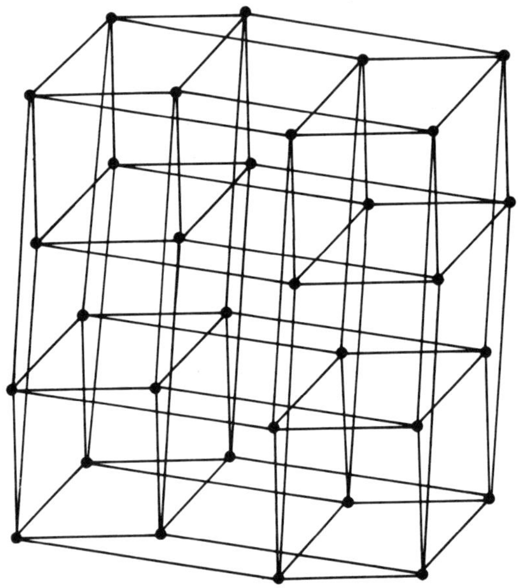

Figure 4.1-4. CHOPP, 32-Processor Configuration

4.1.5 DCS

DCS is a distributed computer system designed and developed by David J. Farber and Kenneth C. Larson [4-11]. Every processor is controlled by its own antonomous operating system and is attached to a single unidirectional communication ring via a ring interface, RI. The ring can be considered as a series of message slots. The RI consists of buffers, a shift register, and an associative store which can be written into by the attached processor.

The associative store contains the names of all processes active on the attached processor. Virtual addressing is used; i.e., messages are addressed to processes, not to processors. To transmit a message, the RI places the message at an empty slot in the ring. When a message arrives over the ring, the destination process name is matched against the RI associative store. If a match occurs, the message is copied and passed over to the next RI. The messages are removed from the ring at their original RI's. Figure 4.1-5 shows a 7-processor example of a DCS.

A prototype was developed at the University of California, Irvine has three Lockheed SUE and two Varian 620/i minicomputers.

4.1.6 AN/UYK-7

AN/UYK-7 is a thrid-generation, general-purpose computer developed by Univac for military applications [4-12, 4-13]. The processor architecture is based on processor, memory and I/O building blocks. By different combinations of basic building blocks, a large family of computer configurations can be generated to meet a variety of processing requirements. The basic architectural building blocks are:

- Central Processor Unit (CPU)
- Memory Unit with 16K words
- Input/Output Controller (IOC)
- Input/Output Adapter (IOA)

The CPU has the capability of referencing a maximum of 16 memory units. Instructions are obtained from memory via an instruction bus; operands via an operand bus.

The memory has eight access ports with fixed priority. The word size is 32 bits. The IOC can access up to 15 memory units through its own IOC/Memory bus. An IOC can be controlled by a maximum of three CPU's. External peripheral devices interface the IOC through an IOA. Each IOA can have 4, 8, 12, or 16 I/O channels.

The minimum AN/UYK-7 computer consists of one CPU, one memory unit, one IOC, and one IOA. A functional layout of a multi-processor system with three CPU's, four IOC's, and sixteen memory units is depicted in Figure 4.1-6.

Several hundred different systems have been deployed for a wide spectrum of military applications.

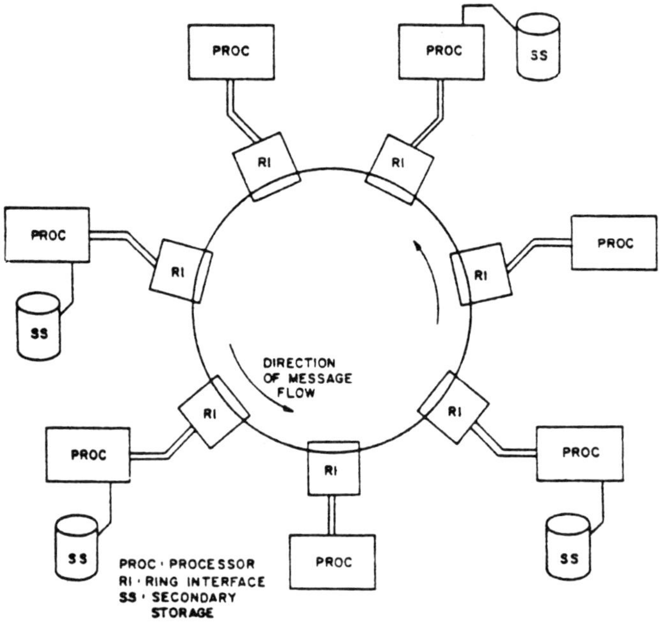

Figure 4.1-5. An Example DCS

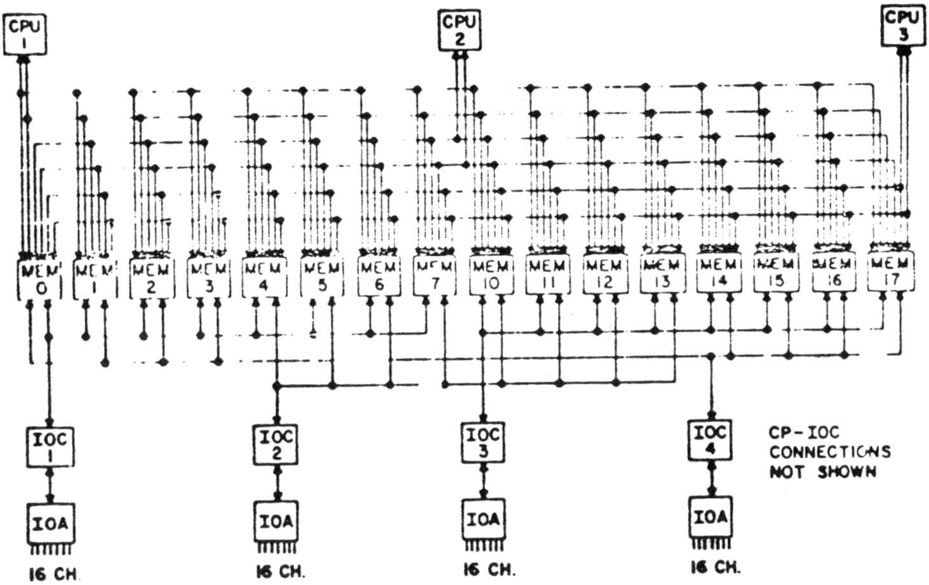

Figure 4.1-6. An Example of AN/UYK-7 Systems

4.2 FUTURE DISTRIBUTED ARCHITECTURE TRENDS

If the technical issues of distributed control and data base management can be resolved - and all indications are that they will. The use of distributed systems will become more dominant. As this occurs we will see major architecture changes in the computer building blocks of these systems. Most all conventional computers which serve as the network building blocks of today have been designed for stand alone, batch or timeshare, centralized configurations and not distributed networks. Their internal architectures emphasize the applications software which will be supported - e.g., business, scientific, control. Future architectures will commence to emphasize the architecture features which can offer the potential of altering/shifting the law of diminishing return associated with network proliferation. Such architecture changes will center on data handling including external message handling and data base management. In addition, we will expect to see architectures with improved external visability for global network fault detection and diagnosis. The need for network time synchronization to support replicated file synchronization, error recovery, and dynamic reconfiguration will also result in processor architectural changes. A few of these architectural features are discussed in more detail in the subsequent paragraphs.

4.2.1 Processor Data Handling Features

The handling of inter-processor message traffic and local data base management, is a major overhead cost factor for bus networks of conventional, off-the-shelf processors. Even with the use of semi-intelligent input/output (I/O) channels which support direct memory access (DMA), there can be a substantial message handling cost within the CPU for moving data and setting up the DMA tranfer and sorting/editing input messages. Once the transfer is set-up, the I/O channel will perform the transfer directly into memory while the CPU can resume processing the applications software. Once the channel transfer commences, the only CPU degradation would be memory contention which in general is negligible (i.e., 2-5%) for most architecture designs. However, the increased message traffic can be a significant cause for lost CPU timeline to the applications.

In a radar command and control system typical processor I/O message rates could reach as high as 7.5 - 12.5K messages per second. These messages typically are small (20 - 50 words per message) compared to the type of data traffic observed for general purpose SW development networks whose I/O message traffic is characteristic by much larger message blocks (512-4096 words) typically resulting from disk I/O. Because of the normally high memory bandwidth (relative to instruction rates), the driving overhead cost factor for communications is the message frequency - not the bandwidth (words per second). Current commercial minicomputers and array processors cannot handle this message traffic load (Figure 4.2-1).

For conventional mini computer systems, I/O message traffic and data base management are typically handled via operating system service requests and system level interrupts. The contemporary approaches to communications pursue applications SW transparency to the HW architecture, which requires the operating system (ØS) to translate logical messages issued by the applications, into physical addresses and memory locations. Such approaches enhance the flexibility of the applications software, and its portability at the expense of increased message handling overhead. Since most of the I/O

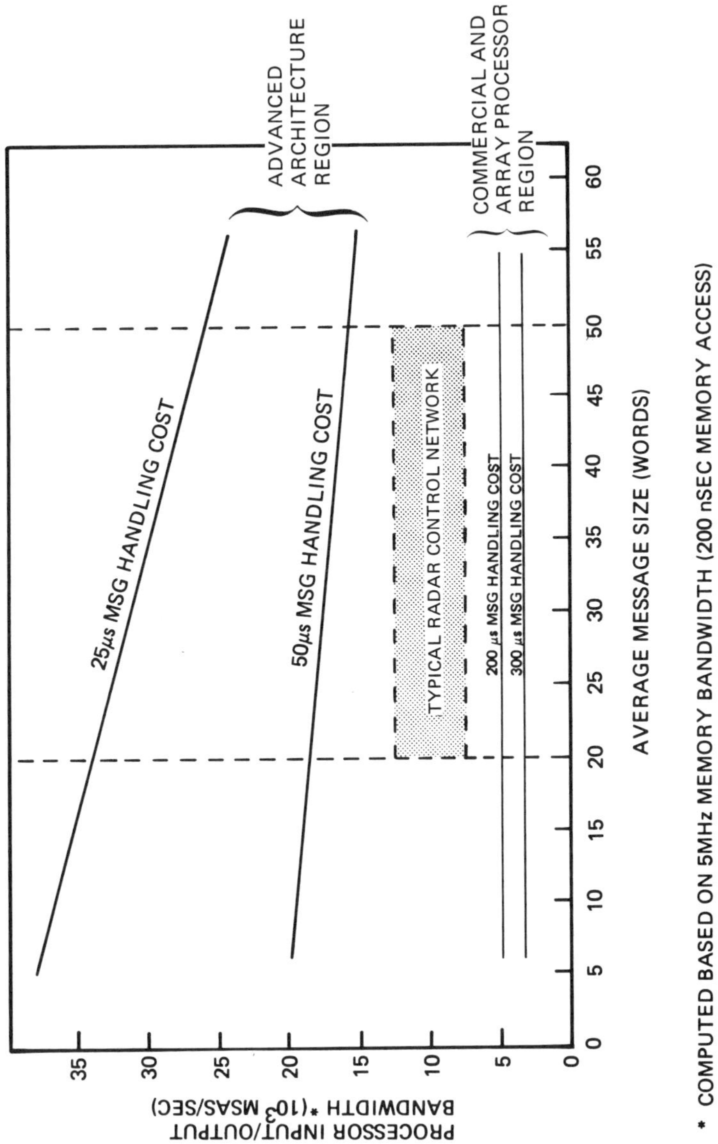

Figure 4.2-1. Processor I/O Sensitivity

message handling is implemented via SW in the real time ØS, message handling costs can typically run several hundred instructions per message transfer. For mini computers networks the CPU timeline cost can run 200-300 microseconds per message interrupt. The only viable alternatives for distributed systems using commercial architectures is to block transfer multiple messages. However, such approaches lead to degraded system response, which for stringent real time applications may become unacceptable.

Advanced processors will soon recognize this deficiency for data handling and will implement HW/SW features which reduce the impact of I/O message handling and data base management on the applications.

These architectures will exploit microprocessor and chip technology to distribute the decision making and hardware control features internal to computers. With the continuing decrease in hardware costs, such new architecture features will add little to the overall computer cost. For example (Figure 4.3-2), advanced computers of the mini-computer class could include such features as:

(1) Special instructions which can be added to the native instruction set to enhance the CPU speed of message handling.

(2) Intelligent I/O channels which can be implemented to presort input messages for the CPU.

(3) Special functional HW which can be added to support the data base management aspects of I/O message handling.

With such additional HW, the computer itself becomes internally distributed. The same basic concepts of internal computer concurrency, which lead to higher performance processors and super computers through instruction level concurrency and parallelism, will result in concurrent and parallel execution of the control functions which tend to dominate distributed systems.

In the candidate architecture postulated (Figure 4.2-2), an instruction preprocessor unit (IPU) prefetches and decodes instructions and routes all data management opcodes to the data management logic unit (DMLU), while all arithmetic operations are routed to the arithmetic logic unit (ALU). In distributed systems the data management functions will include writes to global files. Therefore, once a file write op-code is fetched by the IPU, the DMLU will perform the logical to physical transformation of the write and will handle all the data movement within the data memory. The DMLU will operate out of the data memory completely moving data from temporary storage locations and buffer areas to permanent files within the memory. The DMLU will also format outbound messages and enable the I/O channel for outbound message processing. The DMLU will perform its data management functions in parallel with the ALU execution of applications logic.

All input/output message handling will be performed by the I/O channel controller (IOC). The IOC will have at least the conventional intelligence to retrieve outbound message requests from the data memory, place the messages in the I/O channel buffer and control the transmission of the message over the external bus. The IOC could use a polling scheme to retrieve outbound messages from the internal data memory if messages of varying criticality were used. The controller would pre-sort all incoming messages and transfer the messages to pre-designated buffer areas ("mail

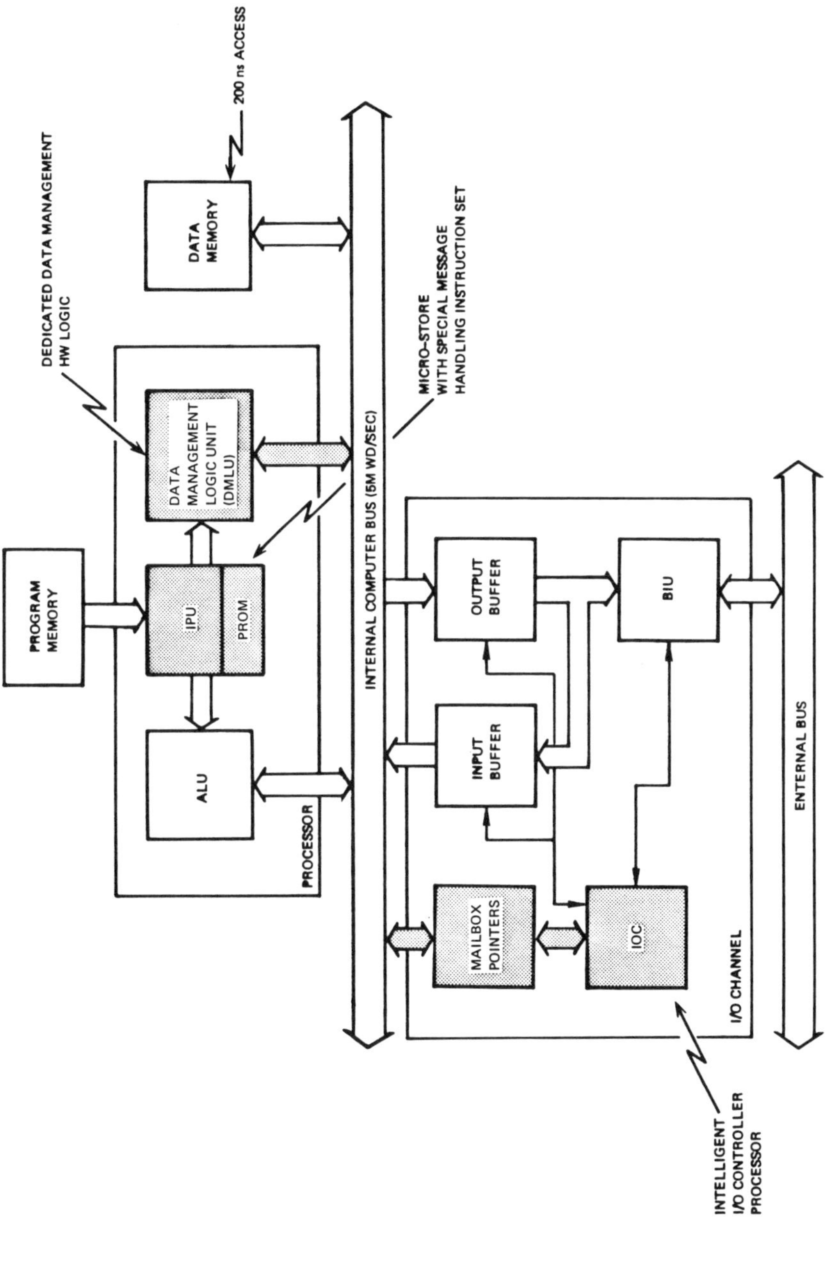

Figure 4.2-2. Advanced Processor with Special Data Handling Features

boxes") within data memory. The mail boxes would be used as the mechanism for communications between the DMLU and IOC'S. The mail boxes could be handled as wrap around FIFO queues with the read/write pointers maintained in a special RAM accessible by both the DMLU and IOC. Separate "mail boxes" could be used for outbound and in-bound messages. The DMLU would manipulate only the write pointers for outbound mail boxes, and the read pointers for inbound mail boxes. The IOC would only manipulate the read pointers of outbound mail boxes, and write pointers for inbound mail boxes. In this manner, internal data base consistency can be insured during the asynchronous, concurrent executions of the DMLU and IOC. Multiple I/O channels and IOC'S would require adidtional and unique mail boxes for each I/O channel.

There are several issues to be worked out for such an architecture, for example, synchronizing the ALU and the DMLU data manipulations to insure that the local data base does not become corrupt or incoherent. A second would be the generation of the logical to physical data base tables required for the DMLU to perform the necessary translation of updates by the local applications tasks. These tables would be initially generated at system generation and could be revised during system dynamic reconfiguration.

4.2.2 Processor Fault Detection & Diagnosis Features

The ability to detect faults and diagnose hardware failures at the point of the fault/failure, and to inhibit the propagation of corrupted data through the network is a major hurdle for insuring the success of DDP. Such a capability will prove to be a major necessity if the integration and test of DDP systems is to be performed within acceptable cost. In addition, hope of dynamic reconfiguration for DDP systems requires that such fault detection, diagnosis and isolation exist.

During system development, the integration and test activity will require the ability to detect failures, usually from abnormal symptoms of system performance, during test operations. The hardware must support the isolation of the failure cause from that of the symptom - where the cause may be hardware, software or a combination of both. Without the addition of new architectural features, the ability to manually trace error sources through a distributed network will be complex and extremely costly.

During real time operation, error trace of hardware failures to support dynamic reconfiguration must be based on hardware. The use of software for error detection, isolation may lead to unacceptable reconfigurations delays.

Meeting these requirements for improved fault detection and diagnosis, will require new features within the processors and their interconnection network bus (Figure 4.2-3). For example, advanced processors could include such architectural features as:

(1) Remote (read only) access to processor working registers to capture time histories of processor execution.

(2) Universal network interrupts which permit uniform and complete network mode changes upon command; which, for example, permits (a) halting the network execution, or (b) stepping through the network processors under global command, or (c) changing from real time to expanded real time execution.

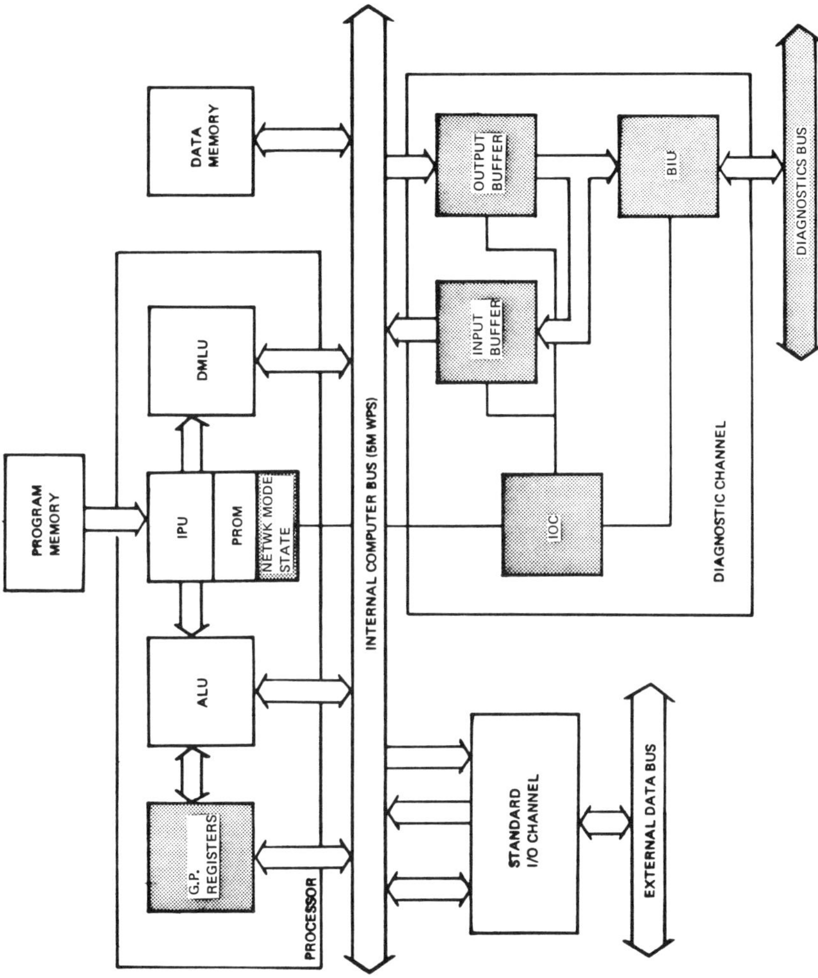

Figure 4.2-3. Advanced Processor with Special Diagnostic Features

(3) Automatic broadcast of processor status and maintenance of network status tables within each network processor.

These features currently must be inplemented in software when using commercial processors, and usually create totally unacceptable overhead. The use of hardware for the generation of automatic processor status table is a feature which will support network dynamic reconfiguration and load balancing.

With these additional architecture features, each network processor has inherent capabilities previously attained through costly software - software which degraded processor performance. The processors general purpose working registers could be tied into the internal computer bus thus allowing access, on a read only basis, by the external network. The processor would have a dedicated I/O channel which supports all diagnostic message traffic. The channel would periodically or upon command (IOC interrupt) read the contents of the GP registers and broadcast over the external bus. The same diagnostic channel would also handle periodic broadcasts of the processor status and loading conditions via messages over the diagnostic bus. The channel IOC would operate in the same manner as the standard I/O channels; i.e., via mail boxes maintained within the random access data memory. Processor status and loading infermation would periodically be placed in the output mail box (FIFO queue) of the diagnostic processor. The diagnostic processor would read the status data from the buffer area within data memory and transmit the required status message over the diagnostic bus. The diagnostic IOC would present inbound messages to determine whether the message was a demand for a "network mode change" in which case the IOC would write the mode change directly into the network state register of the IPU. If the message corresponded to a periodic status update of another network processor the IOC would determine the significance of the message (e.g., processor status update, processor HW failure notice) and write the contents directly into the inbound mail box(es) for the channel. The DMLU would merge the newly received status message into the network status table, which would be used by the local applications task responsible for performing the local component of resource management function (see Section 3.3).

Unlike the standard data bus, which is based on asynchronous and unpredictable message traffic between network processors, the diagnostic bus will be characterized by periodic message traffic originating from each network processor. The diagnostic bus protocol could be quite different from that of the network data bus. Where the data bus objective was to minimize message transmission delay, the diagnostic bus will be driven by the need for message predictability. In fact the predictability characteristic of the bus serve as a major criteria for detecting processor failures and faults within the network.

4.2.3 Advanced Processor Clock Synchronization

The establishment of a global network time source, its distribution throughout the network, and its real time maintenance/synchronization can demand special HW features not available with commercial processors. The time source will typically be used by the ALU, DMLU and I/O channel controllers for global synchronization of such data processing decisions, as computational results, data base updates, external message transmissions, and hardware error detection times. The required accuracy* of the global time is dependent on the network message delay times if the universal time tags are to aid in network with reconstruction. In order to enhance network fault traceability and event reconstruction over the network, the accuracy of the clock should be substantially less than the average network message delay.

Advanced time sorces (e.g., atomic clocks) can provide a time accuracy of 1 part per 10^9 - 10^{12} depending on the stablization technique. This accuracy would insure that once synchronized the time source (with an LSB of 1 Msec) can maintain a 1 bit (1 Msec) accuracy for a period of from 1 hour to over 10 days. However atomic time sources are too costly to maintain within each processor. One alternative is to use the precision time source as a single Universal time source which initializes and maintains special registers within each of the network processors. The universal source would require a direct, dedicated line to each processor's universal time register - the uncertainly in message transmission and handling delays over conventional buses would preclude higher accuracy clock synchronization across the network. Once the network processors' registers have been initialized, the Universal source can either continually maintain the registers, or the local processors can maintain the Universal time with periodic synchronization from the Universal time source. Because of the inaccuracies and drift of internal processor clocks (1 part per 10^6) the synchronization pulse from the Universal time source would be required at least once per second to maintain the 1 Msec accuracy.

In the advanced processor architecture postulated (Figure 4.2-4), the processor has a special access register which contains the Universal time standard. This time standard is typically initialized during network generation by a precision time source. Because of the accuracy required for the universal time source, the initialization and synchronization pulse/strobe must occur over special lines - the processor network can not support an accuracy any better than 35 variance in the network message delay. Once initialized the register is maintained by the processors internal clock. Because of the drift in the processor's clock, the universal time would typically be resynchronized every .5 seconds for a 1 Msec clock accuracy or every 8 minutes for a clock accuracy of 1 Msec.

---

*Accuracy requirement is defined here as the acceptable difference in any two processors' simulataneous reading of the universal time, within the time source is centralized or distributed with synchronizations from a common clock.

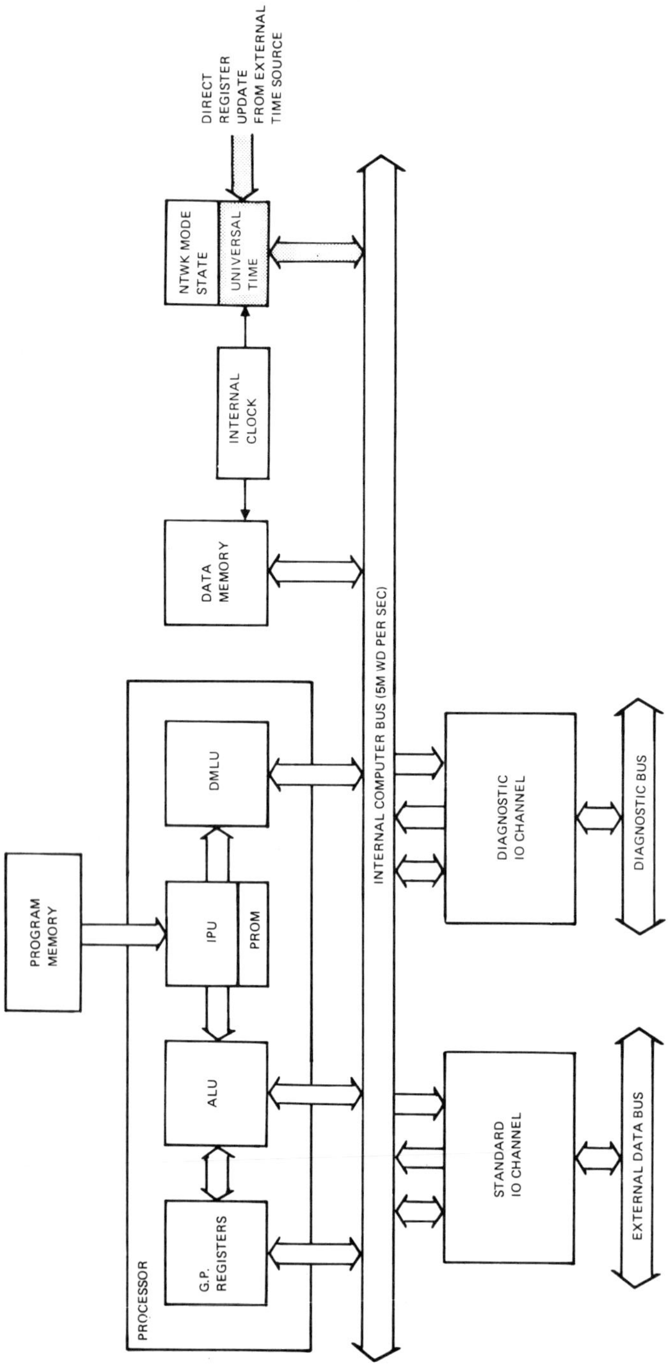

Figure 4.2-4. Advanced Processor with Universal Time Register

4.3. REFERENCES

[4-1A] Flynn, M.J., "Some Computer Organizations and Their Effectiveness", IEEE Transactions on Computers, Vol. C-21, No. 9, Sept. 1972.

[4-1B] Feng, T., "Survey of Interconnection Networks", IEEE Computer, Dec. 1981.

[4-2] Anderson, G.A., and Jensen, E.D., "Computer Interconnection Structures: Taxonomy, Characteristics and Examples", ACM Computing Survey, Dec. 1975.

[4-3] Thurber, K.J. and Freeman, H.A., "Architecture Considerations for Local Computer Networks", Proceedings of the 1st International Conference on Distributed Computing Systems, IEEE Cat. No. 79CH1445-6C, Oct. 1979, pp. 131-142.

[4-4] Wulf, W. and Levin, R. "A Local Network", DATAMATION, Feb. 1975, pp. 47-50.

[4-5] Swan, R.J. et al., "Cm* - A Modular Multi-Microprocessor", AFIPS Conference Proceedings, Vol. 46, 1977 NCC, pp. 637-644.

[4-6] Rudolph, J.A., "A Production Impelmentation of An Associative Array Processor - STARAN", AFIPS Conf- Proceed., Vol. 41, Part I, FJCC 1972, pp. 229-241.

[4-7] Goodyear Aerospace Corp., The STARAN E. System, An Overview, Code Ident. No. 25500, 1976.

[4-8] COMTRE Corp., Multiprocessors and Parallel Processing, P.H. Enslow, Jr., Editor, 1974.

[4-9] Sullivan, H. and Bashkow, T.R., "A Large Scale, Homogeneous, Fully Distributed Parallel Machine, I", 4th Annual Symposium on Comp. Arch. Proceed., 1977, pp. 105-117.

[4-10] Sullivan, H., Bashkow, T.R. and Klappholz, D., "A Large Scale Homogeneous, Fully Distributed Parallel Machine, II", Ibid, pp. 118-124.

[4-11] Farber, D.J. and Larson, K.C., "The System Architecture of the Distributed Computer System - The Communications System", Proc. Symp. Computer-Communications Networks and Teletraffic (New York: Polytechnic Press, 1972), pp. 21-27.

[4-12] SPERRY UNIVAC, AN/UYK-7 Technical Description.

[4-13] DED Education Dept., UNIVAC, AN/UYK-7 Study Guide, Vol. 1, Functional Description, 1972.

]4-14] Gehringer, E.F., The Cm* Testbed", IEEE Computer, Oct. 1982.